Studies in
library management
volume seven

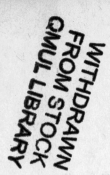

Studies in
library management

volume seven

edited by

Anthony Vaughan

 CLIVE BINGLEY 🅑 LONDON

First published 1982
by Clive Bingley Ltd, 16 Pembridge Road, London W11 3HL
Set in 10 on 12 point Press Roman by Allset
Printed and bound in the UK by
Redwood Burn Ltd, Trowbridge, Wilts
Copyright © Clive Bingley Ltd
All rights reserved
ISBN: 0-85157-322-3

British Library Cataloguing in Publication Data

Studies in library management. — Vol. 7
   1. Library administration — Periodicals
   025.1   Z678
  ISBN 0-85157-322-3

Contents

5

Introduction
ANTHONY VAUGHAN

Librarians are facing the remainder of the decade with mixed emotions. A feeling of gloom probably predominates, at least in Britain, for librarians are still being told to reduce their costs and their services; no hint that this state of affairs will shortly be alleviated has yet been expressed. However, while librarians are struggling to preserve their libraries from irreparable damage, they are aware, to a greater or lesser degree, of the possibilities of libraries becoming 'information centres' in an altogether new way. Some, impressed by the new technology, have misty visions of a so-called 'information society' where librarians or information specialists play a key role. Others, believing that the future may see as rapid a development in the means of controlling, distorting or suppressing information as in disseminating it, conceive of libraries becoming community information centres helping the so-called 'information poor'. Both groups believe in a redefinition of the purpose of libraries, and for them the questioning of library values brought about by budget cuts can actually help to move libraries in new directions. Meanwhile life in the library must continue, and to the feelings of short-term gloom and long-term aspiration are added present-day worries.

The articles in this volume of *Studies in library management* are intended to provide relevant and practical contributions to these various discussions. They all deal with issues of the moment, of matters that are, or should be, preoccupying library administrators.

In Part 1 of the volume a number of major topics are given an authoritative treatment. Sheila Ritchie opens the volume with one of the first detailed examinations of the position of women in British libraries. She abundantly documents the extent to which women librarians are underrepresented in senior library positions, and dismisses, after careful analysis, the reasons sometimes advanced to justify this state of affairs.

7

By looking at other countries and at comparable professions in Britain she shows that British librarianship discriminates against women at senior levels quite remarkably, and concludes by asking why librarianship demonstrates such an extreme conservatism when society in general shows signs of change.

It seems very likely that in the next few years women librarians will make known their dissatisfaction with the present position more and more forcefully to their male colleagues and to libraries' governing bodies. The male library manager, recession or no recession, will be obliged to recognize these aspirations.

In recent years some professional librarians have talked about the 'problem' of non-professional staff in libraries. Donald Davinson examines education and training for non-professional staff in some detail, and he considers the problem, if problem there is, to be one of the professionals' own making. Before the growth of full-time library schools virtually anyone working in a library could 'have a go' at the Library Association examinations, and the humblest junior knew that by dint of part-time study over the years he or she could eventually become chartered. The introduction of full-time study and a graduate profession effectively closed these opportunities to many non-professionals, erecting a barrier in the staff structure and consequently creating, for professionals, the 'problem' of non-professional staff.

Davinson writes not only as head of a library school but also (and this is rare among library school teachers) as someone actively involved in non-professional training through chairing the working party revising the City and Guilds Library Assistant's Certificate. Davinson discusses this certificate and the BEC librarianship modules and makes a plea for librarians to stop contemplating their professional navels for a moment and to remember the other fifty per cent of library staff and their career needs. He suggests that a career structure for non-professionals is also good management, and would lead to a more interested, more motivated junior staff.

Bob Usherwood's contribution looks directly at motivation and at the whole meaning of work. He criticizes the theories of motivation conventionally taught at library schools and widely accepted amongst the profession, and considers that a better appreciation of work as it appears to the person actually doing it can bring new awareness and understanding. His article is timely as many libraries are faced with a static staff complement in the years ahead, and will need to make the most of it.

Usherwood discusses one or two new practical approaches in this field, notably in South Glamorgan County Library. He is well aware of the possible influence of new machine-based techniques on librarians' motivation, and comments that 'with the increased use of technology the challenge to library managers to provide a satisfying, motivating environment will become greater', and he adds, perhaps somewhat ominously, 'part of this challenge is to understand what it means to perform repetitive and routine work'.

The most pervasive of these technical changes in libraries is undoubtedly the switch to automated cataloguing. This is the subject of Stephen Massil's paper. The change to automation has been more dramatic and disturbing in Britain than in, say, North America. There, many libraries had for decades 'bought' centralized cataloguing in the form of Library of Congress cards or proof-slips, which provided all cataloguing information for them — LC and Dewey class numbers, added entries and subject headings. To get exactly the same information on an OCLC catalogue card, or even on a microfiche was far less revolutionary a change for them than the changes which are taking place in Britain, where rugged individualism in cataloguing was far more widespread and the change to standardization and new formats seen as much more difficult or even painful.

Massil's detailed and comprehensive review examines all aspects of the administrative side of automated cataloguing, and should be read not only by chief cataloguers contemplating automation, but also by library managers who may be only vaguely aware of what actually happens to the cataloguing department when automation arrives, and also, indeed, by reader services librarians, for Massil frequently describes the new interplay between reader services and technical services resulting from the automation of cataloguing.

Part 2 of the book includes two studies of rather more general significance to librarians and library administrators. Christine Oldman looks at the 'value' of libraries. At a period when all public services are being obliged to justify their existence the importance of this topic is evident. But Dr Oldman points out the inadequacies of many of these attempts at justification. They work, she says, with a mechanistic model of a library, measuring supply and demand and perhaps costs and effectiveness, but ignoring the political and social dimension. Better, she says, to start such studies with the question 'How much good is the library doing?'. This cannot be answered just by measuring use or recording

9

users' expectations. She illustrates her approach by examples drawn from her Cranfield study which she can look back on more dispassionately now that, as she says, 'the dust has settled'. Oldman points out that the value of a library means different things to different people: it can never be 'objectively' measured. She reckons that perhaps the best way of demonstrating the value of a library to funding bodies is for the librarian to adopt a proselytizing role, and engage in a little consciousness-raising.

McLean writes on 'New technology in academic libraries'. He looks principally at attitudes to automation and to technological change. He reviews what has happened so far very soberly: speaking of computerization in the 1970s he considers that 'the failures in many cases outweigh the successes'. He draws attention to the widespread though rarely reported scepticism among library staff about the benefits of automation and explains why, despite these doubts, librarians continue to automate their operations.

Still stressing the importance of attitudes, McLean looks at likely developments in the next decade or so, and also how far librarians are aware of the possible changes. He identifies among the various attitudes the enthusiastic technological determinist who engenders the opposite conservative reaction of 'well, anyway, we'll aways need books'. McLean's perceptive essay, though written with academic libraries particularly in mind, is of relevance to librarians in all kinds of libraries.

Part 3 presents some more specialized studies of interest to librarians and library school students. The first article in this section is a study of the British Library Reference Division by its director general. The Reference Division is Britain's biggest library by far, but the managerial problems of running such a huge and complex operation are surprisingly little known. Indeed, much more has probably been written in the last twenty years on the youthful Lending Division than on the Reference Division. Alexander Wilson brings home to the reader how the sheer size of the library and the extraordinary variety of its operations make administrative change a qualitatively different matter from change in a smaller library. One is reminded of a huge oil tanker endeavouring to change course in order to get back into a main shipping lane. Such a change of course, a simple matter for a small boat, has to be done by the oil tanker with care and prudence; to end up on the rocks would cause a disaster and public outrage. So with the BLRD; it is gradually moving into the main current of British librarianship, but it is not a

10

process which can be hurried. Wilson describes the past and present organization of the Division and documents the many organizational changes which have already taken place since the British Museum Library became part of the British Library nine years ago.

British public librarians have long looked at Scandinavian libraries as representing the epitome of good design and a pleasing aesthetic environment. Poul Andersen and Børge Sørensen describe some organizational changes which show that British librarians might also look to Scandinavia for some promising experiments in new managerial systems. Andersen and Sørensen examine 'collective management' in Danish public libraries. They describe the principles of collective management, and then those practices in Denmark most nearly approximating to them. It would seem from their account that a relatively genuine type of 'industrial democracy' can be set up successfully in a public library. It is interesting to read that the collectivity includes all who work in the library, professional and non-professional alike, and that the system, once established, is popular with the staff.

The final contribution comes from France. British librarians tend to be ill-informed about the French library system, and this is partly due to a lack of authoritative general analyses written by French librarians for British readers. This lack is remedied in Henri Comte's study of the administrative setting of French libraries, a study which not only describes the system but explains how it arose.

Throughout his paper Comte's focus is on that most crucial of aspects of library management — the relation between libraries and their funding and policy-making bodies. In Britain it is becoming clear that publicly funded libraries are affected far more profoundly by decisions made by the central government and its agencies than by those made by their local governing bodies. France, at least for the period 1945 to 1975, had something which Britain has never yet had — a national libraries policy, sustained by a small specialized department within the central government administration.

Comte considers that, on balance, this period was a fruitful one for French publicly funded libraries, and he thinks that with the abolition of this department in 1975, and the splitting up of responsibility for libraries and information among several separate units, prospects for further progress are not good. Yet he also points out that even with such a policy there remain problems about the level of funding and about the influence that past traditions and powerful interests can bring to bear on the policies established. In the last few years the Library

11

Association, SCONUL, and House of Commons Committees have been pressing for the British government to develop a national libraries and information policy. A reading of Comte's paper will show something both of the possibilities and of the drawbacks which the establishment of such a policy in Britain would bring.

(*Editor's note* — The paper by Henri Comte was translated by the editor, and any infelicities of style are his responsibility and not that of the author.)

Part one

Women in library management
SHEILA RITCHIE

The library profession in the United Kingdom is in composition predominantly female. It is only at the higher levels of seniority, in terms of job status, that this numerical superiority becomes reversed and the majority becomes the very scarce minority. This paper is an attempt to review some aspects of this paradox; to present factual information on library manpower statistics according to gender, and to investigate briefly some possible reasons for women's low status. The sections on manpower statistics are fuller than those on the reasons for women's lack of advancement: such reasons are complex and under-researched. It is easier to identify trends and facts than to ascertain causes; unfortunately, possible solutions more often result from causal analysis than from mere statements about a problem. My own current research is concerned with these causes and what follows is a mixture of fact and conjecture, each labelled appropriately.

STATUS AND SALARIES
Salaries and status have a strong positive relationship in all types of employment: usually, the higher the one, the higher the other. It is to be expected that, if women hold fewer high status posts than men proportionately, they will also tend to have lower salaries. Sadly, both suppositions are true.

Status
Women are not included in the present establishment of senior library posts in proportion to their numbers in the profession. This is true of public, university, polytechnic, colleges of higher education, and large industrial libraries. For public libraries in particular Table 1 gives the numbers and proportions of each sex at the top three levels of the hierarchy in 1977.[1]

13

Level	Men	%	Women	%	Total
1	106	98.1	2	1.85	108
2	98	85.9	16	14	114
3	353	72.5	112	27.5	487
1-3	557	79	152	21	709

Table 1 Men and women in senior posts (public libraries in England – 1977)

In case 1981 might be thought to present a very different picture, the figures are given below in Table 2 for levels 1 and 2 only.

Level	Men	%	Women	%	Total
1	105		3		108
2	96	84.2	18	15.7	114

Table 2 Men and women in senior posts (public libraries in England – 1981)

The bare figures are depressing enough, but when the actual numbers of women working in the profession are taken into account, the situation looks even worse. The census figures which match the 1977 survey results are those for April, 1978.[2] These state a figure of 6,536 qualified librarians working in English public libraries. A rough check of the Library Association yearbook for 1978 reveals that about 60% of professional librarians working in English public libraries were female. Applying this proportion to the census total gives 3,922 females and 2,614 males, which is spuriously accurate, but usable for construction of Table 3 below showing the percentages of each sex holding senior posts at levels 1, 2 and 3.

It can be seen that men, with 21.3% of their numbers in senior posts, are represented in greater proportion than women, with only 3.9% of theirs. The most glaring differences are seen at the top two levels. With 4% of men in a level 1 post, there is a roughly 25:1 chance of success for a keen young male librarian. For women, with .05% reaching the top, the chances are 2,000:1 — keenness is not likely to

14

Level	% of males	% of females	% of total
1	4	.05	1.6
2	3.7	.4	1.7
3	13.5	3.4	7.4
1-3	21.3	3.9	10.8

Table 3 Senior postholders, percentages of men and women working in English public libraries, 1977

be present in enough quantity to overcome odds of such magnitude. To update again to 1981, with 3 women in top level posts, the odds shorten to 1,307:1 against, for a female librarian. Such chances have the flavour of the lottery rather than allowing for objective judgement on the abilities, experience and qualifications of the candidate.

Analysis of the 1977 results by type of public library points to metropolitan districts as the largest employers of women at senior levels: 24.8% of levels 1, 2 and 3 posts are held by women in such authorities, compared with London boroughs which employ only 13% in similar posts. Researchers into other types of library, notably Slater, have found that this inequity is repeated. She states: 'the trend for men to be more prevalent at the top and women at the bottom of the job status scale was constant and consistent in all four studies'.[3] A recent study by Pankhurst found that women occupied only three of the level 1 posts in thirty-one polytechnic libraries.[4]

A calculation of the present establishment of senior public library posts on the basis of proportional representation of each sex would give the result below in Table 4:

Level		Men	Women	Total
1		43	65	108
	(Actual)	(105)	(3)	(108)
2		46	68	114
	(Actual)	(96)	(18)	(114)

Table 4 Proportional representation by sex in senior public library posts in England, compared with actual representation

15

Comparability with other countries

The USA is the crucible of the second wave of the women's movement in western countries and many studies have been undertaken there of the role, status and history of women in libraries. The latest analysis of top jobs there yields the following figures.[5]

Level	Men (% of posts)	Women (% of posts)
1 – Director	84.7	15.3
2 – Associate/ Assistant Director	94.8	5.2
3 – Dept Head	82	18

Table 5 Proportion of senior posts held by men and women in libraries in the USA, 1980

In Canada a national sample taken in 1975/1976 gave, at first sight, a more heartening picture. Forty-nine of the women in the sample and forty-seven of the men were in top level jobs. Unfortunately, two-thirds of the sample were female and relative proportions produced a figure of only 11% of the women compared with 21% of the men.[6]

Hungary, with a woman in charge of the National Library, and fifty-four out of sixty-three public libraries attached to the Budapest Municipal Library managed by women, scores higher on the equity scale.[7] Even here though, proportional representation is not achieved. A check of the *World guide to libraries* for 1980 shows that of sixty-eight chiefs of university and college libraries, only thirty-three are women.[8] With 70% of the profession female, 48.5% is not proportional representation.

A better record is demonstrated by France where between 70% and 80% of qualified librarians joining the scientific staff (ie the highest level) are women.[9] Of this highest grade of staff, 73% were female in 1973.

On a league table Britain would probably rank level with Australia as the worst appointers of women to senior library posts.

Historical perspective

It is worthwhile to set the present low status of women in libraries in its historical context. After all, if previous years have seen no women appointed to senior posts, then even a handful represents a great leap forward. Sadly, the converse appears to be true. The position of

16

women has worsened over time and both the numbers and the proportion of women in senior posts has declined. This is studied most easily for public libraries, perhaps because of the existence of usable published data. In 1976 there were six female chief librarians in public libraries in England and Wales — 5.5% of all posts. In 1971 there were sixty-one — 18.1% of all posts. For true comparability, many smaller authorities existing in pre-reorganization 1971 must be excluded from the calculation. If all libraries employing fewer than twelve chartered librarians are excluded, forty-four urban boroughs and districts remain, compared with thirty-six after local government reorganization. On this basis, of larger libraries only, women occupied fourteen of the top tier posts — 11.6% of the total.[10]

In 1976 there were nine women at level 2 — 9.3% of the posts. In 1971 this figure was 28.2%, but estimates based only on the larger library authorities produce a figure of 9.3%. There is not sufficient suitable data available for comparisons to be made on posts at level 3.

Entry into the profession has stabilized at a ratio of 80:20, women to men, since the 1960s. The proportion of personal members of the Library Association has hovered around 60:40, women to men, from the end of the Second World War until recently. In the first half of the century the figure was closer to 50:50, but now it is 68:32.

A rather depressing comparison can be made with France where the position of women in senior library posts shows gradual improvement over time. Boisard remarks that 'more than 70% of the scientific staff, the top staff category in libraries, are women. This percentage has continued to increase regularly since 1946 . . .'[9] The trend is shown in the table below, extracted from Table 3 of the Boisard study:

Year	Proportion of women
1946	61.78
1950	67
1959	68.29
1962	68.34
1966	69.86
1971	70.29
1973	73.18

Table 6 Women as proportion of postholders at the
scientific level in French libraries

We cannot make an exact comparison between France and the other countries which have been mentioned as the French scientific staff are recruited, for the most part, directly from the French state library school, which in turn draws most of its students from those who have recently completed their university studies. But the figures do indicate the high, and increasing, proportion of women in senior positions in French libraries.

The reasons for the decline in numbers and proportion of women in senior posts in Britain are the subject of much popular theory. One explanation is that library committees were willing, in the days of flexible salaries, to give the job to a woman if she could be got more cheaply than a man, other things being equal. This became less easy with the development of trade union influence and the negotiation of national salary agreements. Another theory for the larger number of senior women librarians in the 1940s and 1950s is that men's career progression had been interrupted by war and, later, national service and that women thereby gained a momentary advantage.

Comparability with other professions
The teaching profession bears close resemblance in terms of manpower structure to our own — and also in terms of its public image and its residence in the domain of the social professions.

A recent report issued by the National Union of Teachers pointed out that although nearly 60% of all teachers are female, only 38% of headships are held by women.[11] It brings our own problem into focus when we realize that in public libraries, where about 60% of professionals are female, 1.85% of 'headships' are held by women; in polytechnics, about 6% are; and in universities, about 4.4%. The teachers are in a far better position.

The Medical Women's Federation has actively campaigned for more posts for part-time hospital consultants, so that married women can continue their careers at more senior levels. In 1980 it also organized the election of three women doctors to the General Medical Council. The parallel with libraries is clear. More part-time posts at senior levels would benefit many women in the profession. There is also evidence that elected representatives could be fostered, and sponsored, by an organized women's movement.

Salaries
Figure 1 shows the salary distribution for men and women in the pilot survey of 1978.[1] Differences between salaries paid to men and women

18

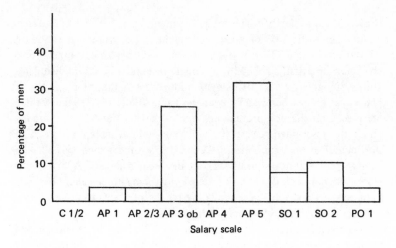

Figure 1A Salaries, men

Figure 1B Salaries, women

KEY: C 1/2 Clerical grades 1 and 2   AP 1 Administrative and Professional Grade 1   AP 2/3 Administrative and Professional Grades 2 and 3 below the bar (for qualification)   AP 3 ob Administrative and Professional grade 3 over the bar (for qualification)   AP 4 and 5 as above Grades 4 and 5   SO 1 Senior Officers' Grade 1   SO 2 Senior Officers' Grade 2   PO 1 Principal Officers' Grade 1

19

show up quite clearly. The mode for men is grade AP5 local government scale, with 34% of male respondents. For women the mode is AP3 over the bar (ie the minimum NALGO negotiated grade for a chartered librarian), with 45% of female respondents. More disturbing still is the large number of women, about 28% of the sample, who are placed on grades below AP3 over the bar. About 12% of the women are placed on the non-professional grades Clerical 1 and 2, even though all of the respondents were chartered and with at least three years of post-qualification experience. Whereas 85% of the men earned AP3 over the bar and above, only 72% of the women did so. A larger scale study of polytechnic libraries, currently being undertaken by Rita Pankhurst, is revealing very similar salary distributions to those of men and women in the public library sample.[4]

American research on status and salary differentials between men and women in libraries has been well established since the early 1970s, and tables now appear annually. These also include data on the funding and support of public library authorities according to sex of director. Mean salaries for women in the 1980 tabulations vary by type of library between $14,236 and $14,850, whereas those for men vary between $18,692 and $20,520. Support and funding for public libraries also varies according to sex of director. In 1979 the mean *per capita* support for libraries with male directors was $7.37; for female directors it was $6.05.[12] A cynical view is that poorly funded libraries and parsimonious committees are likely to offer low salaries and, therefore, are also likely to employ female chiefs. It seems that the mean salary for female librarians is exactly that.

Promotion
In the 1978 public library study a slightly higher proportion of men (71%) had been promoted at some time in their careers than women (57%). The same number of each sex (53%) expected to be promoted from their present job in under five years. Just over half of both sexes thought that promotion was likelier in libraries other than their present one, and 38% of both men and women felt that their chances of promotion would be lower in outside libraries.

Although the number of women actually promoted is a little lower than that for men, and prospects for senior posts are far gloomier for them, only 4% of the women surveyed stated that they were currently looking for a job out of librarianship. This compares with 25% of the men. This is paralleled by Slater's finding, 'Women may have shorter
20

professional lives than men . . . But an employer tempted to employ a man instead for this reason should also take into account that a woman seems more likely to stick with the profession than a man'.[13]

On that note, the question of mobility and career commitment, it is worth looking at the profession as a whole to see if there are significant differences in the survival rates of men and women.

SURVIVAL AND CAREER COMMITMENT

The membership of the Library Association in 1980 was composed of women and men in the ratio 68:32.[14] Entry into the profession has been at the ratio of 4:1, women to men, for some years. The proportion of those registered as Associates of the Library Association in 1980 was 20.8% men and 79.1% women. The actual figures were 223 men and 845 women.[15]

The difference between the proportions of those entering the profession and the proportions of those who are members of the Association raises some interesting questions, and, usually, some shakily based answers. Investigation into the causes of the difference reveals a more complex picture than the simplistic assumption that young female entrants just don't stay. The first stop on a fact-finding mission is to look at survival rates for both men and women and try to ascertain if there are differences, and what features such differences might display.

Constructing a survival curve is ideally done on a population of librarians followed through their membership (and employment) over a period of years: in short, a longitudinal study. For ease, and without significant loss of validity, a survival curve can be constructed by taking different populations of librarians at the same point in time. The curves reproduced in figures 2A and 2B below took a 'snapshot' analysis of all librarians still in Library Association membership in November 1977 who had become chartered in six previous years – 1964, 1967, 1969, 1971, 1974 and 1976. Gender could be used as the basis of division since the Library Association publishes annual figures of the number of newly chartered librarians by sex. To derive the number of men and women remaining (or surviving) in membership, and in employment in libraries, the 1978 Yearbook of the Association was analysed for the relevant years. (FLAs had to be traced back through previous yearbooks to reveal date of chartering.)

Table 7, overleaf, gives the proportion of men to women surviving from each of the six years selected.

21

Year of chartering	% Men	% Women
1964	43	57
1967	49	51
1969	49	51
1971	39	61
1974	27	73
1976	27.5	72.4

Table 7 Men:women remaining in library profession and employment, November 1977

Survival curves are commonly S-shaped, but the scatter of the points in figures 2A and 2B is such that there is no justification for forcing an S-shaped curve through them. It could be argued that the scatter of the last three points on the survival curve for women indicates the point at which some women leave work for family reasons, returning to the profession later. However, it must be remembered that the points represent different populations at a single moment in time, and not the same population followed through time. For this reason too much meaning cannot be read into the curves.

The curves plotted represent the best fit of any simple function to the points. They were derived using the 'Forecast' command of the computer-based financial planning system FCS. Using this command it is possible to find the best fit from a range of simple types of function (eg straight line, quadratic, exponential). The curves drawn represent the quadratic functions:

$$y = 100 - 3.1422x + 0.2747x^2 \text{ for the total population,}$$
$$y = 100 - 3.2944x - 0.0272x^2 \text{ for the male population,}$$
$$y = 100 - 10.0691x + 0.3818x^2 \text{ for the female population,}$$

where y = % remaining, and x = length of employment. The fit of all three is significant at the 95% level.

It is not surprising that, as women form the majority of the profession, there is a marked similarity between their survival functions and that of the total population. The male survival curve is *very slightly* concave upwards, but is more approximate to a straight line. This indicates that the rate at which men leave the profession is roughly constant, increasing only slightly with length of employment. The female survival curve is concave upwards. This indicates that the rate

22

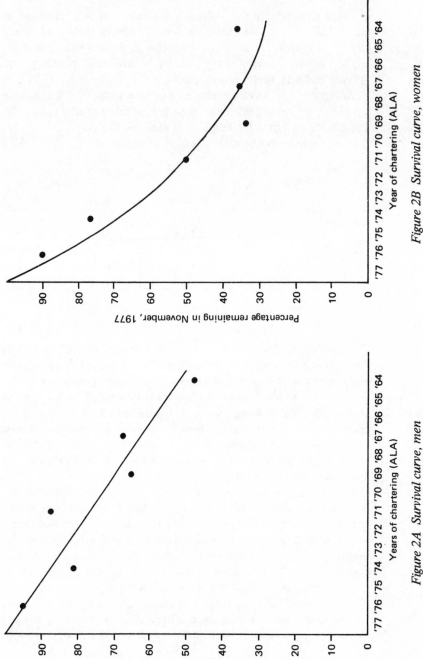

Figure 2A Survival curve, men

Figure 2B Survival curve, women

at which women leave the profession decreases with length of employment. This does not immediately explode the popular myth that women cannot be counted upon to stay long enough to be worth promotion, but it does suggest that the myth should be broadened to include both sexes as 'bad bets' for long-term reliability.

Analysis of the curves themselves could support the view that women are likelier to leave than men in their first seven years after chartering. Table 8, below, gives the numbers of each sex likely to remain in the first and second seven-year periods of employment.

| | Surviving | | Leaving | |
	Men	Women	Men	Women
Years 1-7	87	57	13	43
Years 8-14	47	37	40	20

Table 8 Leaving pattern of men:women (each 100)

The most interesting feature of this is that women do seem to be less likely to stay in their first seven years, but men seem to be twice as likely as women to leave in their second seven-year period of employment. What a library/leisure committee is to make of such a trend is questionable, but it does seem that women discriminated against for promotion, on the grounds of their lower survival probability, should expect reverse discrimination to apply during the middle management career years. There is evidence that the first case operates, but not many examples of the second.

It is possible, of course, that women may not be responsible for their early high casualty rate, to the extent that, if women's promotional chances are very low (whether or not because of fears of their instability), then they are likely to become demotivated and to seek opportunities elsewhere. Slater spotted the potential ambiguity of such causes and effects and cautioned that women should beware of giving domestic reasons for leaving a job as a cover for other reasons.[16] It may be thought easier to resign and cite a domestic cause rather than tell the truth about the uncongenial job without prospects, but the excuses of the few will be paid for by the many and unfavourable

24

stereotypes will be reinforced. On the question of intention to remain in the profession, 63% of the men and 56% of the women in the 1978 public library survey said that they would remain until retirement.

Qualifications

Another possible measure of career commitment is the number, and type of qualifications held by men and women in libraries. Slater remarked that 'men emerged as the better qualified sex in a dual sense. Numerically . . .' and by level.[17] In her study men averaged 2.6 qualifications, women averaged 2.

My own 1978 public library survey showed men to be slightly better qualified (if more equals better) than women at each comparable level of experience. 44% of the men had taken a further qualification since chartering, compared with 27% of the women. On the other hand, only 7.4% of the men were currently enrolled in a course leading to a further qualification, compared with 12% of the women. On the question of intention to take further qualifications, 74% of the men and 70% of the women replied in the affirmative. Perhaps this last question produced over-optimistic replies; intention is not actuality.

Analysis of present senior postholders' qualifications cannot be done by gender as the numbers of women at levels 1 and 2 are too small for significant conclusions. Of the 264 men at level 3 whose qualifications were known, 27.6% have the FLA. Of the 102 women at level 3, 20.5% have the FLA. For other types of qualification, eg ALA only, BA plus ALA, there is no evidence of gender difference.

It seems that it is in qualifications beyond first professional level that gender differences show most clearly. This is dramatically demonstrated in the USA, where 90.2% of first professional level librarianship students are women, but only 50.6% of students at the doctoral level are women.[18] Our own doctoral enrolments at schools of librarianship are too low for meaningful analysis. There is no doubt, however, that many more men than women hold the FLA.

Professional activity

There are several accepted yardsticks for measuring involvement in professional activity. The most obvious is that of membership of committees and other bodies representative of the library and information science professions. The Library Association Council for 1981 comprises 52 men and 10 women.[14] It could be that elected offices are a different class of appointment and that women have only themselves to blame if they are not well represented. This would have more force as an argument were it not for the appointed (as opposed to elected) posts in the Library Association where both top jobs are held by men, that of Secretary-General and of Deputy Secretary-General. Women appear in tertiary-level positions and below, where they predominate numerically.[15]

In 1965 Eric Moon noted with spirit that 'the presidents-elect of both the American and British Library Associations . . . are women.'[19] The vigour of this assertion fades a little when it is remembered that, had he been writing in any other year this century or last, he would have been unable to make the claim. There have been 91 male presidents of the British Library Association and one female.

There is more evidence of women's activity in professional matters in America, not only resting on the fact that the ALA president is a woman (Elizabeth Stone) but also supported by the rise of numerous organizations and groups representing women's interests, many of which are professionally based.[20] Unfortunately, 'professional visibility', as Kathleen Heim aptly terms it, still shows a predominance of men at every level of involvement, with the most obvious variance at the national level. In elected or appointed positions at national level, 31.7% of ALA men are involved, but only 14.6% of ALA women.[5]

Boisard remarks that 'in France, between 1906 and 1964, the Association of French Librarians had thirty male presidents and only three women presidents, the first time [for a woman] being in 1945'.[9] She goes on to say, though, that women are tending to take more part in the work of the council and its sections and that their numbers in office are beginning to parallel their representation among the membership.

Another measure of professional involvement is publishing activity in librarianship and related fields. Estabrook and Heim found that, 'men publish roughly three times as many books and book reviews and four times as many articles as women.'[5] A study of authorship in five major American journals in library and information science showed that men were responsible for about two-thirds of the articles.[21] (The citation of this work I find interesting in its own right.)

The 'People' column of the *Library Association record* lists the doings of twice as many men as women: 68% of its entries are about men. This proportion is an exact converse of their true professional representation.

Women's lack of professional visibility relative to men is one area

26

that is open to change from within. It may be true that council membership requires that a candidate first stand for election and that the publication of articles and books depends on third party approval, but both of these activities are open to contenders without the complex and hidden obstacles which make the job market and promotion so difficult for women. In other words, professional visibility is largely voluntary (especially in the case of that 'People' column, where the editor assures me that entries are self-submitted) and women can alter the adverse variances in professional representation by their own efforts and a little less marketing modesty.

ASPIRATIONS

One of the commonest myths about women at work is that they are not ambitious. Sometimes this is taken further to the belief that women should not be ambitious, that it just isn't nice, or feminine, or that a woman should only be ambitious for someone else. The first assumption is capable of challenge; the second belongs in the realms of what ought to be and is part of that class of argument which, like compost rotting, generates more heat than light.

Chambers' twentieth century dictionary defines ambition as 'aspiration after success or advancement'. For measurement purposes, such a definition is virtually worthless. One example of the problems which can arise from attempts to measure such a difficult concept comes from my own 1978 study of public librarians.[1] Survey respondents stated the highest level of post they aspired to, according to a seven-grade scale on which chief librarian was graded 1 and 'no ambition at all' was graded 7. The distribution is given below, in figure 3A for men and figure 3B for women. (As the scale runs from left to right, the more ambitious respondents figure further to the right.)

There is a tendency for men to aspire to the highest level of post, 44% of the men indicated category 1, chief librarian, and this is the mode of the distribution. Category 3, district librarian, came a close second with 39% of the men. For women the mode is at category 3, district librarian, with 51% of the respondents. Just over 15% of the women aspired to category 1, chief librarian. With all the usual reservations about sample size and confidence limits, there is more than a hint here that women are less ambitious.

But, to return to the ambiguity of the quality under measurement, ambition is not an attribute which is stable over time and of which the magnitude can be confidently assessed. It is likely to fluctuate markedly

27

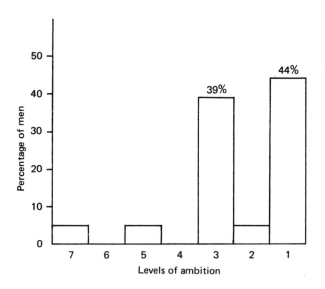

Figure 3A   Absolute aspirations, men

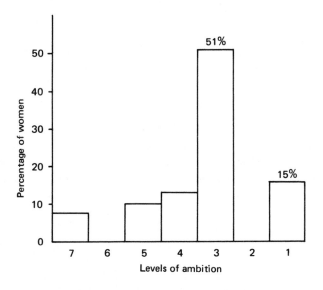

Figure 3B   Absolute aspirations, women

according to a person's motivation, self-image, perceived likelihood of advancement, present status, and numerous other variables and imponderables. Taking just one of these variables, present status, and recalculating the survey responses in the light of this, allows a different distribution to be arrived at. Each respondent was assigned to a status category, graded 1 to 7, the 1 corresponding to chief librarian and the 7 to that of student or unemployed librarian. Each person was then awarded 'points' as follows:

	Points awarded
Remain at present level	0
Aspire 1 level higher	1
Aspire 2 levels higher	2
Aspire 3 levels higher	3

and so on to a maximum of 7 points.

The maximum score possible, 7 points, was for a student or unemployed librarian to aspire to be a chief librarian. On the basis of this interpretation of ambition, women are more ambitious than men, as can be seen in the table of responses below:

	Men		Women		Total	
Points	Number	%	Number	%	Number	%
0	2	7.4	5	7.5	7	7.5
1	1	3.7	7	10.6	8	8.6
2	7	25.9	7	10.6	14	15
3	2	7.4	19	28.7	21	22.5
4	3	11.1	6	9	9	9.6
5	3	11.1	9	13.6	12	12.9
6	1	3.7	1	1.5	2	2.1
7	–		2	3	2	2.1
No answer etc	8	29.6	10	15.1	18	19.3

Table 9 Relative career aspirations of men and women

Too much should not be read into table 9, but it is a fairer measure of true ambition than that of absolute aspirations. The claim that many women have 'no ambition' is not supported by this survey:

both sexes have equal proportions in this category. What can be stated is that women aspire to better things, relative to their present inferior status. The fact that many do not covet the very highest posts should not disqualify them for consideration for intermediate levels, nor should the minority who do aspire to reach the heights be disregarded. It is, of course, possible that those who say that female librarians are not ambitious base their assumption on the fact that very few are in senior posts. Circularity of this nature is not amenable to argument.

MANAGERIAL QUALITIES

Opponents of women in senior management positions, in libraries as well as other organizations, often claim that women do not possess 'managerial qualities'. Such assumptions are worth challenging.

Management itself is the subject of thousands of books, journals, and reports, the concern of countless organizations throughout the world, and, in the UK alone, the 'common denominator' of 68,000 members of the BIM. There is no agreed universal definition, no defined and limited subject area, and not one of those BIM members has a job exactly like another. The search for the qualities which make for successful leadership has ranged over decades and continents and taken up much time, energy and scholastic application. It has resulted in nothing of use for predictive purposes. Even the ultra-conservative Sandhurst Military College abandoned the 'born leader' concept in the 1960s when John Adair identified its weaknesses.

In the light of such universal vacuity on the exact qualities needed for leadership, and where the only lasting theories base their predictions on contingency — ie that everything depends on the circumstances of the task, the team to be managed, and the leader — how can anyone seriously insist that a man is better as a manager/chief librarian?

Even worse, apart from the Sheffield study on manpower by Sergean, no attempt has been made to establish the nature, purpose and content of professional and senior librarians' jobs.[22] With such a poor state of job analysis it seems rather high-handed to pontificate with solemnity on the best person to do the job, when the job itself is unspecified. It is more than high-handed to categorize two-thirds of the profession as immediately disqualified by virtue of their sex.

In 1979 I conducted a study of the nature, contacts and content of senior librarians' jobs in London boroughs.[23] The highest level, that of borough librarian, had a markedly external orientation: there was much contact with local authority departments other than that including the library service. In addition, many organizations outside the local authority were contacted by chief librarians and a good deal of time was spent in functions, meetings and formal and informal conversations. None of these activities are gender-specific. If anything, popular prejudice would classify most of these as 'feminine'.

The claim that women cannot do a job is hard to support if very few have been given the chance in the first place. Low validity is the inevitable result of studies analysing performance on very small numbers. Such studies become even more difficult where the job itself has not been properly analysed and specified.

EDUCATION

One broad field of interest in education and training for women in libraries is the study of women in society and history, including their role and status in the library professions. This is rightly termed education and is fast acquiring a body of literature and a defined subject area. Another field of interest, more rightly termed training, is concerned with those skills and abilities which women are allegedly lacking, and which are assumed to be the prerequisites for success in management. Under this heading come such courses as interviewing skills, self-presentation and marketing, assertion training and all forms of interpersonal skills training directed specifically at women.

A problem with this second approach is that it is based on unsound and untested hypotheses. The question of whether or not women should be trained in the skills of corporate gamesmanship should be preceded by the question of whether such characteristics should be encouraged and developed as the benchmarks of success in organizational life. Before massive training programmes for women are run on assertion skills, it might be wise to consider first whether men could be trained in the skills of co-operation and non-competitiveness.

Popular myth assigns sexual stereotypes to personality characteristics, and avowed feminists can be as guilty of generalization as those they decry. According to one writer, women 'do not wish to be involved in the competitive, aggressive, rigid hierarchies which constitute top management positions because, as women, they are less likely to have those "male" characteristics — aggression, competitiveness and so on — which supposedly make good managers. Instead they stay in middle level posts where their "female" characteristics — caring, collectivity, non-competitiveness and so on — will be put to best use'.[24] Behavioural scientists would be very surprised to hear that women are less aggressive

31

or less competitive. The magnitude of the quality is one thing, its direction is another. It has never been demonstrated that aggression makes a good chief librarian, nor that the best district librarians are caring and non-competitive. There is mounting evidence that our corporate society needs to encourage and reward team building and co-operation amongst its workers, but any move to outlaw aggression would need first to provide a definition of it and then to find a suitable substitute for its energizing, stimulating and goal-directed properties.

The most positive steps in education for librarianship in women's studies have been made in the USA. A report of the first 'Women in Librarianship' course to be run on a credit-earning basis, as part of the curriculum, appeared in 1979. The purposes of the course were to trace the feminization of librarianship within the context of the history of women in America; to examine a number of topics of particular importance to contemporary women in librarianship; and to consider the future of women librarians in the United States.[25] The major result of the course was increased awareness of the discrimination suffered by women in American librarianship, and suggestions by participants included a list of further possible courses including guest lectures, role playing of senior jobs, workshops on writing for publication, and interviewing techniques.

This recognition of women's need for skills-related training with a behavioural basis is a common theme in participative workshops on the role of women in libraries, almost regardless of the original subject under discussion. It emerged as a strong theme at the United Kingdom 'Women in libraries' inaugural conference in February 1981 at the Polytechnic of Central London. It was also discussed as a positive way forward in three of the four workshops following the Margate seminar in September 1981; the Women's Group that organized the workshops is hoping to be incorporated formally as a Group of the Library Association soon.

One ingenious, but flawed, argument in the *Australian library journal* in 1973 was invoked to prove that women were less likely to be leaders of tomorrow's libraries because of their mathematical incompetence relative to men.[26] The writer suggested that computing skills would be at a premium in the new computerized library and that, as women score lower than men on tests of mathematical ability, their changes of promotion would be affected by this handicap. One problem with this argument is that mathematical skill is not required for mastery of basic computing techniques. Another is that it is necessary to show that senior posts in libraries would require mathematical skills of a high order before women's relative incompetence is admissible as a reason for their exclusion. Contrary to this, there is evidence to show that the more senior the library job, the less likely it is to include tasks depending on technical skills. In my own study of senior librarians in London boroughs, technical expertise began to lose ground to political and behavioural skills at levels of principal officer and above. Chief and borough librarians hardly involved themselves at all in the 'oily rag' side of administration, concentrating instead on external politics and interpersonal dealings.[23]

REASONS FOR WOMEN'S LOW STATUS

The most honest statement on the reasons for women's low status in libraries is to admit ignorance. There are plenty of theories which seem, at first sight, to offer an answer, but none of them identify the major cause of the problem.

What can be said with some claim to factual foundation is that the reasons are *not*:

— that women are less ambitious;
— that women do not stay in the profession;
— that women are less committed, as evidenced by qualifications and intention to remain in the profession;
— that women do not possess managerial qualities.

Unfortunately, the *belief* that women are guilty of all these 'faults' could very well be a major reason. The truth or otherwise of a belief rarely influences attitudes.

What has not been investigated properly, nor even seriously suggested as a possible reason, is the effect that poor career chances have upon the female librarian. Women often have great difficulty finding a first post at a reasonable salary. Many settle for a job that sounds as if it includes some tasks suitable for the application of their hard-won librarianship skills, even if the salary is lower than that supposedly agreed to be the minimum by the relevant trades union. The position is even worse for a mid-career woman returning to the profession after family commitments. Once in post, the new recruit realizes that nearly all the senior posts are held by men, including those at neighbouring libraries. A combination of these two factors, even if there were no others to exacerbate the problem, should be enough to daunt the most motivated person.

Although such a theory needs careful testing, it is not unreasonable to turn around the sequence of logic which states that 'women are less ambitious and capable, and this causes their career chances to be affected', and render it into: 'women have lower career chances, so that they become alienated and demotivated'.

The reasons for women's low status in libraries will probably continue to be expounded vigorously, usually with very little factual basis. Rebuttals of such reasons will also be in plentiful supply, and will just as often be based on very slender foundations. Such exchanges could be much improved by a little research: each 'reason', when investigated systematically, seems to give way. Perhaps the gradual isolation and exposure of the myths, one by one, will leave no platform on which discrimination can base itself. This optimistic view does not leave much room for wilful prejudice, which has never needed a factual foundation, but it does allow for attrition of the fabric of conjecture which shores up outdated attitudes.

In my view librarianship must be a microcosm of the social world in which it operates. It is not only firmly set in context by society's delineation of its role and place, but is a social profession itself, bounded by the limitations of the media it harnesses for society's ends. It draws it rationale, its philosophy, its funding and its employees from the society it serves and cannot be other than a reflection of that society's culture, traditions, norms and failings. Therefore, it must also exemplify society's attitudes towards employees, work and the natural order of organizational life. The real puzzle then, for me, is why librarianship demonstrates such an extreme conservatism in its employment patterns, when society shows signs of change.

References
1 Ritchie, S F C *Career aspirations of female librarians in English public libraries: a pilot study of attitudes towards work and career ambition, comparing male and female chartered librarians in public library authorities in England* London, ELM publications, 1978.
2 'Public library staff establishment and grading census' *Library Association record* 80 (4) April 1978, 150-151.
3 Slater, M *Career patterns and the occupational image: a study of the library/information field* London, Aslib, 1979, 122.
4 Pankhurst, R 'Women in the library profession: the present position and strategies for the future' *Information and the library manager* 1(3) December 1981.

5 Estabrook, L and Heim, K M 'A profile of ALA personal members: findings of a new, wide-ranging study of ALA as distinct from the field at large, with comparisons of data for male and female full-time workers' *American libraries* 11 (11) December 1980, 654-659.

6 Wasylycia-Coe, M A 'Profile: Canadian chief librarians by sex' *Canadian library journal* 38 (3) June 1981, 159-163.

7 Jobórú, M 'Women librarians and documentalists in Hungary' *Unesco bulletin for libraries* 29 (6) November-December 1975, 315-318.

8 Lengenfelder, H *World guide to libraries* 5th ed. München, K G Saur, 1980 (Handbook of international documentation and information, vol 8).

9 Boisard, G 'Do women hold the reins of power in French libraries?' *Unesco bulletin for libraries* 29 (6) November-December 1975, 303-314.

10 *Libraries, museums and art galleries yearbook* Cambridge, James Clark, 1971 and *ibid.*, 1976 edition.

11 National Union of Teachers *Promotion and the woman teacher* London, NUT, 1980.

12 Heim, K and Kacena, C 'Sex salaries and library support . . . 1979' *Library journal* 1 January 1980, 17-22.

13 Slater, M *op. cit.*, 131.

14 *Library Association yearbook, 1981.*

15 Library Association *Annual report, 1980* London, Library Association, 1981.

16 Slater, M *op. cit.*, 71.

17 *Ibid.*, 115.

18 Heim, K 'Women in librarianship' *ALA yearbook: a review of library events 1980, volume 6* Chicago, American Library Association, 1981, 299-303.

19 Moon, E E 'Tokenism at the top? Women in minority' *Library journal* 1 October 1965, 4019.

20 Mallory, M and Heim, K *Directory of library and information profession women's groups* Chicago, American Library Association, Standing Committee on the Status of Women in Librarianship, 1981. A new directory, which will be international in scope, is in preparation.

21 Olsgaard, John N and Olsgaard, Jane K 'Authorship in five library periodicals' *College and research libraries* 41 (1) January 1981, 50.

22 Sergean, R *The Sheffield manpower project: a survey of staffing requirements for librarianship and information work. Final report*

Sheffield, University of Sheffield Postgraduate School of Librarianship and Information Science, 1976.

23 Ritchie, S F C *Management training needs of senior public librarians in London boroughs* London, ELM publications, 1979 (Occasional publications, no 2).

24 Jespersen, S 'The problems faced by women in libraries: why we formed a group' *Librarians for social change* 9 (1) no 25, 1981, 3-5, 10 (Special issue entitled 'Women in libraries').

25 Boucias, K 'Been down so long it looks like up to me' *Journal of education for librarianship* 19 1979, 273-278.

26 Cass, F M B 'W(h)ither a female profession?' *Australian library journal* 22 (2) March 1973, 49-55.

Non-professional library staff education:
a state of the art report and proposals for the future

DONALD E DAVINSON

In almost every other professional field clear lines of demarcation, a *modus vivendi* and a qualification structure have been worked out between professionals and their supporting staffs. Whilst it would be wrong to claim that there have not been problems with, say, legal executives vis-à-vis lawyers, accounting staff and accountants and the various auxiliaries to the medical profession and doctors, the system as it has been worked out has operated reasonably smoothly and logically. An important characteristic of most of the developments of technician/ para-professional/auxiliary (the activity is a terminological minefield) has been the active participation of the senior professional bodies in developing associations, qualifications and standards for their support staff.

Until very recently professional librarians in the United Kingdom have taken great care to have nothing at all to do with non-professional staff education, qualifications or associations. As things stand (in 1981) the degree of recognition and assistance to the growth of a separate non-professional staffing category on the part of the professionals as they are represented by the Library Association is small and rather grudging. There is a strong feeling abroad amongst professional librarians in the United Kingdom that non-professional staff are merely people inadequate in some way — educationally or socially — to be professionals and that professional status is the only status that ought to matter. There is, of course, a strong streak of professional protectionism in the attitude and this is a theme which will be returned to later.

In almost every country in which librarianship has developed into a professional (or quasi-professional anyway) activity there has developed a clear system of staffing structures. In North America and Australia library technicians/graduate librarians relationships are, if not always cordial, then at least co-existing. In much of Europe and especially Eastern Europe, the high, middle, low structure of staffing and qualifications is well established. Why is it then that in the United Kingdom

37

there has been so much unwillingness to recognize a stratified system of library staffing structure? It must be suspected that the answer to that question can never fully be understood, so deeply buried is it in professional politics, the incredible maze of professional and graduate qualifications in librarianship in the United Kingdom and the sheer culture of British professional education generally, where the professional associations and corporations have traditionally been so dominant. Whatever the cause the effect has been to degrade almost to the point of total extinction any consideration of non-professional staff training and qualification.

The history of professional education and the non-professional
One of the principal effects of the existence of professional bodies in the United Kingdom holding Royal Charters as independent corporations charged with the regulation of professional qualifications and registration has been that the status of the university graduate *qua* graduate has been distinctly lower than it has traditionally been in many other countries. The operation of educational systems, examinations and qualifications of their own, which even university graduates in appropriate disciplines must take at least part of, has given the British professional corporation a strong independent role which they have not been afraid to prosecute even at the risk of offending the universities.

In any case until recent years the British universities assiduously avoided any teaching which smacked of connections with the world of work and of trade directly. The idea that degree level teaching and qualification could be carried out in vocational areas (other than the Church, law and medicine) came late to the British universities. As a direct consequence of this the characteristic which so frequently has distinguished the line between professionals and non-professional library staffs in other countries has been missing in British practice until recently. It has not been possible to distinguish simply between graduate and non-graduate and be sure of, at the same time, distinguishing between professional and non-professional. In librarianship, as in many other professional fields in the United Kingdom, a great deal of time and energy has been expended upon 'proving' that non-graduates are as good as, if not better, professionals than graduates.

Until the 1960s the number of graduates employed in librarianship in the United Kingdom was very small and principally confined, in terms of proportions compared to other staff, to university libraries. In order to become professional librarians all library staff — even graduates – were obliged to follow courses of study and examinations prescribed by the Library Association. These courses and examinations were designed in such a way that it was the expected thing that they would be pursued part-time and would result in a slow, part by part, accumulation of what modern educational jargon would now term 'credits' or modules. It has to be remembered that until 1946 with the single small exception of the University College of London School of Librarianship there was no full-time education for librarianship. Even after 1946, for many years full-time study at one of the various small, low status schools of librarianship was not common. It was thus the case that a 16 year old entering a library direct from school and a 21 year old graduate straight out of university would be expected to embark upon the same programmes of study to become professionals. It is true that graduates were exempted from a preliminary examination, known at different times as the Entrance, Elementary or First Professional Examination, but that was the only difference and a bright 16/17 year old could complete that preliminary hurdle in one year. The rest of the examinations leading to the Library Association's Registration qualification could then take three to five or more years.

The importance of detailing the historical situation of the aspiring professional librarian so fully is to make the point that from the inception of the Library Association's examining system in 1885 until about 1965 library staffs in the United Kingdom, speaking very generally, consisted of two categories. There were professional librarians, most of whom were non-graduate accumulators of the professional qualifications in the mode described above, and there were library assistants, many of whom were in the process of accumulating their professional qualifications. There was, in other words, a homogeneity of interest and aim in all library staff. Those who were not professionals were aspiring professionals (or anyway had the means to be; it would be wrong to imply that all took up the option, but many did). Library assistants in pursuit of professional status acquired, as the years passed and their 'credits' grew, increasing knowledge, expertise and, most importantly, increasing professionalism of approach and attitude. They were, it was true, still library assistants but they were library assistants who had in common with the professional staff an approach, a study system and a knowledge base comprehensible to all. They knew each other's minds as it were. The professionals had emerged from the same chrysalis of evening classes, summer schools and correspondence course study. The library assistants knew that, given attention to their studies they would

39

ultimately emerge into the full plumage of the professionals they worked with.

There was another and even more significant condition which arose out of the historic qualification situation. This was that the aspiring professionals giving up leisure time, spending their own money which was not available in any great quantity (library assistants were very poorly paid) tended to be contemptuous of any of their number who, for whatever reason, decided not to do so. An *esprit de corps* arose amongst the dedicated which set them somewhat apart from the rest. This had two important effects upon staffing structures, one immediately in the 1940s, fifties and sixties when they were studying and one delayed as a culture effect until the present day. The immediate effect was that library staffing structures had in their lower ranks a valuable cementing force of people who were fully acceptable to their peers and their superiors. To the one group they were the vanguard of a category to which they all potentially belonged — aspirants to professional status — and therefore an inspiration and a source of assistance and advice. To the professionals the aspirants had an outlook and norms similar to their own and were extremely useful sort of people to have around the library. They were usually adaptable, eager for experience and willing to accept responsibility without any nagging about pay, conditions of service or tendencies to demarcation disputes. They were people to whom the task of day to day library operation and the supervision of their own junior colleagues could, largely, safely be left.

The delayed culture effect referred to above which now so sours discussion about non-professional staff training in many professional librarianship quarters in the United Kingdom is that, despite the manifest changes in the structure of employment, education and society which have been wrought in the past twenty years, many professional librarians are constitutionally unable to adjust to the realization that there are now inevitably two cultures not one. The lack of respect they had twenty years ago for those of their peer group who did not pursue their studies or become activists in professional associations has tended to rub off upon present day non-professionals who, for various reasons, do not have the opportunity to undertake professional studies anyway! Much of the current resistance to the concept of non-professional library staff training which is so manifest could well be subconscious amongst the more senior ranks of professional librarians. Amongst the more junior professional ranks there is not so much a resistance to non-professional staff training as incomprehension of the need arising out of the fact that they have often never experienced the state themselves, for during the 1960s the professional education scene in librarianship radically changed in conformity to more general trends in higher education in the United Kingdom. To the extent that it has tended to remove any incentive for development of the junior levels of staffing it cannot be said unequivocally that the changes have been totally for the better. There is a cleavage between the group norms of profesisonal and non-professional staff in some libraries these days which borders on the alarming.

The present situation of non-professional staff
Changes in society and educational opportunity in the 1960s together with a period of full employment and rising expectations on the part of school leavers had its effect upon library staff structuring. Coincident with the introduction of a new syllabus in 1964 by a Library Association determined to shift the focus on professional education into a full-time setting in strong, large schools of librarianship attached to prestigious educational institutions, was an increase in the number of graduates being produced by the academic system. More of these graduates were finding their way into librarianship and, indeed, as attitudes to vocational education were changing, degree level studies in librarianship were established and grew apace. After a somewhat bloody battle (often fought through the correspondence columns of the *Library Association record* in a way which must have been perplexing to any foreign readers for whom the battle was a non-issue) graduate entry to the profession became the established means and the ability of anyone not equipped by virtue of school-level qualifications to enter undergraduate education to become a professional librarian was virtually extinguished.

As time passed and the new ways became embedded the likelihood that a person employed as a non-professional library staff member having any but the most elementary of school-leaving qualifications became uncommon. No longer were today's perspiring counter assistants tomorrow's aspiring professionals. In these circumstances the need to ensure that library assistants receive adequate training and are provided with the incentives by way of an explicit promotion ladder based upon evidence of commitment and achievement as measured by educational successes could be thought of as essential. In fact not a great deal of effort has been injected into any formal systems of education and qualification for library assistants and it cannot be said that all libraries have recognized that they have any formal obligations for on-

41

the-job training of their library assistants. Perhaps the preoccupation with the way in which professional education was being restructured so occupied the corporate professional mind that there was little time left for thinking about the non-professional in any but the most perfunctory manner in the context of teaching them how to do the particular jobs of the individual library department.

In terms of evolving strategies for the training and development of their non-professional colleagues the record of British professional librarianship is not good. The waste of resources, the damage to the public relations with the library's users and the frustration of non-professional staff arising out of the lack of attention to informing them of the broader issues and role of libraries must be considerable. That there is no lack of enthusiasm amongst non-professional library staff for their own development and finding out more of the 'why's' of the job was evidenced by the private report produced by Judith Bowen wherein she held interviews with a large number of non-professional library staff, all of whom expressed a desire to know more about the reasons why they did things.[1] The way in which many library assistants have undertaken studies leading to the City and Guilds 737 Library Assistants' Certificate, despite knowing that it leads nowhere in particular for them in terms of advancement, is further evidence of the high motivation many of them have for improving their skills.

In academic libraries, especially university libraries in the United Kingdom, there has always been an explicit but limited career ladder for non-professionals in many libraries. They have provided the closest approach to the typical European pattern of tiers of staff graded according to qualification level. In such libraries, it is true, the tendency was to consider all 'professional' librarians qualified under Library Association examination schemes as senior non-professionals presiding over and supervising a clerical grade, usually female, and usually expected to be transient and therefore not worth the effort of training. The university libraries actually expected to be able to pick up most staff in these grades already at least semi-trained through offering better pay and conditions than local public libraries and, thereby, poaching staff from them. This view of the status, training needs and prospects of non-professionals came out very strongly in the proceedings of the one day conference at the School of Librarianship, Leeds Polytechnic in 1976 edited by Davinson.[2] University representatives present appeared to have some difficulty in grasping what the concept of non-professional library staff was, let alone discussing their training needs. That the

42

situation is changing even in such libraries is evident from the work of David Baker and his colleagues in developing, at Leicester University Library, a very elaborate scheme of training for non-professional staff.[3]

Special libraries have, by their nature, a particular need for effective non-professional staff. Their usually small staff size makes imperative the need for all staff whether professional or not to be able to carry out a wide range of functions effectively. The environment in which they exist is often one in which the technologist/technician or manager/ supervisor/clerk relationships are carefully structured and interdependent. It is small special libraries which are in difficulty, however, in relation to releasing staff for formal off-the-job training or even in having the time and resources to engage in a structured programme of in-service training. The uniqueness of the operations of many special libraries means that the skills acquired by non-professional library staff in the conduct of their day to day duties are not always so readily interchangeable as those of, say, public and academic library non-professionals. Without access to an explicit system of training and qualifications the prospects of such staff should they need to move are very limited.

In public libraries the problems of non-professional staff training are many. It is amongst this group that the widest range of conflicting attitudes exist as to the need for any training system. It is amongst this group that there is the most concern that an explicit system of qualification and training for non-professionals would result in a diminution of the opportunities available for professionals. Ever since the Library Association's public library centenary document on standards which postulated a 40% professional 60% non-professional staff complement in public libraries it has been a problem finding suitably professional employment for the 40%.[4] The Library Association has itself somewhat unconvincingly tried to separate out professional and non-professional work.[5]

Some public librarians are worried that formal recognition of some sort of technician grade for library staff would persuade their employers that there was less need for the employment of large numbers of relatively more expensive professionals. In one sense they are right to be concerned. Not every British public library has taken steps to ensure that the various grades of staff are being economically and appropriately employed and their staffing arrangements would not withstand investigation by an impartial outsider. Other public libraries, notably Surrey County Library, have consciously made the move into larger numbers of properly trained and renumerated semi-professionals (technicians/supervisors or whatever title is thought most appropriate in the absence of an accepted one) and fewer, more organized, professionals. It seems to make a lot of sense in the context of public library operations but is bad news for schools of librarianship! It is a concept which has been most rigorously examined in recent years by Charlotte Mugnier, whose remarks, though American in context, are universally apposite.[6]

Other objections to non-professional staff training centre on the fact that many of them are in employment for only a short time and that high turnover of staff implies substantial waste of training resources. It is also argued that in periods when training budgets are so restricted due to an adverse economic climate the resources which are available ought to be devoted to developing professional staff. The fact that non-professional staff timetables are difficult to arrange, given the long opening hours many libraries operate upon, and that any further complicating factors arising out of training release would be intolerable, is also a frequently quoted reason for not undertaking such activity.

The need for non-professional staff training
The apparently strong desires to learn more about the background to their work on the part of non-professional staff discovered by Judith Bowen have already been referred to. What is particularly striking about much of the relatively small amounts of literature available on the subject is that the major theme the literature explores is the mechanisms of training. It is how much training, whether on-the-job or off-the-job, what sort of qualifications, examinations and content of programmes and whether there ought to be a general education component as well as a specifically librarianship component which fills the literature. There is little or no attention given to the purpose and outcomes of such training. It is also noteworthy that most contributions to the literature are by professionals who write about the problem from their point of view and with the implicit feeling that what is best for them will have to be best for the non-professional.

Perhaps it is in the nature of things that almost nothing has been written in British librarianship literature about the problem seen through non-professional staff eyes. This is perhaps understandable because there is no obvious forum for such writing as there is in North America where the various associations of non-professional librarians have their own journals. Until something similar emerges in the United

44

Kingdom the emphasis upon structure and form rather than need and purpose will continue.

Looking at need from a purely utilitarian standpoint is sufficient to justify an adequate programme of on- and off-the-job training. When all kinds of political, economic and technological forces are conspiring to dilute the professional input into the public service aspects of library work it is imperative that the non-professional staff to whom the job is bequeathed, willy-nilly, must be appropriately informed as to their role. On a more elevated plane than the utilitarian it is surely a moral requirement to ensure that employees are given every opportunity to improve their skills, career prospects and, thereby, their job satisfaction. Those librarians who are lukewarm about the need for non-professional staff development on the grounds of their high turnover and low return on effort invested may perhaps be missing the point. High turnover may well be a consequence of low motivation. In its turn low motivation could well arise out of lack of opportunity for development, poor career structures and a feeling of being undervalued by professional colleagues. High turnover may be an effect rather than a causal justification for lack of effort in non-professional staff training.

It seems a fair bet that into the forseeable future there will be no expansion of resources available to libraries. There may be more contraction to come. On the sheer basis that every effort must be made to maximize the effectiveness of the available human resources the case that there is a need for non-professional library staff training is made. What ought to be the nature and purposes of the training to be given is a very complex question.

Nature and purposes of training
It is very tempting to argue that the nature of the training given ought to be such that any non-professional can be facilitated to reach full professional status. A nostalgic and romantic view of the past such as that presented earlier would argue that this would be an ideal to be achieved. It ought certainly to be an objective of all education that it opens doors to other things and facilitates upward mobility. Whether the primary objective of training non-professional library staff ought to be to enable them ultimately to become professionals is very questionable. It is a striking feature of any conversation with library technicians in North American libraries that many of them have consciously chosen that status and have a conviction that it carried itself sufficient satis-

45

faction, job content and, perhaps most significantly, status and career prospects to make it a worthwhile occupation in its own right with no need to aspire to any other status. Perhaps even more striking is the high regard in which their professional colleagues hold the library technicians. Insecurity bred out of the vague and shadowy nature of their own supposedly professional status does not always lead young professionals in British libraries to accord the more senior non-professional staff similar respect.

The nature, then, of non-professional staff training must rest surely upon the conviction that there is an integrity about the work they do which is sufficiently significant for a separate and distinct approach to be made to training and education. There is a great deal of conflicting opinion about the most valuable purposes of training. Whether the stress needs to be laid upon training in the specific drills, skills and routines of a particular library or upon a broader awareness of the scope and function of libraries and the world of information generally is hotly debated whenever the question is raised.

Even more contentious is whether library staff ought to undertake programmes which broaden their general education and stimulate their intellectual development as well as updating their librarianship skills and knowledge. An even more esoteric argument occasionally advanced is that library staff ought to be encouraged only to develop their more general education on the premise that the range of library skills they are expected to undertake are unlikely ever to be too demanding not to be quickly acquired and it is more important for them to work at their general development as people, to widen their horizons beyond a dead end job.

Properly undertaken a programme of library and related studies ought, however, to un-deaden the ends without resorting to the latter expedient and be demanding enough to be stimulating. It was clear in the 1976 Leeds Polytechnic seminar that it was very difficult indeed to legislate for all types and sizes of library in one scheme of non-professional training. Public libraries are, these days, parts of large organizations with central training schemes which, some librarians believe, in concert with their own in-library training, are sufficiently comprehensive to rule out the need for any formal programmes emanating from outside their authorities. On the other hand many special libraries are so small in themselves and so uniquely specialized within their organizations that there is no opportunity for them to carry out all the necessary training in-house. Academic libraries vary in size and purpose

46

so much that it is difficult for a generalized view of their needs to emerge.

Discussions of the nature and purposes of education of non-professional staff almost inevitably degenerate into arguments about means and structures. The lack of any consensus between the representatives of different types of library as to the best means of forwarding a generally applicable formal scheme usually arises out of a desire, which is perhaps natural enough, to ensure that their own needs are made paramount. It is a natural enough desire until it is appreciated that it takes little account of the needs of the individual non-professional assistants involved in these various libraries.

The needs of the individual in the training process

The selfish needs of the individual librarian in the guise of an employer of library assistants would be, if stated at their most extreme, to acquire staff who needed as little time and effort invested in them as possible in order to become competent enough to discharge specific duties satisfactorily. Ideally no time and effort at all would be best! Given, however, that such an ideal is, practically speaking, unattainable the next objective of the selfish employer must be to ensure that any time and effort invested pays off quickly. To this end the employer is likely to argue that the need is for training in the routines of their own library and no more. In the viewpoint of the individual library assistant the perceived need might be wider than that. They might wish to know more about the context in which the individual library is placed – a concept the narrowly self-interested employer might not agree with. The individual might have another need which is unperceived by them until they wish to move from their job for some reason or another. This need could be for some form of training which had fitted them for employment elsewhere and, perhaps, provided them with some form of paper certification of competence recognizable and acceptable to potential employers.

The narrowly self-interested employers who argue that internal, specific job-directed training is all that is required would deny any responsibility for needing to equip an assistant for wider acceptability of their training. They might even argue that any training is a waste of effort if it encourages people to move on. There is, it is true, a certain altruism in all training in the sense that only some of it will rebound to the benefit of the organization whilst the rest benefits the individual receiving it and society in general.

47

At the risk of appearing male chauvinistic it can be said that these days the vast majority off library assistants will be female who are either now, or will at some future date, be mobile as a result of the job of their male partner. In this context the need of the individual is for the acquisition of skills and expertise which can be transferable to other jobs in other places if the need arises. Such transferability is unlikely to arise out of the training programmes of narrowly self-interested employers who train internally for the purposes of their own needs. Transferability is more likely to arise out of the kinds of training programmes mounted by educational establishments and professional bodies who train staff on behalf of employers and, perhaps, provide certification of skills achieved which have a national or even an international currency. It is the structures of how such forms of certification might be made to conform to the needs of employers of librarians which have dominated such debate as has taken place on the subject of non-professional library staff training. The views of the staff themselves or any consideration of their needs and even the objectives of the training have taken second place.

Who shall do the training and how?

When the question of how to organize and operate a system of non-professional library staff training separate and distinct from the examinations leading to professional status was first seriously raised in the mid 1960s the Library Association was in process of disengaging itself from a role it has held for nearly eighty years as virtually the sole provider of certification. Power and influence were being devolved upon the schools of librarianship to examine their own students and indeed to devise their own syllabuses within carefully determined limits in accordance with overall structures laid down by the Association. The schools of librarianship were also in fact laying plans to cut out the Library Association completely by operating their own system of degrees in librarianship. For these, and some other reasons, therefore, the Library Association was not interested in saddling itself with responsibilities for non-professional certification at that time.

One of the problems for non-professional training needs which arose out of the institution of a revised syllabus by the Library Association in 1964 was that the variously named Entrance/Elementary/First Professional Examination was discontinued in favour of direct entry to the Final Parts I and II on the basis of Advanced General Certificate of Education school-leaving qualifications. Although not intended as such

48

the earlier syllabuses with their preliminary examination in elementary library practices had been extensively used as a sort of non-professional staff training scheme. Large numbers of library assistants studied for and ultimately passed the Entrance (etc) Examination who did not proceed any further with professional studies. There was an extensive network of evening institutes and colleges offering this course of study which did not offer preparation for any parts of the rest of the Library Association's examinations.

For many libraries, and especially perhaps small special libraries, this initial Library Association examination was used as a sort of basic training arrangement adequate enough for enabling them to offer some recognition of competence to successful students in the form of limited promotion or additional increments. In effect, the examination was used by some employers of librarians as a self-sufficient, free-standing non-professional qualification conferring some benefits on both student and employer. As it was the only 'qualification' of its kind it had some sort of limited national recognition. Job advertisements, for example, sometimes specified that applicants must have passed the appropriate examination.

With the cessation of the programme by the Library Association a gap developed in the system as many employers were used to seeing it and the demand arose for a repalcement. As indicated above the Library Association was not interested, being concerned to make itself exclusively interested in professional certification of other organizations' educational efforts. With some informal assistance from the Library Association, however, an approach to the City and Guilds of London Institute resulted in the establishment of a Library Assistants' Certificate course under their aegis. The City and Guilds of London Institute has traditionally been the premier examining body for technician-level education and certification in a huge number of fields and it is interesting to contemplate the introductory statement to the syllabus which was ultimately devised by a group under the Chairmanship of Mr K A Mallaber (who was senior member of the Library Association's Board of Assessors at the time, incidentally, and who played a significant part in the production of their new syllabus in 1964).

The introduction opened: 'This scheme for courses of part-time study and related examinations is intended for those people employed in libraries and information bureaux in a non-professional capacity, who do not aim at professional status. Its purpose is to provide a basic qualification in library practice and its underlying principles with

49

emphasis upon practical skills. The scheme is not intended to provide an alternative method of entry to the examinations of the Library Association. In addition to the syllabus General Studies are included in order to develop the student's ability to absorb, interpret and transmit information, whether in spoken or written form, and to contribute to their general education and personal development. The scheme has been designed to be complementary to the training and experience students will be obtaining in their employment'.[7]

This introduction very clearly places the context upon the scheme and also indicates its limitation. Being unconnected with any other scheme of examination or qualification in librarianship there was no means for further advancement, should the student wish it, for which the certificate would be acceptable. To that extent it represented something of a dead end even though it proved to be a demanding enough course. Employers were distinctly variable in their approach to recognition of the qualification. A few were willing to make it an essential requirement for promotion to supervisory grades, others (though not too many) were willing to award extra salary increments to successful students. For most purposes, however, it became simply a course of study the keen well motivated library assistants could take out of interest and personal enthusiasm not recognized in any formal way by their employers other than that in some cases they had been willing to grant time off to students to undertake the studies. In many (perhaps most) cases students have been entirely self-starting and self-supporting in their enterprise.

Perhaps between 500 and 700 people a year have undertaken studies leading to the examination since its inception in 1967 and there is enough steam left in it for the Institute to have deemed it worthwhile to revise the syllabus in 1982. To this end a working party under the chairmanship of the author has been at work since June 1980 undertaking the thorough revision of a programme which has also, in fact, proved attractive to many overseas students.

Given the lack of any overt official support from the Library Association and other related professional bodies and the variability of the recognition by individual employers — evidence, no doubt, of the indifference to non-professional needs by professional librarians in the United Kingdom — the scheme must be rated a modest success even though it leads nowhere in particular for most people. The geographical 'take up' in terms of centres offering courses of study leading to the examinations is distinctly 'spotty' with by no means every large centre

50

of population and library having easy access to a course.

Successful maintenance of programmes in any given centre has often owed more to the energy and enthusiasm of one or two individual working librarians willing to give up large amounts of their free time to the teaching of the programme in local colleges than to any clear commitment on the part of official bodies. To many employers and individual students it has been a course of study better than nothing at all rather than a positively recognized beneficial scheme in its own right. This is unfortunate given the numbers of students who have now been through the programme and the undoubted merits of much of the teaching that has been administered and the support of the City and Guilds of London Institute.

Perhaps the most significant achievement of the programme so far (and as has been hinted above it is still very vigorous) has been to keep the flag of non-professional library staff training flying throughout a period when professional librarians have been involved to the point almost of obsession with professional education and its problems. It has even been possible to demonstrate that the certificate need not necessarily be a dead end. Experimental and tentative moves to enrol a number of mature students with substantial library experience and holding the certificate in the Honours Degree course in Librarianship at Leeds Polytechnic, even though they lacked any other formal academic qualifications have, thus far, proved very successful indeed. Such students have proved well able to cope with the rigorous theoretical approach of a degree course and have considerably more staying power than most students.

The resurgence of interest in non-professional training
The lonely flag flown by the City and Guilds of London Institute has now been joined by others. The growth of interest in the problems of non-professional staff training arose, in part at least, rather paradoxically. During much of the 1970s the Library Association had somewhat tense working parties sitting to determine the future shape of professional education. Two aspects of the problem occupied their attention. Firstly, the future of their own system of qualifications in a world increasingly filled with graduates of all kinds, including librarianship. Secondly, the difficulties caused for professional muscle power in pay negotiations and job opportunities of a surplus of qualified staff leaving schools of librarianship. Both issues led to a considerable amount of discussion about the future shape of the personnel market in librarianship.

51

Inevitably this led to discussion about the need for training opportunities for non-professional staff as a by-product of the consideration of the numbers and nature of staff in various grades which would be needed.

At the time the Library Association's Future of Qualifications Working Party was sitting the Business Education Council (BEC) came into being as a national (England and Wales) agency for sub-professional awards in the business, social sciences and legal fields. A parallel organization for technical education (TEC) was also established and Scottish equivalents SCOTBEC and SCOTEC came into being. They appeared to offer prospects for the creation of non-professional qualifications in librarianship with a wider acceptability and more flexibility than the City and Guilds Certificate. In fact it was the Scots who entered the field first with a Certificate course in Library and Information Science at Telford College of Further Education, Edinburgh, offered under the aegis of SCOTEC. Confusingly it was with BEC, the Business Education Council, that discussions were held in England and Wales.

The Business Education Council initiative and opposition to it
The discussions of the Library Association's Future of Qualifications Working Party had included some consideration of the possibility of the Library Association operating its own system of non-professional library staff certification. The possibility was decisively rejected by the working party on the grounds, firstly, that the Association did not wish to re-enter the field of administering examinations and, secondly, that a greater service would be done to prospective students of such awards through being tied to a nationally recognized system extending beyond the narrow confines of librarianship. To an extent the City and Guilds connection had done that but the great virtue seen in the BEC schemes was that they provided an extended ladder of six qualification steps starting at a level requiring nothing in the way of formal qualifications for entry, known as a General Certificate, and ending at an equivalent of an unclassified degree, known as a Higher Diploma.

With the problem of the apparently closed-ended City and Guilds Certificate before them the Working Party's imagination was gripped by the dual prospect of a progressive scheme of education, training and qualification which offered a viable opportunity for effective and self-sufficient non-professional certification and scope for easy translation of successful students to professional programmes in librarian-

52

ship or indeed, degrees of any kind. It was at the heart of the BEC/ TEC structures that they could easily be related to the kinds of entry qualifications traditionally required for undergraduate study so that their opportunity ladder could, for the very enterprising and determined, stretch out to the top of the academic tree. The two councils had been established to coordinate and make coherent in one set of awards a mass of pre-existing awards. To this extent it implied that the awards would be instantly recognizable wherever presented in the world of business, industry and the government service. Thus, it was felt, that the creation of a non-professional award under BEC aegis would afford library assistants great flexibility in moving from job to job carrying a qualification whose designation and merits relative to other staff in a given organization was instantly recognized in personnel offices. A constant problem to library staff, especially in industry and commerce, has always been that their qualifications and work experience have had an uncomfortable uniqueness not readily assimilated by organizations dealing with few librarians but large numbers of other people with more standardized qualification systems.

The Business Education Council's structure requires that studies should be undertaken in three sections.

1 Common core
2 Board core
3 Options

The common core element is an obligatory study, to be undertaken by all students, in general business studies and organizations. The board core elements refer to a group of more specialized studies related to social services, legal studies etc, depending upon the broad area of activity under which prospective students are employed in their everyday work. The options relate specifically to the specialism of students as, say, police, insurance officials, hospital administrators, social workers or librarians, for example.

The Library Association decided that it was the middle two of the six awards available — the National Certificate and Diploma Awards — which were most appropriate to the needs of library staffs. The National Awards are roughly of equivalent level to the General Certificate of Education University/Higher Education entry standards. The designators 'Certificate' and 'Diploma' have no significance as denominators of attainment standards but are applied respectively to qualifications gained by part or full-time study. The full-time Diploma Studies are in fact somewhat broader having a larger number of option

53

modules in their make-up. A proposed module for the two option modules in librarianship was designed and submitted to BEC for comment. It was at this point that considerable opposition both to the whole concept of non-professional education in general and specifically to the BEC model in particular arose within Library Association politics. The opposition to the BEC proposal was the most serious element and its instigators appealed to the self-interest of librarians as employers which was referred to earlier. Their objections were that the common core/board core obligatory prescriptions within the BEC National Awards meant that relatively little of the studies undertaken would be specifically library orientated. In round numbers one quarter of the total syllabus covered would be general business education. The aim of creating a unified body of experience and training in all non-professional/semi-professional staff in the wide field of business and government which was at the heart of the BEC philosophy has been decisively rejected by the opposition lobby within librarianship. It would have none of the proposition that it was in the best interests of young library assistants to broaden and generalize their education in the interests of increased flexibility of career opportunity now and in the future. The image of a married woman, returning to the world of work after a period of family rearing, carrying with her widely recognized evidence of a general business education meant nothing to the narrowly self-interested, looking for highly specific librarianship-only training. If the Business Education Council could not, or would not, provide this then, said the anti-lobby, it should be dropped and a Library Association sponsored certificate introduced instead.

Rather ironically the main centre of the opposition sprang from the Library Association's own Industrial Group. Of all segments of the librarianship world it had always been special librarians who had had most difficulty in securing recognition of their Library Association-based qualifications in industry and whose assistants were virtually alone, of all employees in a particular business, in having no nationally recognized opportunities for qualification and certification appropriate to their needs. The Industrial Group devised their own proposals for a purely librarianship/information work scheme of study which, of itself, was unexceptionable other than it was rather heavily biased in favour of the more specialist libraries and would hardly have appealed to other types of library. It also required that the Library Association re-establish an examinations section at a cost which was not estimated to undertake a body of work whose size was not quantified.

54

To its great credit the Library Association Council despite fierce opposition (and not only from their Industrial Group) persevered with its negotiations with the Business Education Council and brought the proposal for Librarianship option modules into fruition in 1978-1979 and a number of colleges are now offering them. It is quite true that BEC insists upon a heavy load of general business education in its awards. What the opponents of cooperation with BEC failed to appreciate, or failed to say if they did appreciate it, was that substantial amounts of the supposedly non-librarianship components of the general business core and the board core have considerable relevance to librarianship, indeed they are widely taught in professional librarianship courses as they exist in degree and post-graduate diploma and degree programmes. These components cover such aspects as human relations and inter-personal skills, communications skills, office organization, elementary accounting and financial procedures. None of these items is totally irrelevant to librarianship, some of them are usually carried out badly in libraries. A knowledge of the organizational structures of national and local government and the world of business generally is also taught on BEC courses as an obligatory element but it is hard indeed to argue that it is totally useless knowledge for a library assistant to possess! The opposition was not always fully informed and was sometimes less than honest in its manipulation of its case to fit the known prejudices of some librarians against non-professional staff training.

One element in the Industrial Group's case which did, however, touch a sensitive spot was its point that undesirable duplication of effort was threatened by a proliferation of qualifications and study schemes for non-professionals. This is, indeed, a problem and one which could become worse if successful candidates for one of the existing awards – City and Guilds Certificate, BEC National, SCOTEC National – wish to have a higher award available to them as, indeed, some already would like.

Present and future position of non-professional courses already approved
The situation as it now stands is that the City and Guilds Certificate courses cover a period of approximately one academic year (some courses are slightly longer, and shorter) and although there is a mandatory element of general education studies in the programme amounting to about a third of the whole (a fact ignored or suppressed by the shrill critics of the BEC non-librarianship elements) the programme is princi-

pally of study in librarianship. Although the City and Guilds of London Institute specifies no pre-entry qualifications are necessary they do recommend that candidates should be at least 19 years old at the time of the examination and have at least two years library experience. In effect the programme is one which satisfies the apparent requirement of some employers that it is librarianship and only librarianship which library assistants should study if they are to be released for off-the-job training.

The Working Party set up by the Institute in 1980 to revise the syllabus and reorganize the assessment procedures undertook a great deal of background research to ascertain how the programme was currently taught and to whom. A total of seven hundred and thirty questionnaires were sent out to libraries from which students came and tutors employed to teach them. More than half of the questionnaires were returned − a satisfactory response rate to a postal questionnaire.

The research revealed that the often repeated assertion that the Certificate had a bias towards public libraries in terms of student take up and of syllabus prescribed was borne out by the replies but not decisively so. Some centres taught only non-public library staff and were satisfied that the syllabus was flexible enough to deal with that situation. It was suspected by the working party that the bias, such as it was, may well have been generated by the way the syllabus was taught and as a result of course publicity in some areas generating largely public library staff which made any non-public library personnel recruited feel that the course had a bias even if it did not.

One of the most startling revelations was the wide range discovered in input of teaching hours − from eighty-two to two hundred and twenty. Careful centre-by-centre surveying of the examination results revealed that the wide variations of teaching input did not materially affect examination success rates. The norm of teaching input discovered was one hundred and twenty hours a year. It is at this level that the working party established their marker in determining the amount of material to be included in the new syllabus revision. Many respondents to the questionnaire asserted that the Certificate course needed to be strengthened and significantly added to. Had the extremes of the suggestions for revision been adopted the programme would have needed to be a full-time one of at least one year duration with a very large assessment/examination scheme.

The working party also noted a very strong, if minority, call for an advanced certificate to follow on from the current award and perhaps offer opportunities to specialize in one type of library operation — public, academic or special. The working party was very sensitive to the fact that however desirable a lengthening, strengthening and deepening of syllabus content might be, the various constraints upon libraries was such that it was unlikely that any call for increased amounts of release for off-the-job training would be welcomed and any attempt to do so would be self-defeating. Whilst the call for advanced Certificates was strong, it was not sufficiently so to justify the effort which would be involved in setting them up. It was, in any case, in the minds of the working party that the BEC proposals, which were beginning to come to fruition whilst they were sitting could well ultimately result in an advanced provision being avilable there which it would be pointless to duplicate.

The Business Education Council scheme is, in its general application, now well established. The introduction of a librarianship package has had the full backing of the Library Association's Professional Development and Education Committee who have established an Advisory Panel on BEC. This official adoption of the new BEC scheme by the Library Association contrasts with the somewhat more distant relationship they have adopted to the older City and Guilds scheme where they have had only one nominee (appointed in his own right not as a Library Association delegate) on the revision Working Party. Happily, though coincidentally, this nominee was Derek Jones, Borough Librarian of Richmond-upon-Thames, who was subsequently appointed chairman of the Advisory Panel on BEC and who is a former chairman of the Library Association's Education Committee.

It is too early yet to judge the effectiveness of the BEC approach to non-professional library staff training. The unfortunate circumstance of the programme being introduced at a time of deep economic recession in the United Kingdom which has seriously affected the willingness and ability of all employers to support training programmes anyway has distorted the picture. Ultimately, assuming the eventual up-swing in the economy, it is possible to expect that the BEC approach to non-professional staff training could be successful. Over the whole field of business and technical education there are now few colleges of further education in the country which are not operating BEC/TEC or their Scottish counterpart schemes. One of the problems the City and Guilds Certificate has faced is that as a free-standing programme it runs into difficulties of logistics.

The economics of further education college life and the regulations of the government's Department of Education and Science (DES) Inspectorate of Schools and Colleges dictate that unless a regular and substantial flow of prospective students can be assured over many years it is not possible to establish a teaching centre for any course. The DES Inspectorate specify an intake target of between fifteen and twenty-four students a year as being the minimum necessary to set up a programme in any given centre. Effectively this has limited the prospects of establishing a City and Guilds 737 Library Assistants' Certificate course teaching centre to the very large centres of population with a good hinterland of student catchment. It has been, and will continue to be, a serious constraint upon the development of the programme. Large areas of the country and substantial numbers of potential students will always be outside of the geographical range of viable teaching centres for the free-standing programme. This need not be the case for the BEC scheme.

In terms of logistics the Business Education network (and therefore by analogy the SCOTEC scheme in Scotland) has powerful advantages. Being designed as a compendium programme for the whole of Business Education in the sense of providing, through the common core and board core elements, a basic framework of generally useful business training upon which specialisms can then be hung it greatly improves the ability of even small colleges in relatively isolated centres of population to operate effectively. The core elements are operated in all BEC schemes for the benefit of every student regardless of employment background – insurance, banking, accounting, law, transport, social services, national and local government – and libraries. There can be few centres of population which do not offer the prospect of the generation of large numbers of students in such a wide area.

Only the question of the ability to support relevant specialist options need be considered as a constraint. It is in this area that the DES rules operate in favour of the BEC scheme and against the City and Guilds scheme. It is the whole BEC programme in a particular college which is regarded as the free-standing course for purposes of the operation of the intake numbers constraints. There are regulations for options within a particular scheme which lay down that eight to twelve students will be sufficient to operate any given option in any given year. This implies the possibility of extending the range of centres in which non-professional library staff training is viable especially since it is possible, given the fact that the BEC National Award Programme is a maximum of two years in duration, to offer a librarianship option

58

once in two years only and thus doubling up on the prospective number of students available.

For the reasons of geography and economics indicated above it is possible to infer that despite the vehement opposition in some quarters within librarianship to the attachment of a library studies element to the BEC scheme there are reasonable prospects for its ultimate success. It might be that the success depends less upon absolute conviction that it is the best solution to the off-the-job training needs of non-professional library staff than upon the appreciation that as the only one available in a given area it is better than nothing at all. Since this has been the motivation leading many towards the pre-existing City and Guilds Certificate courses this may seem a somewhat negative thought but geography and educational logistics are against librarianship in seeking other solutions to their off-the-job training needs.

The needs of the job, especially of county public library staff and many special library personnel, often dictate that they be stationed away from the large population centres where viable courses of a more specialist nature would be feasible. There is also the thought, discussed earlier, that the more specialist courses are not necessarily best for the student even if thought to be so by their employers.

Making the best of a bad job with the City and Guilds Certificate as an introductory programme for library assistants with little or no formal educational attainments followed by a BEC National Award, where they might be joined by library assistants with a higher initial level of school leaving qualifications, could perhaps become the pattern for the future. It is too early to tell.

What is not too early to tell is that formal off-the-job education and training for library assistants in the United Kingdom is at least on the move, albeit in a halting, stumbling, confusing way so typical of British education (and, dare it be said, British librarianship?) Taking a line from experience in other countries what is needed now is that a forum be established for the organization of non-professional library staff activity and defence of interests. An informal Library Assistants' Certificate Tutors Discussion Group generated out of City and Guilds Certificate teaching has done valuable work in this context. It is now in process of broadening its interests to cover all forms of non-professional education. Its members have been active in helping to generate much needed teaching texts for the specific needs of non-professionals.

The Library Association itself is considering the possibility of establishing a special membership grade tentatively entitled 'Technician

Grade'. It is a welcome gesture but in view of the history of indifference and considerable disunity of view on the subject within the Library Association membership, library assistants might be advised to have a completely separate organization of their own instead of, or in addition to, such a Library Association Technican Grade.

References

1 Bowen, J *Perceptions about training needs and further qualifications amongst non-professional staff in a public library* Leeds, Leeds Polytechnic School of Librarianship, 1977. (Private report not available for general circulation.)

2 Davinson, D E *Library staff training: the problem of non-professional staff training* Leeds, Leeds Polytechnic School of Librarianship, 1977.

3 Baker, D *Junior staff training* Leicester, Library Association, University College and Research Section (East Midlands Branch), 1980.

4 Library Association *Century of public libraries* London, Library Association, 1950.

5 Library Association *Professional and non-professional duties in libraries*, 2nd ed. London, Library Association, 1974.

6 Mugnier, C *The paraprofessional and the professional job structure* Chicago, American Library Association, 1980.

7 Quoted in L J Taylor *A librarian's handbook* London, Library Association, 1976, 598. The complete text of the regulations and syllabus is reproduced in this work.

Additional reference C Harrison and R Oates *The basics of librarianship* London, Library Association, 1980.

Management and the meaning of work
BOB USHERWOOD

'The belief that money is the sole or even the most important of several motives for work, is so foolish that anyone who seriously holds this opinion is thereby rendered incapable of understanding either industry or the industrial worker.'[1]

'People who speak grandiosely of the "meaning of work" should spend a year or two in a factory ... Work at factory level has no inherent value. The worker's one interest is in his pay packet.'[2]

'Frankly I hate work. Of course I could also say with equal truth that I love work, that it is a supremely interesting activity.'[3]

'For the most part, work for the majority is little more than an irksome pre-condition for the real business of living.'[4]

Most introductory courses in library management introduce, sometimes re-introduce, participants to the motivational theories developed by Maslow, Herzberg and others. My own courses are no exception. There can be little doubt that these theories do provide useful insights as to why people work and that as such they are of real value to the practising manager. However over the years I have become increasingly concerned that these well-known, and often repeated, theories of motivation provide only a part of the answer to the question – 'Why do people work?' In this contribution I want to explain my unease at an over-reliance on motivation theories and to indicate the practical implications and advantages of adopting a broader view of people's work orientation.

The meaning of work
The quotations at the head of this chapter demonstrate the problem of suggesting a definitive meaning of work for the worker. The final statement for example suggests that work, for the majority, is devoid of any intrinsic meaning. It is in a way a restatement of Marx's much

61

quoted view that 'The worker feels himself at home only outside his work and feels absent from himself in his work. Work is thus not a satisfaction of need, but only a means to satisfy needs outside work.'[5] There is certainly some evidence in the literature to support this point of view. The work of Goldthorpe *et al* stresses the instrumental orientations to work held by 'affluent workers'.[6] The Luton car workers who were the subject of Goldthorpe's study were using work as a means to an end. Their concern for 'the real business of living' is reflected in their preoccupation with their standard of living and material position. However, it is important to recognize some of the special factors inherent in the Luton study, such as the age, and social and geographical mobility of the respondents, before drawing too firm conclusions from it.

There are, too, a number of other studies which indicate that instrumental considerations are not the major factor in a worker's life. Stager, for example, found that workers rated a steady job and work they enjoyed higher than their level of pay.[7] This view is of course a contrast to the approach of Taylorism and of so-called scientific management which relied so heavily on stressing the value of money incentives. Today there is considerable evidence to indicate that the 'man/woman works for money' thesis is a gross oversimplification. However, this is not to suggest that one should underestimate the motivational power of money. As Tannenbaum writes, 'people want money, they want to save it, spend it or show it . . . Money is important because it buys things that people value, but the importance of money is as much psychological as it is economic'.[8]

Traditional theories of motivation
Equally it can be argued that the importance of work itself is psychological as well as economic. Over the years behavioural scientists have provided some interesting and valuable perspectives on this issue. Most readers will be familiar with the work of Maslow and Herzberg and there is no need to do more than remind ourselves of some basic points. Maslow in his seminal publication *Motivation and personality* provides some alternative reasons as to why people work.[9] His approach suggests that man lives by bread alone only when there is no bread. He argued that work satisfied a hierarchy of needs. The first of these, physiological need, obviously depends on an economic reward but once these basic needs are satisfied they no longer motivate to a great extent. Safety needs, social needs — the need to belong and be

62

accepted, ego needs for status – for recognition and finally self-fulfilment are, according to Maslow, important for people in their working environment.

Herzberg demonstrated that the motivation to work is often separate from job satisfaction.[10] In developing his 'two factor theory' he found that sources of satisfaction in a work organization were quite different from sources of dissatisfaction. Satisfiers related to the job in terms of achievement, recognition, responsibility and so forth while dissatisfaction arose as the result of poor working conditions, lack of security and inter-personal relations – in Herzberg's term, 'hygiene factors'.

As readers of an earlier volume in this series will be aware, Herzberg's theory has been tested on librarians. The study by Plate and Stone is generally supportive of this theory and suggests that librarians 'respond positively to such motivational factors as a sense of achievement, recognition, and work that is intrinsically satisfying'.[11]

The Sheffield Manpower project while not especially concerned with testing Herzberg also found that for library staff 'factors which acted as "satisfiers" . . . were those which were intrinsic to the work itself (eg variety, involvement with people, a sense of service and social worth, intellectual satisfaction, opportunities for personal development). These factors were quoted at all levels'.[12]

Though some of the behaviourists' views have been challenged, management theory and practice has taken many of them on board (see for example McGregor[13]). Firms, local authorities and other organizations have introduced job enrichment schemes and the like in the wake of such theories. The carrot and stick approach of Taylorism has been replaced by the human relations approach. This is not just because it enriches people's working lives but because it has been found to be a more efficient method of getting people to work. While one may object to this on political and/or moral grounds the fact that such theories have been translated into practice demonstrates their importance in understanding the meaning of work.

Some comments on the traditional view of motivation
However as indicated above, the somewhat simplistic assumptions of Herzberg and Maslow have been criticized. In the first place they take little account of an *individual's* responses and preferences. Vroom in his 'Expectancy theory' of motivation does consider the individual's desires and expectations but this model has not been widely adopted in practice.[14] This is, perhaps, because it does not offer a ready and

63

obvious blueprint for motivating employees. It is, however, of considerable interest in that it investigates the relationship between individual and organizational goals.

A lesser known motivation model is that developed by Porter and Lawler.[15] According to this, effort (their word for motivation) depends on the value of the reward as understood by the individual and the perception by that individual of the probability of his or her effort leading to a reward. The model suggests that performance does not depend on effort alone but also on the individual's traits and abilities and his or her role perception. This approach also reflects the fact that extra effort does not always produce a desired level of performance. This is a reflection of library life; we all know of the member of staff who tries very hard but never makes the grade. As the diagram shows the performance of the worker will lead to both extrinsic and intrinsic rewards. These rewards, together with the individual's perception of the equity of his or her reward influence the level of satisfaction he or she obtains from work.

This view is somewhat different from that of Herzberg and it has important practical implications. According to Porter and Lawler satisfaction can depend as much on the person's perception of a just reward as the actual reward itself. This may offer some explanation as to why job enrichment schemes sometimes fail. (They may for instance be perceived as making the job more complex without offering a fair reward for extra effort.) Secondly while, according to Herzberg, performance depends on satisfaction, Porter and Lawler suggest the reverse; in their model it is only via feedback that satisfaction affects performance. Their view is also significant in that it indicates the importance of attitudes (as to the value and probability of rewards and role perceptions) in determining effort.

The early theories discussed motivation and work in a very broad way. However, as Allport reminds us 'the outstanding characteristic of man is his individuality'.[16] Thus aspects of a person's personality will contribute towards his or her definition of the meaning of work. The individual arrives at work with his or her personality 'given'. Members of staff do not leave their attitudes and prejudices at the library door, they bring them to work with them. The relationship between attitudes and behaviour is a complex one but suffice it to say that attitudes can and do predispose people to perceive and behave in certain ways.

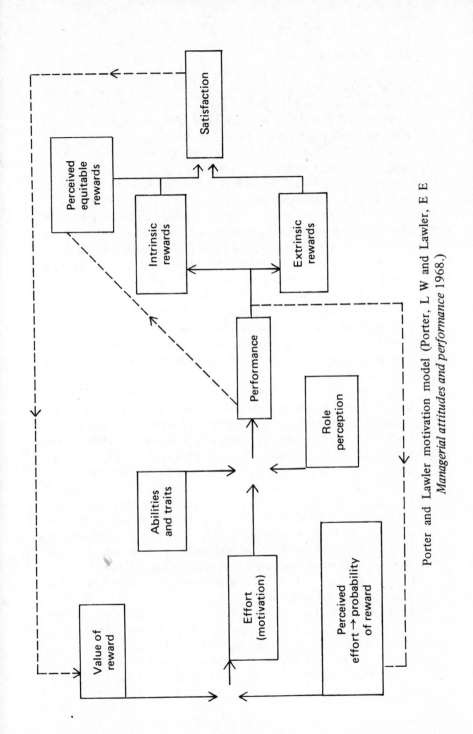

Porter and Lawler motivation model (Porter, L W and Lawler, E E *Managerial attitudes and performance* 1968.)

Personal attitudes to work

Individual attitudes and perceptions may be the result of many and varied circumstances and it is only possible to indicate some of the areas that might help us understand how an individual arrives at a definition of the meaning of work. For example, people in different positions in an organization hierarchical structure may perceive events at work quite differently. Morse, for instance, asked a group of clerical workers and their supervisors: 'How does a person get ahead in this company?'. She found that the supervisors stressed 'merit' while the workers ascribed advancement to 'luck' or 'knowing the right people'.[17]

The beliefs and attitudes acquired by an individual over a period of time: attitudes to work – to authority – to the capitalist system – are part of his or her personality, and will influence his or her view of the work situation. The staff member will make evaluations and judgements from his or her own frame of reference. Liebermann,[18] for example, has shown that a worker's attitudes to the job are likely to change as his or her position changes in the organizational hierarchy. Thus workers who become foremen are likely to adopt attitudes similar to those of other foremen and different from the attitudes of other workers. It would be surprising if similar changes did not take place in those making progress in library hierarchies.

Of course it is not only professional librarians who work in library organizations. The library manager is often responsible for a wide range of occupations. Many of these are important not only for what they do but for the way they can affect the public's perception of a library service. A librarian's managerial responsibility can often bring him or her into contact with porters, caretakers, drivers and clerks as well as professional colleagues. Each of these should be made to feel that he or she matters and that they are making a contribution to the overall service. There are well-researched links between occupation and social class and plenty of evidence to support the view that the meaning of work is closely related to social stratification.[19] This evidence would appear to suggest that for the working class work is instrumental, that it is viewed in extrinsic terms. The skilled working class and the middle classes may on the other hand find a degree of intrinsic meaning. The luxury of self-discovery, self-development and self-fulfilment, beloved of the behaviourists, may be reserved for the privileged few, among which we can probably include many professional librarians – but not, perhaps, all the people who work in library organizations.

Educational opportunities are linked to class and there is again evidence that people who have gone on to further education are more likely to expect and enjoy intrinsic satisfactions in work. Cotgrove, whose study provides evidence for this argument, also confirms that the work situation itself is a significant variable in the analysis of the meaning of work.[20]

The importance of work to the individual is emphasized (albeit in a negative way) by considering the effects of redundancy. The results are both psychologically and sociologically important. For example the effect on the self-image is 'a deep personal shock which can assume the proportions of a natural disaster in people's minds' (Daniel).[21] The first-hand experiences of people from all types and level of occupations reported in *On the dole*,[3] *Workless*[22] or *Stories from the dole queue*,[23] suggest that even if work is little more than an irksome pre-condition for the real business of living, it is pre-conditioning that people, apart from those of hippie persuasion, feel they need.

Social attitudes to work

It can be argued that this 'need' is the result of a wide variety of conditioning factors in society. Most people are exposed to a number of socializing activities which lead them to accept the doctrine of work, indeed to accept a doctrine of work that expects and seeks largely instrumental satisfactions. In fact the hippie philosophy rejects work 'not only for its supposedly dehumanizing content but also for its system of organization and what it implies for society'.[24] Within the strictures of this paper there is time to do little more than indicate some of the socializing factors. Perhaps the most important is the experience of work itself — most work organizations embody philosophies of work. Most of these philosophies are concerned with minimizing costs and optimizing output, though trade unions, professional organizations such as the Library Association and Aslib also play a significant part in the orientation of their members to their particular work situation.

In the larger society it is consumer values that predominate, governments stress the importance of productivity, while growth is a perennial preoccupation. The values of the market, of state apparatus, of international trade are centred around expansion. At the same time, although we can note some cross-cultural differences, which can have important implications for those who teach overseas students or librarians, in industrial societies the major cultural values and ideologies, the sub-cultures, education, church and family and the media reinforce the work ethic. The importance of work is therefore implicit in the social structure. The dominant groups who are often the major beneficiaries of work, also influence people's perception of it. Thus it could be argued that for lower level workers much of the meaning or satisfaction they find in their work is in fact illusory. Argyris has suggested three worker rationalizations of the situation:

1 I must enjoy it (work) in order to live with myself.
2 I must enjoy it or else go through the difficulty of finding another job.
3 One way to live with the job is to enjoy it.[25]

The importance of work is, of course, extended outside the work organization. It is one of the most important parts of a person's social identity. As Hughes says, 'a man's work is one of the things by which he is judged, and certainly one of the more significant things by which he judges himself'.[26] This view of the academic is reflected also in the words of a redundant worker quoted by Stanley Parker. 'It isn't just the job or the money. That isn't what it's all about it's one's life you see.'[27] In fact the link between a person's work experience and his or her view of himself or herself is a very strong one. However, the self-image of a worker can only be maintained in a social context in which others are willing to recognize him or her in his or her work identity. In this sense identities are socially bestowed and must be socially sustained.

Work as a social activity

For many work is a social activity. Work relationships, interests, and activities permeate people's lives out of work. Salaman's study of two occupational communities demonstrates how workers as apparently disparate as architects and railwaymen both, in their own communities, share friendships, clubs and talk 'shop'.[28] For both of these groups work was a dominant and central life interest. Further evidence can be found in Brown who describes how pools winners in no need of money return to work because of its social meaning.[1] Similarly one notes how many retired persons, including librarians, like to maintain contact with their old organization on a social basis.

The evidence regarding the meaning of work is, to say the least, conflicting. It is possible to find empirical data to support those who see only extrinsic values and for those who see intrinsic values in work. Work has been shown to have both sociological and psychological significance for people. There are, in addition, many variables in the

68

situation. Social stratification is the most important of these and, in general terms, it does appear that individuals, such as librarians, with more education and a higher social class are more likely to find intrinsic satisfaction in work. In addition one must note the great variety of socializing agencies that contribute towards people's view of work.

Work in the library
Such considerations about the meaning of work are not only of academic interest — they can be of considerable value to the busy practising library manager. There are, for example, certain costs resulting from a lack of staff motivation. Some of these such as a high rate of absenteeism or staff turnover can be measured. However, it is likely that such visible costs are only the tip of the iceberg. The real and often massive unseen problem is the talent and enthusiasm which may lie dormant in many library staff who have become demotivated or apathetic.

To quote Fox: 'A work environment which offers no or only trivial opportunities for choice decision and the acceptance of responsibility is one which offers no opportunity for growth'.[29]

Obviously the work environment in libraries and elsewhere is affected by the organization's structure and processes. A highly mechanized and formalized structure may not be the best environment for personal growth and development. Today the increased size and complexity of many library organizations makes it even more necessary to support staff and to provide them with satisfying work. This perhaps is particularly true for new professionals.

However, even if in our own organizations we provide for growth and development and satisfaction, we need to remember that our staff may bring with them to our library views and attitudes developed as the result of previous experience and other external factors. In these circumstances an understanding of how they view their work can be a valuable asset for the practising manager. This view has been developed in a recent book by Roger Bennett who is Head of Research at the Thames Valley Regional Management Centre. 'Employee's views of work' says Bennett, 'have considerable impact on behaviour and performance. We must therefore have means of describing the nature of these views. From this knowledge will flow indications for appropriate action'.[30]

Measuring attitudes to work

Taking action, as librarians will be aware, requires information. Bennett provides for this by designing a methodology for acquiring and measuring views of work. This is fully described in his book which is strongly recommended.

Bennett's aim was 'to end up with self-completion measures in the form of a questionnaire that could be standardized and used by other people'. Of the four measures he tested (job descriptions: paired comparison items: rating scales: semantic differentials) rating scales seem to be 'the most promising way of assessing views of work'.[30]

Bennett's 'desire' and 'expectation' scales are reproduced here in Tables 1 and 2. These are given only as examples not as ready made measures for immediate application in libraries. My aim in mentioning these scales is to bring them to readers' attention. Detailed information about their application is beyond the scope of this short contribution – but can be found in Bennett's book.

South Glamorgan County Libraries have used a somewhat related approach in their management training and development programmes for professional staff. On these programmes, 'Maslow's motivation theory is explained by getting members to answer a whole series of questions about their present job indicating how many of Maslow's motivations:

a are present now
b they would like to be present
c how important each motivation is to them personally.

... Each question is numerically scored and the totals transferred to a tally sheet. Each individual then compares his score with mean averages for different types of occupation ...This exercise highlights the variety and complexity of reasons people have for working and what each individual wants to get out of a job, even within the same organization'.[31]

Other exercises utilized by South Glamorgan include a 'blockage questionnaire' and a rating scale for interpersonal relationships.

On the blockage questionnaire participants are asked to decide if some 110 statements about the libraries department are true, vaguely true or false. Statements to be considered include:

'The Libraries Department seems to recruit as many wasters as efficient people.'

'Unconventional ideas never get a hearing.'

'Only top management participates in important decisions.'

'The boss believes that people are basically lazy.'

Instructions to respondents Please read carefully each of the statements printed below and consider how *desirable* they are to you, that is how much you may or may not want the things they describe. Then read each of the possible answers given opposite the statement and put a circle round the answer that best indicates how you feel.

How desirable it is that you:	Extremely undesirable	Undesirable	Don't know	Desirable	Extremely desirable
D1 Are able to use your own common sense? (P)	1	2	3	4	5
D2 Are sure of having a job in difficult times? (E)	1	2	3	4	5
D3 Have friends who would help you out when you're in a spot? (S)	1	2	3	4	5
D4 Have a job that doesn't require too much thought? (−P)	1	2	3	4	5
D5 Earn more money than you get now? (E)	1	2	3	4	5
D6 Get the credit for doing a good job? (P)	1	2	3	4	5
D7 Work with friendly people? (S)	1	2	3	4	5
D8 Keep yourself to yourself? (−S)	1	2	3	4	5
D9 Save and invest some money? (E)	1	2	3	4	5
D10 Have an interesting job of work to do? (P)	1	2	3	4	5
D11 Earn just enough money to get by? (−E)	1	2	3	4	5
D12 Live next door to friendly people? (S)	1	2	3	4	5

Table 1 Bennett's 'desire' scales

71

Instructions to respondents Although we all want different things from life, some of them are more frequently obtainable than others. Read the list of statements printed on the left-hand side of the table below and consider how frequently you expect to have opportunities to achieve them. Then place a tick in the box under the heading which best indicates how often you expect to have what each statement refers to.

How frequently do you expect to have these opportunities	Not at all	Very seldom	On some occasions	On most occasions	All the time
E1 To be given more responsibility at work (P)					
E2 To earn more money (E)					
E3 To have a secure job (E)					
E4 To be with people you like (S)					
E5 To have interesting work to do (P)					
E6 To save some money (E)					
E7 To get credit for doing a good job (P)					
E8 To have friends who will stand by you (S)					
E9 To work with friendly people (S)					

Table 2 Bennett's 'expectation' scales

NB The letters following each statement in Tables 1 and 2 indicate the view of work represented by the statement. [E (Economic); P (Psychological); S (Social)].

'People feel as though they work in a "second-class" organization.'
'People would welcome more challenge in their jobs.'
'I, personally, feel underpaid.'

This particular test was adapted for library managerial purposes from one provided in Woodcock and Francis *Unblocking your organization*.[32]

Values, clarification tests and other self-analysis questionnaires are used in staff training sessions in Baltimore Public Library, Maryland.[33] The aim of these is to create an awareness among staff about the ways personal attitudes to work and other topics can affect the quality of library service.

Enough has already been said to indicate the dangers of generalizing about people and work and the meaning it holds for them. Motivation theories provide a useful but only partial perspective. Other research has indicated that for any individual the meaning of work can depend on a wide range of factors. These can include his or her place in the organization, beliefs, attitudes, previous experience, age, professional socialization, social class, external responsibilities and a range of other variables.

The importance of understanding attitudes to work
There is then a vast amount of evidence (albeit at times conflicting) available to the library manager. This information can be of practical value in a number of important areas of library management. In general terms there is a relationship between people's view of work and their behaviour. The more we know about the former the greater our chances of understanding and improving the latter. As we have seen it is possible to measure and assess staff's view of work. Techniques of this kind are already being used in library training and development programmes.

The working environment we provide, both in terms of the physical setting and inter-personal relationships, should be related to what we learn about people's view of work. If it is found that staff will do a better job when they are involved or committed it is only sensible to provide appropriate opportunities in the library environment. In addition such information has relevance for other managerial considerations including the shape and structure of the organization, the style of management adopted, job design, staff selection and promotion and the introduction of change. Of course the decisions managers take in these areas will in themselves influence worker behaviour.

Because the views of different groups of workers may well be different it is not practical to rely on one set of theories but an analysis of these different views will enable the library manager better to understand some of the problems he or she faces and to plan and act accordingly. Traditionally it has been assumed that manual workers and white collar workers have different views of work. However, there is now some evidence to suggest that this may not be as true now as in the past. Certainly the impact of technology has meant a blurring of the differences between some blue-collar and white-collar employment. Computers have succeeded in making some white-collar jobs as routine and unsatisfying as some manual work. In the library environment it is not unusual to hear counter staff, used to Browne charging, complain that computer charging systems make their job less interesting and rewarding — because they fail to provide the personal contact that the Browne system allowed. At a professional level many cataloguers feel that automation has 'de-skilled' their particular job. With the increased use of technology the challenge to library managers to provide a satisfying, motivating environment will become greater. Part of this challenge is to understand what it means to perform repetitive and routine work.

In order to understand those who work with or for us, we need also to understand ourselves and our own attitudes to work and work people. The real value of McGregor's X and Y theory is not in the 'rightness' or 'wrongness' of either approach but that it makes us face up to the basic assumptions we hold on human nature and motivation. If we believe that our staff are naturally lazy and don't want responsibility then we are likely to adopt a management style based on the threat and the bribe. Likewise if we go along with Y our approach is likely to reflect that belief.

There are a wide range of tests and other materials available that can help us assess our own attitudes and managerial style. Some of these, as we have noted earlier have been used in library training programmes. South Glamorgan for example have used self-scoring sheets to relate participants' decisions to McGregor's X and Y theory.[34] Self-discovery can be a painful process and I have had particularly mixed reaction to one 'game' which endeavours to discover the way people deal with conflict in organizations.[35] Nevertheless despite such problems self-evaluation techniques can provide us with useful insights about ourselves and people at work.

In fact relatively little is known about librarians' orientation to work.

74

We need to find out much more about how library staff members experience their job, not just at the professional level but at the library version of the shop floor. A library equivalent of *Working for Ford*[36] could reveal much more about the people who look after library and information service points.

Throughout I have drawn on a wide range of sometimes conflicting literature and theoretical positions. No one source can provide a total explanation of how people view work. Some readers will favour one approach more than others, most, it is hoped will be able to relate some of the ideas and concepts to the practice of management in their own library or information unit. Both the study and practice of management should take people into account. Practitioners in the field and in the lecture room need to consider the human component in terms of staff's value systems, hopes, fears and aspirations.

Conclusion

In this paper I have concentrated on people's motivation and orientation to work in the belief that these affect their performance. Of course performance also depends on professional or other skills and abilities, but the quality of that performance will in turn depend on how far staff are motivated to use their talents. Further, we would argue that in developing effective managerial strategies and programmes designed to *encourage* people to work to their full potential, we must first obtain some understanding of their view of work and the meaning it holds for them.

References

1 Brown, J A C *Social psychology of industry* Harmondsworth, Middx, Penguin, 1954.

2 Johnson, D 'Factory time' *in* R Fraser, *ed. Work* Harmondsworth, Middx, Penguin, 1968.

3 Keenan, J 'On the dole' *in* Fraser, R *ed. op. cit.*

4 Fox, A 'The meaning of work' *in* Open University. People and Work Course Team. *Occupational categories and cultures 1* (DE 351, Block 3 Part 1) Milton Keynes, Open University Press, 1976.

5 Marx, K quoted in Fraser, R *ed. op. cit.*

6 Goldthorpe, J H *The affluent worker in the class structure* Cambridge, Cambridge University Press, 1979.

7 Stager, R 'Psychological aspects of industrial conflict; II: motivation' *Personnel psychology* 3 1950.

8 Tannenbaum, A S *Social psychology of work organisations* London, Tavistock, 1966.

9 Maslow, A H *Motivation and personality* New York, Harper, 1954.

10 Herzberg, F *The motivation to work* Wiley, New York, 1959.

11 Plate, K H and Stone, E W 'Factors affecting librarians' job satisfaction: a report of two studies' *Library quarterly* 44 (2) April 1974, 97-110. Reprinted in Shimmon, R *ed. A reader in library management* London, Bingley, 1976.

12 Sergean, R, McKay, J R and Corkill, C M *The Sheffield Manpower Project: a survey of staffing requirements for librarianship and information work* Sheffield, Postgraduate School of Librarianship and Information Science, 1976.

13 McGregor, D *The human side of enterprise* New York, McGraw-Hill, 1960.

14 Vroom, V H *Work and motivation* New York, Wiley, 1964.

15 Porter, L W and Lawler, E E *Managerial attitudes and performance* Homewood, Ill., Irwin, 1968.

16 Allport, G W *The nature of prejudice* Reading, Mass., Addison-Wesley, 1954.

17 Morse, N *Satisfactions in the white collar job* Ann Arbor, University of Michigan, 1953.

18 Liebermann, S 'The effects of changes in roles on the attitudes of role occupants' *Human relations* 9 (4) 1956.

19 See, for example, Emery, F E and Thorsrud, E *Form and content in industrial democracy* London, Tavistock, 1969, or Morse, N C and Weiss, R S 'The function and meaning of work and the job' *American sociological review* 20 (2) 1955.

20 Cotgrove, S 'The relations between work and non-work among technicians' *Sociological review* 13 (2) 1965.

21 Quoted in Parker, S 'The effects of redundancy' in Esland, G *et al People and work* Edinburgh, Holmes McDougall, 1975.

22 Marsden, D *Workless* Harmondsworth, Middx, Penguin, 1975.

23 Gould, T *Stories from the dole queue* London, Temple Smith, 1972.

24 Hills, R *Young outsiders* London, Routledge and Kegan Paul, 1973.

25 Argyris, C *Integrating the individual and the organization* New York, Wiley, 1964.

26 Hughes, E 'Work and the self' in Rohrer, J H and Sherif, M

Social psychology at the crossroads New York, Harper and Row, 1951.

27 Parker, S 'The effects of redundancy' in Esland, G *et al People and work* Edinburgh, Holmes McDougall, 1975.

28 Salaman, G 'Two occupational communities' in Weir, D *ed. Men and work in modern Britain* London, Fontana, 1973.

29 Fox, A *A sociology of work in industry* London, Collier-Macmillan, 1971.

30 Bennett, R *Managing personnel and performance* London, Business Books, 1981.

31 Edwards, I and Day, M 'Management training in libraries using experiential learning techniques: a case history' *Information and library management* 1 (1) June 1981, 10-12, 21-22.

32 Woodcock, M and Francis, D *Unblocking your organization* San Diego, Calif., University Associates, 1979.

33 Examples can be found in Edsall, M S *Library promotion handbook* London, Mansell/Oryx Press, 1980.

34 'Supervisory attitudes: the X – Y scale' in Pfeiffer, J W and Jones, J E *eds. The 1972 annual handbook for group facilitators* San Diego, Calif., University Associates, 1972.

35 'Conflict management: dyadic sharing' in Jones, J E and Pfeiffer, J W *eds. The 1979 annual handbook for group facilitators* San Diego, Calif., University Associates, 1979.

36 Beynon, Huw *Working for Ford* London, Allen Lane, 1973.

Acknowledgements
I am grateful to *Management services* for allowing me to reproduce the diagram of the Porter and Lawler motivation model. This first appeared in the article by Tony Vitalis 'Motivation to work – some current theories' *Management services* 22 (11) November 1978, 16-19.

Also to Roger Bennett and Business Books for permission to reproduce the 'desire' and 'expectation' scales that appear with this article. These are taken from R Bennett, *Managing personnel and performance*, London, Business Books, 1981.

Thanks also to Ieuan Edwards for providing details of the South Glamorgan training and development programmes.

Administrative, organizational and economic effects of automated cataloguing

STEPHEN W MASSIL

Automated cataloguing has been under development, and in some cases has been a fact of life in libraries, for over ten years. It is timely to be writing now about the new cataloguing for we are on the brink of introducing on-line systems and the first phase, therefore, of automation in cataloguing can be reviewed. We shall examine some of the pressures and problems that were faced, and the opportunities that were taken up when computerization was applied to cataloguing. We shall also discuss the organizational and operational adjustments which arose out of the use of automated methods in both batch and on-line systems. There have been enormous benefits, and many of the difficulties encountered have been resolved, but there have also been shortcomings and the displacement of some inevitable problems from cataloguing to other points of endeavour. The costs of cataloguing, the impetus for greater productivity and the consequences of the new catalogue outputs for reader services will all be encompassed by this overview.

The automation of cataloguing is not an end in itself. But, as an area of new development it is often treated and experienced as a complex phenomenon in its own right. The challenges which it presents can seem to be self-contained, and much writing on the subject tends to ignore the implications of the new processing systems on reader services. It merely takes for granted the fact that cataloguing is a tool for better bibliographical and stock control, and that reader services are boosted by up-to-date and improved cataloguing systems.

This study will examine the patterns of automated cataloguing most commonly adopted in British libraries; it discusses the use of computer output microform (COM) as the principal physical form of the automated catalogue and the retention of the classified catalogue as the means of indexing the collections by subject.

PATTERNS OF DEVELOPMENT OF AUTOMATED CATALOGUING

The existence of the MARC data base has become the most significant factor in the automation of cataloguing in recent years, and its development and deployment have attempted to fulfil by modern means the century-old aim of central bibliographical control. Computers were, however, brought into cataloguing before the British National Bibliography's MARC service got going, and the example set by these first libraries adopting automation has been repeated by some others in the last fifteen years. In this respect the reorganization of local government in London in the mid-1960s and throughout the rest of the country in the mid-1970s had a great impact. There was a need to provide a union catalogue for the newly amalgamated library services of previously separate authorities, and this was the single most compelling reason for the introduction of computers into cataloguing in such library systems as Camden, Barnet and Westminster in London in about 1965, as well as in several county library systems in 1974. Why some London boroughs did not follow this example at the time, and why certain county or city libraries like Shropshire, Cheshire, Cornwall and Coventry had already begun to automate their catalogues well before the local government reorganization is another question, one more of attitudes towards the progress of automation. The need for a union catalogue in multi-site libraries was also felt by the new polytechnics brought into being in the period 1969-73. For these academic institutions, even more than the public libraries, have been concerned about the retrospective conversion of the catalogues of the existing collections in the component institutions, and this has affected their operations as much as the need for a union catalogue.

At the same time as certain London public libraries were implementing their first automated cataloguing systems, the British National Bibliography, following the lead of the Library of Congress, whose MARC I project was being analysed, began to involve itself in the development of MARC and the exchange network. The various phases through which the MARC data base was gradually built up are now mainly of interest in respect of bibliographic standards; they are described and discussed later on. With the establishment of these files came the possibility of national bibliographic records being available for exchange and for use locally. With the publication of the first edition of the Anglo-American Cataloguing Rules (AACR 67), which were adopted by the British National Bibliography in 1968, the prerequisites of cooperative automated cataloguing had been established.

Cooperative bureaux were soon in existence and these prompted the sharing of resources amongst libraries united by a need for common files and with a common purpose, and therefore requiring common systems to achieve that end. During this development period, the research grants from the Office of Scientific and Technical Information (OSTI) for cataloguing (as well as for other activities of library automation) were a great boost, and these continued when OSTI became the Research and Development Department of the British Library.

What we have seen in the last decade has been the desire of cooperatives as well as individual libraries to get automation going, and to get involved in it. There has been success in terms of individual catalogues and of union catalogues, and in file-handling and systems development. The fruits of automation in terms of reader services and access to wider resources have yet to be enjoyed, but recent developments among the cooperatives have pointed towards this.

I have stressed the practical needs of newly amalgamated library authorities, and I have stressed the MARC data base, but with no intention of drawing a distinction between academic and practical interests. If a cataloguing cooperative like BLCMP was formed in order to use the newly promised MARC files, the initiative for it came from the University of Aston, one of the then newly created technological universities, and also, perhaps, from the 'AMCOS' project at Aldermaston Atomic Weapons Research Establishment Library. The last ten years have seen libraries joining cooperatives in response to their practical needs, notably the polytechnics; libraries like Camden Public Library have also joined cooperatives after quite long periods of 'going it alone'. More recently libraries have followed up their initial developments in cataloguing with extensions into circulation systems, or by going over to on-line cataloguing, or by changing from their own system to that provided by a cooperative.

The pattern, therefore, has many strands and can be summarized as follows:

a   the felt need for a union catalogue in a multi-site library system;

b   the pressures from a new readership, with perhaps a new building as well;

c   the strains experienced by a manual cataloguing system;

d   the prospect of coordinated systems and resource-sharing for cataloguing and for wider purposes, leading to the emergence of cooperatives as the dominant focus of automated cataloguing services;

e   the opportunity to develop by changing to new systems and by extending automated cataloguing into on-line cataloguing or into circulation systems.

As a background to all this, we should not ignore the existence and the potential of the computer systems themselves, for the introduction of computerized cataloguing has been a challenge in itself, not just an answer to practical problems.

THE ROLE OF THE COOPERATIVES

Cataloguing services based upon the MARC data base and format have grown impressively; the details of their growth can be traced through early reports in the journal *Program* to recent developments and news in *Vine* and *Catalogue and index*. The cooperatives have moved from an experimental state, dependent on grants from OSTI and the British Library Research and Development Department (BLRDD) to a fully productive state. Commercial services and the competition of the market-place are now affecting the broader matter of network development and various possibilities now confront the library manager attempting to choose a new way of cataloguing. There have been studies both in Britain and North America on the major cooperatives that amount to consumer reviews of a *Which?* sort. Issue number 28 of *Vine* (May 1979) reviews the cooperatives and LOCAS over the preceding ten years.

The nature of the cooperatives

It is useful to draw attention to some of the distinctive features of the various cooperatives and to make some observations which can guide the library manager when making his choice. Their growth has not been uniform; they operate across a wide spectrum of activities, and if one wanted a 'total scheme' one would find that some libraries and some services are not being catered for by the present services of the cooperatives. For example regional coverage of the United Kingdom is not complete; a cooperative for the national and copyright libraries has not come into being; there is no consortium of libraries offering a service like that offered by the London and South East Regional bureau (LASER), but right across the country; and special libraries, by and large, have not sought cataloguing services from the cooperatives. These examples show that the present pattern of the cooperatives has been an organic, not a planned development.

The various cooperatives can be briefly characterized as follows:

a *BLCMP* — originally Birmingham Libraries Cooperative Mechanization Project. It has more than thirty members — academic, public

81

and special libraries in almost all parts of the country including Northern Ireland, plus one in Denmark. The system maintains a large MARC data base, and produces a union catalogue and catalogues of the member libraries. It has recently introduced an on-line component of on-line support services called BOSS in a dispersed network linking mini-computers in Birmingham, Manchester and London. Circulation and acquisition subsystems are now under development. BLCMP runs the British National Bibliography's card service under contract from the British Library Bibliographical Services Division. It includes serials and music union catalogues on its files.

b *SWALCAP* − the Southwest Academic Libraries Cooperative Automation Project. This cooperative draws its membership of over fifteen libraries mainly from the south-west of Britain but including London and the South. It has developed a comprehensive on-line circulation system and an on-line cataloguing service which maintains union files but not as yet a union catalogue; not all its members take both the circulation and cataloguing services. Searches are made on the BLCMP data bases on a customer basis.

c *LASER* − the London and South East Region operates systems for a very large number of libraries within its area, at first as a union catalogue for inter-library lending purposes, but now extending this into a cataloguing system with on-line capacity. Some of the participants in the interlending scheme may, like Barnet, operate their own cataloguing systems, while others may use other cooperatives, thus Camden and Richmond public libraries go to BLCMP and Hillingdon public library is a customer of LOCAS.

d *SCOLCAP* − the Scottish Libraries Cooperative Automation Project serves libraries in Scotland and the very north of England and maintains the Scottish union catalogue. It numbers the National Library of Scotland among its members, a copyright library requiring access to the full MARC file. At present it derives its cataloguing from LOCAS and its members are BLAISE/LOCAS subscribers, but it has proposals in hand for the establishment of its own hardware and systems so as to run a more strictly regional network linked to the British Library for access to the data bases, but not dependent on its services.

e *ULSCS* − the University of London Shared Cataloguing Service is confined to member libraries of the University of London. It has nine active participants and others due to join. Like the members of SCOLCAP these libraries are subscribers to BLAISE/LOCAS. Both cooperatives are served by 'union files' held within the LOCAS file
82

structure and it is intended that these will be made available on-line to participants. The ULSCS is perhaps the most strictly cooperative-minded of all these systems as it has a long-term programme for the coordination of resources in all aspects of library service.

f INTERLIB — the shared cataloguing system of a group of government libraries who intend to operate it in a similar manner to SCOL-CAP and ULSCS, that is, by taking coordinated services from BLAISE/LOCAS.

g *BLAISE/LOCAS* — the British Library's Bibliographic Services Division operates in a dual capacity. On the one hand it produces the *British National Bibliography* and supports the cataloguing services of the component parts of the British Library (eg the Department of Printed Books and Science Reference Library). On the other hand it is the source of a service to individual customers and cooperatives around the country through its BLAISE/LOCAS system. It maintains separate catalogue files for all these subscribers, internal British Library departments and outside customers alike. It maintains the UK MARC data bases and provides a MARC Exchange Tape Service, and is the national centre for the International Serials Data System (ISDS). The linking of LOCAS (the Local Cataloguing System) to BLAISE is not a clearcut thing and it makes necessary an administrative separation of the BLAISE information retrieval service from the on-line search service used as an extension of LOCAS.

In addition to the cooperatives described above, mention should also be made of Oriel Computer Services which has customers in the Low Countries and at least one in the United Kingdom. There is also the prospect of the big American cooperative OCLC offering services in Europe by networking arrangements to be negotiated in part with BLCMP. As well as on-line cataloguing, OCLC will be able to provide serials control and inter-library lending subsystems and other facilities of its home system.

Libraries participate in, are *members* of BLCMP or LASER, but they are *customers* of LOCAS. But there is flexibility among the co-operatives and the libraries. Some libraries have joined BLCMP with the long-term aim of setting up their own systems, as Leicestershire County Library has done, using software from the North Yorkshire system, or as Glasgow Public Libraries' Mitchell Library has done, in the expectation of eventually transferring to SCOLCAP, while Hatfield Polytechnic Library started as a LOCAS customer and has now joined SWALCAP. We can, however, make certain general distinctions: in

83

BLCMP and SWALCAP the cooperative aspect is of a basic practical nature, the strict sharing of systems as systems, for circulation, cataloguing, common hardware and data bases; with LASER, SCOLCAP and ULSCS, however, the benefits in common of the results of the shared systems are paramount, that is to say they go for resource-sharing in the widest sense — a common access to greater bibliographic coverage so as to obtain better deployment of funds, better readers' services, easier inter-library loans and a collective self-sufficiency. However, these distinctions should not be stressed too much for all the cooperatives are still engaged in establishing their systems and the projected benefits have yet to be fully experienced. Nevertheless, the potential of, for example, the ten-year old BLCMP files that are so rich in non-MARC material should not be underestimated. The differences among the cooperatives can be seen most clearly in the field of bibliographic standards (which I deal with below), in their accounting procedures, the methods of payment for membership and the manner by which libraries are 'inducted' into the system. For managers making an evaluation of the various systems on offer and taking stock of the administrative demands of membership of a cooperative, these differences carry some weight. The differences among the cooperatives, and the interaction among them are also worth mentioning in respect of recent moves towards the establishment of a national data base, a matter which I also discuss further below.

Choosing a cooperative
The library which is considering joining a cooperative should examine the details of membership closely, look at the physical proximity of the library to the cooperative's headquarters and seek the opinions of existing users of the cooperative. Ultimately, however, the decision as to which cooperative to choose will depend upon a variety of factors within the library and its controlling authority as much as upon the nature of the cataloguing service offered by the cooperative. The library considering automation of its cataloguing service will soon have to look at the related questions of using MARC data and of joining a cooperative. However, there may be pressures to use 'local' computer services, that is to say, to use the computers in the Treasurer's Department or the Administrative Offices of the controlling body. Such an invitation may be beguiling but is to be examined even more closely than the comparative analysis of the virtues of the various cooperatives. Computers which are provided for universities through the Computer

84

Board are not available for the 'production' usage of libraries. So while the costs of the hardware are declining relatively fast and the installation of mini-computers might seem to be coming within the grasp of individual libraries, the present financial climate and the embargo on recurrent if not capital expenditures as well, will still inhibit new initiatives for libraries to automate on their own.

Even if the need to centralize cataloguing or to produce a union catalogue is not paramount, libraries are concerned at the ever-higher costs of manual cataloguing and this has led them to consider adopting machine methods, so that they have been brought to the same point as libraries with other reasons for automation. The questions which libraries must answer for themselves when they examine the whole question of automated cataloguing are as follows:

a Whether local original cataloguing can be supplemented with copy cataloguing from 'cataloguing in progress' (CIP) entries, from the National Union Catalog or from other printed sources, or from fiche services like MARCfiche or *Books in English* – the output remaining on cards.

b Whether MARC services will cover a high proportion of the library's acquisitions.

c What sort of automated cataloguing to go for: what sort of customer or subscriber, what sort of service to seek, bearing in mind the standards of cataloguing which may have to be met and the further opportunities for automating other library operations besides cataloguing; and whether to adopt a commercial package for local implementation.

d How to handle the existing card catalogue or printed catalogue – by closing it, or by absorption into the new automated catalogue.

e Whether to adopt the second edition of the Anglo-American Cataloguing Rules (AACR2) alongside the first edition (AACR 67), or any other code in use, and what level of description to aim at.

f What forms of output for the catalogue, and how great an extent of catalogue provision for the users.

Recently the problems that bedevil batch systems – the questions of input and the delays in producing and up-dating the catalogues – have not been so contentious as they were, but file failures, a lengthy response-time and corrupt systems discs will increasingly afflict on-line cataloguers. Concern over such problems may deter would-be subscribers; some of the difficulties encountered have greater impact on cataloguing productivity and on the quality of catalogue service to

85

library users than others. It is to be hoped that mutual understanding will prevail between library and catalogue agency when they arise.

BLCMP, SCOLCAP, ULSCS and SWALCAP have quite effective committees of users where these kinds of difficulties can be discussed and dealt with in the course of considering ordinary business relating to developments within the cooperative. LOCAS subscribers can belong to the LOCAS Users Group (itself a subgroup of the MARC Users Group), and the British Library maintains good customer relations with individual libraries and with the Users Group. It is, however, perhaps able to respond less flexibly than the cooperatives, where there is a direct community of interest among the participants.

To sum up, the general purpose of the cooperatives has been to develop systems for the common use of bibliographic records and to bring to individual libraries the benefits of operating shared systems for a variety of users. This is done by relying on common hardware and operating systems and by attempting to maximize the use of software, data and expensive resources. These cooperatives started by offering batch systems, but these are being reworked and extended as on-line systems; their full impact and operation have yet to be experienced. The common data base furnishes records for different operations like cataloguing and circulation systems. The goal of cooperative cataloguing has been reached by the generating of individual catalogues according to the library's needs from union files and union catalogues.

LOCAS and the cooperatives provide these catalogues as basic products, tailored to specific requirements – author-title or name-title catalogues and various classified catalogues. There have been some experiments with keyword catalogues and members of cooperatives may retain a local subject-index file on their 'local' computer system independent of the MARC data base, as will be mentioned later. Where the cooperatives produce union catalogues these are author-title or name-title catalogues (the latter more useful as a cataloguing authority). Where libraries participating in cooperatives use classified subject catalogues a union catalogue of subjects is not possible amongst those with different classification schemes. Shelf-lists and 'notifications' to external, subject or area local union catalogues are also produced from the data bases. Where the cooperative services fall down is over the ready production of departmental or single subject listings that members might require as occasional by-products of their input. The way the data base file is 'handled' usually militates against an easy or inexpensive method of producing these, for the systems are geared to wholesale catalogue runs. Other by-products are sub-files for the generation of annual bibliographies, circulation files and records of material on order. In the last named case an automated acquisitions system is not in operation, but the catalogue data base can function as a 'hold-all'.

Reference has already been made to the relationship of the cooperatives with the British Library in connection with a national data base for cataloguing. The burgeoning of automated union catalogues and the problems of making notifications from automated files to a union catalogue which is still based on cards has drawn attention to the relationship of the traditional national and local inter-library lending procedures with these automated union catalogues which can be distributed easily. Further reference will be made to this situation below.

PROBLEMS IN AUTOMATED CATALOGUING

The management of automated cataloguing raises the following problems:

    a The logistics of the use of a cooperative or catalogue service agency;

    b The specification of catalogue requirements and the operation of the service;

    c The standards of cataloguing to be maintained, and the problems of MARC data;

    d The integration of the old catalogue with the new;

    e The choice of COM catalogues, COM readers and the impact of COM on the library service as a whole.

Using a cooperative service

The change from a manual card cataloguing system using original cataloguing to an automated system is a change from self-sufficiency to a state of dependence upon external agencies. Even where an in-house computer service is used, where the relation can be recognized as close, the reliance on files remote from the cataloguer sets up the same dependency with the same need to meet deadlines for input and output as the member of a cooperative experiences using long-distance delivery. On-line systems will vary the nature of some of the cataloguing operations, and it is true that dependence on outside agencies will be reduced with an on-line operation. While it will still be necessary to depend on the files of data themselves, the areas of input and output can come again under the immediate control of the library itself.

87

Specifying the nature of the catalogue

Having decided on the sort of cataloguing service to take, the library will have to go through an intensive phase of specification for the catalogues and must train staff in the new system as well as establishing timetables to meet the deadlines for input and processing. On the questions of input and output the cooperative usually prescribe equipment or a bureau for key-punching, and manage the negotiations with a COM bureau as a matter of course. The local requirements, however, will need to be fully satisfied before the chains of the operation are properly fitted together. Local staff will need to be appointed or designated to liaise with the cooperative and to bear the brunt of discussions about the library's requirements. A major matter in managing an automated system is its cost: the library must investigate the cost of equipment (terminals as adjuncts for searching MARC files and for input, a printer attachment, and microform readers for the COM catalogues), the cost of subscribing to an external service, and the cost of paying any bureaux used for key-punching and COM services.

What is expected from the adoption of an automated system are the immediate benefits of improved rates of cataloguing, easier up-dating and the amending of entries, and the easy production of several copies of the catalogue for distribution around the library and to other service points in the system. The automated system may also transform related aspects of the traditional cataloguing system, such as the production of accessions lists, published bibliographies and the like. For libraries which have not hitherto used subject-headings in a dictionary catalogue, the automated system may allow the generation of a subject catalogue arranged alphabetically by Library of Congress subject headings, direct from MARC. One can be flexible and provide variations in the content of different catalogues: full entries in the name-title catalogue, for example, and briefer entries in the subject catalogues — the specification is all. 'Profiles' for catalogue content and layout can be easily varied, although the cooperatives impose some rules about too frequent changes in this area. As benefits, these may seem sufficient in themselves, and the wider advantages of sharing resources may not rate as priorities, but the catalogue is not an end in itself, only a tool of further service.

Standards of cataloguing with MARC

In cataloguing the condition of participating in a cooperative or of using MARC tapes requires a new approach. Otherwise some of the

88

requirements of the machine-based system may take on the character of drawbacks and disadvantages. The sharing of data presupposes common standards, and the MARC AACR 2 standard is high, higher perhaps than some libraries have been used to. While the use of MARC records in this context may be a simple matter, the residue of original cataloguing for the library's non-MARC material may require greater cataloguing effort than before. The flexibility of computer output and the selection of data elements from a machine record arise out of a full and articulated output.

CATALOGUING WITH MARC
Automated cataloguing, therefore, is no rapid panacea. It makes its own demands. The achievements have to be worked for and the problems resolved. Cataloguing under an automated system faces the following points of contention:

the complexity of MARC data and the variability of the MARC data base;

the questions of currency and coverage of MARC data;

the implications for original cataloguing and local data;

the standards adhered to within a cooperative and the purpose of the 'union catalogue';

the probable existence of split catalogues;

the timetables for input and up-dating the files.

The MARC files
The full MARC record created for British National Bibliography entries is complex and substantial, and is intended to meet level 3 of the AACR 2 levels of description. The bibliographic record itself, the descriptive information, is backed up by considerable subject, classification and coded information together with relevant headings and access points including references. Taking MARC tapes a system or a cooperative may strip away a fair amount of the data provided, for holding the full bibliographic record might be a problem in machine terms as the nature of the variable-length data presents its own problems of storage and manipulation not directly of concern to cataloguers. To meet the standard set by MARC as suggested above may seem daunting.

The experience so far has been largely that of using MARC for current monograph publications. The MARC-based serials files, while notable as achievements, have not had general impact or usage. The creation of MARC files for audio-visual materials, maps, music and pre-1800 publications has not been extensive, so the experience of using centrally produced records for these items has been very limited; so far these categories of materials are to be considered mostly as non-MARC items.

The development of the MARC files and of the format itself has been a drawn out and variegated process. If the international MARC developments are not of relevance here, nevertheless the divergence of the UK and Library of Congress formats needs to be stressed because LC MARC tapes are distributed in Britain, and the British Library files include a substantial part of the Library of Congress files. Even with the enhancement of MARC made necessary by the adoption of AACR 2, the Library of Congress and the BL Bibliographic Services Division have gone different ways. The use of LC records has always been a mixed blessing. The LC format is not articulated so fully as the UK format, particularly as regards uniform titles, and it lacks references and analyticals. The Library of Congress was late in adopting the revised rule 4 of AACR 67 and always adhered to the North American text so that to British cataloguers LC records have always been suspect. SCOLCAP and BLCMP devised routines for neutralizing the problems presented by LC MARC. From this point of view the difficulties of using LC records alongside those from the BL arise out of the idiosyncrasies of LC's tagging of data elements, though ultimately the differences are due to a different underlying philosophy of the use of MARC files for cataloguing. It is a view that has steadily given primacy to the card catalogue in North America, and the transition to on-line catalogues may see it retaining its potency more readily. The North American view may come across rather better now that OCLC is hoping to attract customers here. In the case of UK MARC, the libraries using these files have had to grapple with the integration of records for a national bibliography into a local catalogue.

The successive enhancements to the central MARC files have given members of cooperatives and individual users of the tapes problems of reconciliation of data. The UK MARC data base has gone through several stages. The UK MARC II format was designed in 1969 for AACR 67 records, but MARC I files for the years 1968-71, and subsequent revisions to AACR 67 introduced in 1975 represent further records which were created to different states of the standards. The profile of the MARC data base available to users in Britain can be studied in figure 1. It is to be hoped that the adoption of AACR 2 will

1	BNB data 1950-1968	Achieved by partial retrospective conversion to AACR 67 and MARC II
2	BNB 1968-1971	AACR 67 and MARC I
3	BNB 1972-1974	AACR 67 and MARC II
4	BNB 1975-1980	AACR 67 revised and MARC II
5	LC data 1968-1980	AACR 67 (North American text) and LC MARC II
6	BNB 1981-	AACR 2 and MARC II enhanced
7	LC 1981-	AACR 2 and LC MARC II enhanced

The British Library has converted files 1 to 5 to an AACR 2 'form of heading' according to an automatic specification.

Figure 1 Profile of the UK MARC data base

at least result in a unification, although in certain respects even the enhancements to MARC show certain shortcomings for music and other materials. The files in which the cooperatives integrate non-MARC data with MARC data from the BL approximate most closely to file 4, and include extensive enhancements of records which have been drawn in by retrospective conversion of older stock.

The currency and coverage of MARC data
The currency of BNB and MARC records has always been a matter of contention between libraries and the BNB, and not just for the business of cataloguing. It has been a critical factor for libraries when deciding whether to implement MARC-based systems or whether to set up their own systems. The situation may have begun to improve since the aftermath of the implementation of AACR 2, and the Centre for Catalogue Research at Bath can now study the matter and publish figures on currency and coverage, but cataloguers still find the late arrival or the non-appearance of records which should have been included in the UK MARC service to be an acute problem. The computer systems can easily arrange automatic searching of MARC files over successive weeks, but in the cataloguing departments themselves books hang around waiting processing while the searching goes on. Books have to be left on the shelves arranged in weekly batches, or else integrated into a single sequence and some distinguishing mark added such as a coloured strip to distinguish them by the number of weeks

91

they have been waiting. The shelves have to be weeded at the time-limit for the searches. Where repeated searches are not undertaken, then original cataloguing is necessary. SCOLCAP have instituted a 'waiting for MARC' category of records which can be input at a minimum standard pending the arrival of the eventual full MARC record.

Libraries expect that items that they have ordered from abroad will not arrive before the MARC data arrives on the LC tapes. Unfortunately, irregularities in the despatch of the tapes and consequential delays imposed by the BL in putting them up to users means that this is often not the case.

Related to currency is coverage. Until the BLBSD markets the British Catalogue of Music and its audio-visual and serials files, MARC records consist only of monographs, atlases, new periodical titles in English and that material in Germanic and Romance languages included in the LC MARC. The BL does not put up Australian and Canadian MARC records, nor the tapes provided in the Exchange Network by European agencies, so that records for all these materials, as well as older materials in all languages, audio-visual and non-book materials are regarded as non-MARC or Extra-MARC ('EMMA') materials which require original cataloguing. So too do the current British imprints which elude the BNB. The establishment of a national data base incorporating the extensive EMMA records in the cooperatives' files, those in the LOCAS files of the British Library's Department of Printed Books and Science Reference Library, together with the MARC data bases themselves will bring into the open the extent of the cataloguing pool that is at present so difficult of access.

Another aspect of the coverage of MARC relates specifically to the search mechanisms operated by the cooperatives. The searching routines for identifying, matching and reporting as well as the transferring of MARC records (the 'hits' on the data base) from the MARC file or the Potential Requirements File (PRF) to a transaction and catalogue file are rendered more effective by the scope of the indexing of alternative control numbers. These are held not merely in the main field 001 in the MARC record. In batch systems the cataloguer is assisted by an approach that permits all available control numbers (ISBN, LC card number, BNB numbers or local control numbers including any alternative ISBNs) to be tried wherever stored. However, under a system where the cataloguer has to predict which file to address on field 001 only, that is ISBN for the UK, LC card number for the US, a search may have to be repeated by a second input to the other file if it is not found on the first, and this delays the processing of the item. Cross-indexing on control numbers is also helpful for controlling the growth of a file, and for monitoring and reducing duplication of records from BNB (with the ISBN in 001) and LC MARC (with the LC card number in 001). Catalogue searching, too, is assisted if the searches on the separate files listed in figure 1 above are at least directed automatically from one to the next. On-line searching on BLAISE using other keys, such as author, title or subject, may be effective, but the charges levied for such searches put up the costs of the operation considerably.

In conjunction with an effective Potential Requirements File some cooperatives manage a priority system for accepting records into the catalogue file. Priority is given to the data with the highest standards, and is a consequence of the different strata of the MARC file. Figure 2 gives a typical priority system against which the cataloguer can pit his wits for recognizing how to treat MARC and other records retrieved.

1 BNB data 1981-
2 Union file data of the cooperative
3 BNB 1975-1980 (under the BNB AACR 2 conversion)
4 LC 1981-
5 CIP records 1981-
6 LC 1968-1980
7 CIP pre-1981
8 BNB 1950-1974
9 Union file data entered below the 'minimum input standard'.

Figure 2   A priority system for MARC records

Original cataloguing
The use of MARC records entails the subsidiary activity of adding holdings data to the bibliographic record — the 'local information' comprising call-marks, accession numbers and other proprietorial notes; this is straightforward given standard practices for inputting. In LOCAS the local data are integrated into the structure of the MARC format which can cause problems when bibliographic data are amended but the local data remain the same. In the union catalogue systems the local data are packed as a separate record linked to the bibliographic data and can be addressed independently.

Precis strings, subject headings and classification remain an 'extra-

MARC activity, especially the classification. Even where libraries use Dewey Decimal or Library of Congress classification schemes local practice may have diverged when applying the schedules — and BLBSD does not always come up with the same LC class numbers as the Library of Congress does . . . And no other schemes, not even UDC which has a MARC tag assigned in the format, appear on MARC records.

The most important activity in a MARC-based system is the input of original cataloguing for the non-MARC intake: the EMMA records, as already described. Both to permit the sharing of such records in a cooperative and to ensure their viability in complex files the input of EMMA records is usually subject to a 'minimum input standard'. In the case of the cooperatives and the LOCAS union systems, these minimum standards are quite high, equivalent at least to the level 2 of description laid down by AACR 2.

Standards

The minimum input standard relates equally to the use of the MARC records from the data base as to new input. As was clear from figure 1 and from statements concerning the complexity of the format and data elements, participating in MARC systems entails a high level of cataloguing. It is this aspect which is constantly under discussion when questions are raised about the automatic acceptability of centrally produced records and about cataloguing productivity. To scrutinize MARC records excessively reduces the benefits of taking centrally produced records as found, yet at the same time their level is manifestly not uniform, hence the need for priority tables of the sort given in figure 2 above.

The basic duty imposed upon the practitioners in cooperative systems has been to adhere to standards for the creation of MARC records. It is an essential requirement in union catalogue systems. Members of SWALCAP and individual LOCAS users have not been under such an obligation. In a union catalogue, or in a large library catalogue, records taken from the various strata of the MARC data base do not fit together in an acceptable filing sequence because of the different rules pertaining. Even after the machine conversion of records to AACR 2, discrepancies amongst records will show in a long series, and may lead to duplication of input and the need for *ad hoc* amendments.

Control of standards is central to the creation and use of cooperative data bases. The nature of the standards relate directly to the nature of the cataloguing service provided. The shortcomings associated with the

LC records, from the point of view of British librarians, have already been alluded to, and in North America MARC has been used mainly to continue the card catalogue. In Britain, the development of MARC-based services has been associated with the introduction of new forms of catalogue, especially computer output microform or COM. British practice, too, has seen the need to marshal large files and structured catalogues under common standards to ensure a semblance, at least, of editorial respectability. BLCMP, SCOLCAP and ULSCS have established priorities among the records as already noted, and as illustrated in figure 2. Included in the priority list are CIP records which may be used in the expectation of their being replaced by full MARC records, and also certain categories of substandard records which participating libraries are licensed to put in for 'other' purposes, such as on-order records, circulation records and retrospective conversion data. Both BLCMP and LOCAS market records for the stated purpose of retro-spective cataloguing at a lower rate, in recognition of the inferior quality of the earliest MARC records. The effectiveness of the priority system is increased by making its automatic operation rely upon the internal evidence of the records themselves.

BLCMP, SCOLCAP and ULSCS operate an *editorial policy*. So too, of course, does the British National Bibliography whose staff respond to innumerable requests concerning problems of establishing headings and of cataloguing practice. The ULSCS has a cataloguing coordinator on its staff, BLCMP has an editor with assistants, part of whose work is to monitor the quality of the records, to sort out problems, to record difficulties and to seek their resolution. BLCMP goes so far as to con-vene meetings to discuss problems of interpretation with BNB; both BLCMP and ULSCS arrange meetings of their cataloguers to thrash out common approaches. These are expensive procedures and this adher-ence to standards adds to the staff costs of participating in the system. There are costs, too, in handling the files for the automatic intervention in records and the operation of the system of priorities.

It is expected that with on-line catalogues many of these demands may be relaxed, but where the output format is COM the burden has to be borne. The on-line catalogue will be more accessible to different search techniques, and the collocation of entries retrieved should be more easily browsed through and more varied, so that discrepant head-ings may not conceal or obfuscate in the way that they do in card catalogues and COM frame catalogues.

Split catalogues

British cataloguing management over the last fifteen years has tended to use the advent of automation as the opportunity to close the card caralogue. Output on cards is not, of course, unknown with automated systems, and it has been retained with ulterior motives in certain cases. But with the advent of automation formats other than cards quickly predominated: printed page catalogues at Camden and other public libraries, followed by cassetted microfilm and then microfiche with the COM bureaux.

After the arrival of the COM catalogue in the library, the maintenance and fate of the old card catalogue has had to be considered. The matter has not been neglected and various measures have been tried to mitigate the problems of having to look in 'two places' when using the catalogue. The minimal approach is to do no more than to explain the coverage of the two catalogues and their respective subject or classified counterparts. Full retrospective conversion would eliminate the card catalogue – in time, and at considerable expense.

For large libraries the elimination of the card catalogue has certainly not been practicable although smaller libraries have joined cooperatives with this as a prime goal: the opportunity to consider the matter further comes when large-scale on-line circulation systems are implemented. Some libraries have started MARC cataloguing by taking cards as their initial output and interfiling them in the card catalogue (at least where the rules have remained the same), and have at a later stage gone over to COM when the proportion of stock represented by pre-MARC cards has been reduced by withdrawal, or has otherwise been superseded or converted to MARC.

The alternative favoured by some of the largest libraries like the National Libraries of Scotland and Wales and the University of Birmingham Library, as well as Exeter University Library and some smaller libraries, is to microfilm the card catalogue by conventional methods and reproduce it on fiches so as to offer their users fiche catalogues at all locations for both old and new stock. A problem of use still remains since the microfiches for the old catalogue will outnumber the COM fiches and cause difficulties of storage. If partial retrospective conversion or withdrawal of old stock take place then the old catalogue fiches become out of date, so the microfilming exercise may have to be undertaken again.

A further question to answer is whether the split in the catalogue should be made by date of publication or by date of acquisition. It may be more helpful to the user if it is made by date of publication, so that only items published after a certain date will appear in the new catalogue, but for libraries, and in the long run, it is easier to split the catalogue by date of acquisition regardless of date of imprint. Other problems arising from the existence of split catalogues derive from a change of cataloguing practice between the old and the new, and from the existence of new editions, series and multi-volume works in progress represented in part in both the old and the new catalogues. Extensive cross-referencing is inevitable, though in practice libraries have usually converted existing entries and brought them into the MARC-based files.

On the subject side, wherever a classified catalogue is in use, the problem of the split catalogue is especially acute, but the situation seems to carry its own solution. Automation, while it may be accompanied by a change of cataloguing rules (eg from AACR 67 to AACR 2) can stimulate new outputs, like a Keyword-out-of-context (KWOC) listing or a subject heading catalogue as complements to the classified file, and does not readily call for a change of classification scheme. An index to the classified card catalogue will then serve quite well as the index to the COM classified catalogue, though it will need up-dating, and will need to be duplicated for an effective subject service if the new catalogue is to be found at several locations in the library.

The maintenance of indexes to classified catalogues has been an area for considerable local independence both amongst libraries which are members of cooperatives as amongst those who have developed their own systems. The automation of the index can be a separate exercise within an automation project. The MARC agency should be able to cope with Precis if necessary, and with Library of Congress subject headings, MeSH (Medical subject headings), or other terminology, but many libraries do opt to rely upon their institutional computer service to undertake this phase of the system. With classified catalogues on cards or produced by COM it is quite useful to have the subject index in printout form. After its initial creation by the computer its rate of up-dating will be slower than the rate of growth of the catalogue itself. The size of the file is not excessive and it is not difficult to manipulate or maintain. It keeps the library in good standing with the local computer manager, particularly when the library goes outside the institution for so many other computerized projects.

The reader services aspect of split catalogues is paramount. As well as just providing guidance on the use of the different catalogues, librarians

97

should remember the need to remind users of the existence of the two catalogues so that neither category of stock is neglected.

COM catalogues

The earliest COM catalogues, for example those at Westminster Public Library and LASER at the end of the 1960s, were on cassetted film, although at the same time Shropshire County Library had already chosen microfiche. After the various trials and reports of the Bath University Comparative Catalogue Study (1975) between 1975 and 1977, BLCMP and libraries like those at Southampton University and Trinity College Dublin went over to COM fiches, sometimes at the point when the film readers were coming to the end of their useful life and were due for replacement. Microfiche is the predominant form at the moment. Although it was seen at first as an interim form, before the arrival of on-line catalogues, COM may hold its own longer, thanks to its portability and may be succeeded by videodisc up-dating before on-line proper.

The great advantage of the COM catalogue is its availability in multiple and cheap copies which can be easily up-dated and readily distributed within a single campus or a large building, or over multi-site institutions like many polytechnics and public library systems. However, in the larger libraries the size of COM catalogues after more than seven years is beginning to become a problem and an expense. To offset the cost of microfiche, libraries are resorting to less frequent up-dating and to a system of supplementary up-dating of a cumulated file. The latter measure only exacerbates the problem of the split catalogue which the move to automation created at the outset.

The Centre for Catalogue Research at Bath University Library and the studies on the form and layout of catalogues at the Royal College of Art have provided an extensive overview of COM systems. Without these studies there would have been no enquiries into the purpose of catalogues, and no review of catalogue layouts. As it is, the COM era can pass into the on-line era with much information from which videodisc and on-line output will benefit enormously.

The use of COM catalogues requires the installation of microform readers on a large scale. There may be apprehension that queues will form to use individual machines, and this may lead to studies on the use made of catalogues and the amount of possible congestion at the machines. Such analyses can lead to the provision of machines for technical services staff, cataloguers and acquisitions staff at their workplaces, thereby reducing pressure on the machines in the public areas. Any review of the ideal number of machines to install in a library to cater for median use would also have to take into account such matters as the availability of plug points in older buildings and the possible lack of space at existing service points for new equipment. The arrival of COM readers in open view may be the first outward sign of the 'new technology' in many a library, and serves to give the use of microforms in libraries the biggest boost since the first reading machines were installed in darkened rooms twenty years ago or more.

Initial resistance from staff to the idea of COM was an aspect of a more general resistance to microforms in libraries and to be overcome. COM has revolutionized the market for microform readers as a product, so that one problem exercising catalogue departments is to decide which of the many models to choose. Other practical problems for these departments include maintaining the machines, distributing the catalogue up-dates to the various catalogue locations, finding a way to store the fiches, and supervising them as they grow into perhaps hundreds for each catalogue. The National Reprographic Centre for Documentation (NRCd) and Library Technology Reports produce evaluative studies on new readers as they come onto the market. COM users are limited to some extent by the local or favoured bureau of their cooperative; features of indexing and labelling available to SCOLCAP users seem to be beyond the ingenuity or interest of bureaux south of the border!

By placing COM catalogues at locations in the library not previously served by a catalogue, use of the catalogue is dispersed, which entails a parallel broadening of reader service for the catalogue, since advice and guidance should no longer be confined to one 'catalogue hall'. However, where the old card catalogue has not been filmed such decentralization of reader services can only be partial.

Summary
To summarize the questions discussed in this section is to cover the matters that surround the actual cataloguing process under an automated system. Preparation for automating the catalogue will involve an extensive specification of catalogue requirements, which will include the working out of the logistics of taking services probably from a remote cataloguing agency which works with fixed schedules and a fixed delivery service both for input data and for products. The basic operations of input, processing and output, however they may be

99

coordinated, may be handled by three different agencies: a key-punching bureau which tackles cataloguers' input sheets, the cooperative proper with its central processor which holds the data bases and catalogue files, and the COM bureau which receives formatted tapes and which generates the catalogues required in the correct number of copies.

Once a library has chosen a catalogue service and has specified the type of catalogue required and the frequency of its up-dating, then it must turn its attention to gearing the library as a whole to this intrusive new technology, visible in stark form as microfiche readers and the like. Of course, the fact of automation, and the presence in the library of the new technology, should not be felt as an intrusion but as something basic and normal; so, by the management of change, librarians should endeavour to make the new system at home in the library as early as possible, as something as familiar and ordinary as the telephone and other tools of the trade.

MARC-based systems require an adherence to standards. They also necessitate using a core of externally provided records that need 'handling' before they can serve as entries in a local catalogue. More manual intervention is necessary than one might expect at first, because of the variability of the data bases, the inadequacy of coverage and the limitations of editorial control. In fields where coverage by MARC is low, then, of course, original cataloguing will bulk particularly large.

Adoption of automation brings the advantage of greater flexibility of catalogue outputs, but usually gives rise to the problem of a split catalogue in an extreme form. The decision to have a COM catalogue means that decisions must be taken on the particular make of microfiche reader to be bought, the number of copies of the catalogue required, the location of the individual copies of the catalogue, and the manner of organizing their maintenance and supervision. While cataloguers will remain responsible for the production of the catalogues, their physical dispersal means that reader services staff will make greater use of the catalogues and will be concerned with their physical maintenance. The filing of cards, which may have been a shared activity amongst a whole range of staff in the days of the card catalogue, will give way to such chores as distributing the fiches and ensuring that the machines are dusted and in working order.

THE PROCESS OF AUTOMATED CATALOGUING
The organization of cataloguing in an automated system has to accommodate various sets of activities. There will be variations due to the

nature of the system – in-house and therefore relatively self-contained, MARC-based and operational under a cooperative, with or without partial on-line components – but all will require decisions and a commitment of resources. They are likely to include:

a Setting up workflow procedures to separate MARC-type and non-MARC materials.

b Pre-searching for MARC records and related listings of control numbers.

c Checking a union catalogue or other MARC authority.

d Establishing a balance between off- and on-line searching and between off-and on-line input.

e Reviewing the extent of checking necessary for data going into the system, and the point of entry into the system.

f Providing a suitable environment for new equipment.

g Establishing timetables for regular procedures.

h Devising emergency measures for breakdowns in the systems.

Armed with the cataloguing code which will be annotated with the local or the cooperative's interpretation of options in the rules, with a set of input forms, with the input manual which must be mastered and kept up to date in every detail, the cataloguer in an automated system is involved in a more specialized and compartmentalized set of activities than before. To proceed most effectively automated cataloguing needs to be centralized cataloguing. By using MARC, and by participating in a system founded on a union data base, the cataloguer is bound by conditions which modify the nature of the tasks to be undertaken in cataloguing, and these conditions may give more specific roles for different levels of staff than was formerly the case. The categorization of books as MARC or non-MARC, the need to search for records of the former and to consult the union catalogue for the latter, and the use of other authority tools impose stages upon the processing of materials which do not apply so rigidly in self-contained and manual cataloguing systems. Figure 3 displays the probable line of processing in a manual cataloguing system with a classified catalogue. It is self-contained, though it may show loops where BNB or other external card services are included similar to the flow in a MARC-based system. The library doing original, manual cataloguing, while it may use external printed tools, remains nevertheless its own authority. The diagram would also apply to a library implementing its own automated system, though here the need for a timetable for the computer side of operations would change the diagram in some respects.

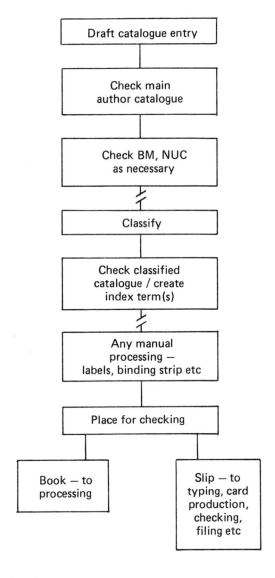

Figure 3 Scheme of a manual cataloguing system

Figure 4 tabulates the general set of questions faced in a MARC-based system using AACR 2 and participating in a union catalogue project. The conventions of input and codings of data affect the filing order, punctuation and the layout of entries in the catalogue, so that the onus is upon the cataloguer to complete the input form correctly in all respects.

One variant approach to the model occurs at the outset and is followed quite commonly. This is to list control numbers for the searching either on-line or at least ahead of the other processes which may be started at the accession stage or even the ordering stage. The search and the match result in a transfer of records from the PRF (Potential Requirements File) to the catalogue file, while non-matches are indicated automatically as EMMA items. Where there is an automatic recycling of control number searches books are left 'pending', that is left on the shelves of the catalogue room (which, as we have seen above, has its own practical implications), and those still unmatched at the end of the set number of weeks are catalogued as EMMA items. Files of 'short forms' are often established; the forms are prepared for MARC items before they have been matched with control numbers, and the file can be maintained against the notification of a MARC entry. In a batch system this comes through weekly, and the match is confirmed by a diagnostic print of the MARC record. Where on-line access exists the printout of the record (in full or in brief) can be rapidly produced. The finicky attention which must be given to the quality of the records arises out of the need to maintain standards and consistency in the 'union' catalogue, and relates to the system of priorities found in the union catalogue, the need to follow AACR 2 precisely, and the rules laid down by the cooperative. As the proportion of original AACR records increases after 1981, the number of items requiring this high quality supervision should decline. It is possible to delegate to junior staff the first checking to be made in the union catalogue and in *Books in English*, but EMMA cataloguing, and classification, require professional skills. So too does analytical cataloguing and the cataloguing of audio-visual materials, music and sound recordings. These are particularly complex in MARC input because the inadequacy of the format to meet the requirements of AACR 2 means that special provisions apply. The creation of references may also be a problem depending on the conventions followed by the cooperative.

The streaming of the work-flow, notably by the division of books into MARC and non-MARC items will result in a parallel division of

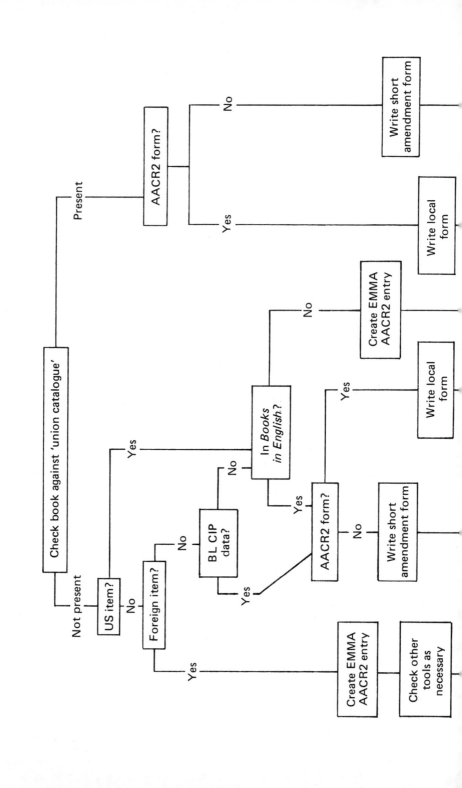

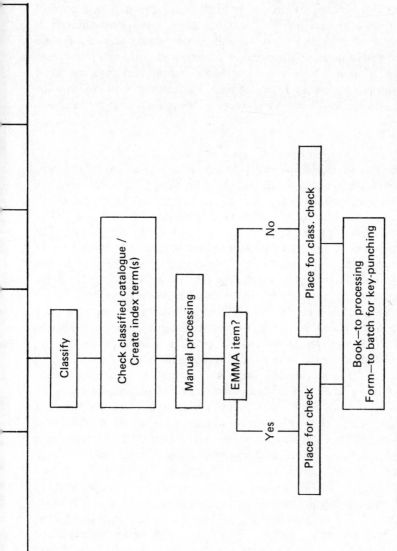

Figure 4 Scheme of an automated cataloguing system using MARC and AACR 2 with participation in a union cataloguing scheme, and with a classified subject catalogue

staff duties. As has been suggested, the use of MARC records as such is a limited part of the whole operation: to find that a large proportion of one's acquisitions are covered by MARC is a boon and a vindication of the whole process, but it is the 'other half of cataloguing' which needs the effort. The integration of machine records into a particular file and the management of the stock of a library collection require considerable effort and a plethora of decisions and tasks are involved, all of them more specialized than before. For libraries in cooperatives the dimensions are broadened because of the greater need to adhere to standards.

Input
The transition from paper tape to discette or to on-line input is now well under way, but still, for the most part, involves the keying-in data from completed worksheets. The library will have to muster a decision on whether to undertake this work within the library or to subcontract it to a bureau directly or through the cooperative. The advent of the intelligent terminal makes it possible for the library to retain input as its own responsibility using designated staff to key data onto magnetic tape or disc for dispatch to the cooperative or for direct on-line transmission. On-line input is expensive and the need for it is limited if the catalogue file itself is up-dated only monthly. But where the file, or part of it, is on-line in conjunction with a circulation or acquisitions system, the relevance of on-line up-dating is obvious.

Standard practice with paper-tape production includes double-keying for verification purposes, editorial checking being arranged when the library receives the printout diagnostics of records after the monthly catalogue runs. With input through a visual display unit (VDU), hard copy output could be available directly; alternatively a verification stage can be interposed before the data are sent off. In either case visual checking and proof-reading are available if necessary. By printing brief records selectively from the terminal it is possible to reduce checking to just the essentials such as headings and class numbers, those being the most important parts of the catalogue entry for accurate retrieval. The advantage of using a VDU, whether on-line or via discette, is that corrections can be applied before records are processed and therefore before anything appears in the next up-date of the catalogue.

The use of terminals has implications for the cataloguing process. There is the trade union interest in new technology agreements; there are ergonomic aspects of working conditions; there is the scheduling of the operators' time. There should also be continuous refinement of the searching and input techniques themselves, where faster and more efficient methods can be developed as experience in the system is gained. Once mastery of the system is achieved, the only limiting factor may be the constraints arising out of the handling of the data base.

Output
The COM frame catalogue is less flexible than a sequence of cards, but a COM catalogue is easier to manage. The filing, of course, is automatic, corrections made from one input record apply to the whole set of headings, and copies of the catalogue are easy to produce. The library has to be equipped with microform readers, and these have to be maintained in good order, their focusing kept right and spare light bulbs kept in stock. They may need special tables, some to enable consultation from readers standing up, others for users who prefer to be seated, especially for longer consultation. Instructions on the use of the machine are necessary as well as guidance on the catalogues themselves. Files for the fiches, or special 'pigeon-hole' shelving for cassetted film have to be provided. Up-dates of the catalogue need to be quickly made available and the discarding of superseded copies organized; the latter may go to subordinate locations in other departments of the library, or to neighbouring institutions, in which case responsibility for their despatch may be taken by the reader services department.

We have already noted above that the relationship of the new COM catalogue to the old card catalogue needs to be explained. As the COM catalogue becomes more extensive, users may have to be reminded of the records remaining in the card catalogue. The actual content, labelling and layout of the COM catalogue can be reviewed after a time. The profiles of entries, and the frequency of issue can be changed if the cooperative is responsible. Variations in short and full entries can be made to the name-title, subject and classified catalogues as an experiment.

By the time that the COM catalogues have grown into hundreds of fiches, it may be necessary, as mentioned earlier, to reduce the frequency of the up-dating for the sake of economy, and to institute monthly supplements to an annual or three-year cumulation. And while a single microfiche reader may suffice when the COM catalogue is first instituted, serving both author-title and subject files, as the catalogue grows the different catalogue sequences may each have their separate readers:

such a move has implications for both space and reader service to the catalogues.

With the growth of on-line cataloguing the COM catalogue may become the 'old' catalogue, and the current component of the data base introduced as the on-line public catalogue. An alternative to this is the provision of videodisc up-date in place of COM and used on-line from an in-house mini-computer, still being up-dated regularly from the external cataloguing agency. These developments will bring new preoccupations, but also, where on-line circulation systems exist, new scope for services to users by integrating the catalogue with the loan file.

One minor aspect of output is the matter of notifications to subject or area union catalogues. Most of these union catalogues are not automated files themselves, but are increasingly being up-dated by contributing libraries who are using automated cataloguing. To meet its commitments the library may have to continue to produce cards for supply to the union catalogue. This is relatively expensive but the various cooperatives can generate them.

Summary

For the library using batch systems only it is important to establish timetables for searching, input, processing and output. Dates for the input and for the despatch of forms for key-punching must be established, and a mechanism set up for clearing 'on-order' files after entries get into the catalogue. The main timetable has to be coordinated with the operations of the cataloguing agency, which in turn depend upon the times of up-dating the MARC files and the arrangements made for operating the computer.

The apprehension that there might be large-scale failure of computer systems has not been realized, but all users and cooperatives will admit to difficulties with their systems, starting with the teething troubles during implementation and including times when the system is not working properly. Strikes at computer centres, power failures (which affect terminals, library lighting and COM microfiche readers), rail and postal delays all become hazards of the operation. So long as the data base maintenance by the cooperative can proceed without interrupting the daily operations of the system, the library should not be bothered by this aspect of using an external service. Cataloguing management, however, has to face these problems as they arise for they include interruptions to the MARC service, failures of the system and corrup-
108

tion of the data, all of which may affect the currency of the catalogue. Shortcomings in the MARC records themselves and poor MARC coverage of acquisitons lead to a greater amount of original cataloguing, which is likely to be input less rapidly. Otherwise the chief problem to be faced is probably the tracing of books between the accessions stage and their appearance in the catalogue. When things go well, the time saved on current cataloguing can be used to eliminate the backlogs and make a start on the retrospective conversion of the catalogue.

THE COSTS OF AUTOMATED CATALOGUING

The costs of traditional cataloguing are almost wholly staff costs. Some external payments may be necessary for card cabinets, stationery, BNB or Blackwell's cards and for bibliographical tools like the *National union catalog*, MARCfiche or *Books in English*. An automated cataloguing system incurs substantial capital costs at the outset and various recurrent costs.

Capital costs may include:

a Hardware, such as computers, terminals and telecommunication equipment;

b COM catalogue readers and related equipment;

c Key-punching machines

d Training programmes

Recurrent charges arise from two sources. There are firstly the costs of the cataloguing service, and secondly the traditional costs of staff salaries, bibliographic tools, stationery and office supplies. In the first category can be included:

a Subscription to a cooperative or catalogue agency;

b Charges for MARC records, file handling and catalogue production;

c Searching charges;

d COM production;

e Key-punching charges;

f Charges for the maintenance of equipment.

The second category would include, besides salaries and the traditional bibliographical tools, supplies of input forms and discettes.

The various cooperatives levy their subscriptions and charges according to different criteria, and the factor most talked of at the moment is that of 'first time use' (FTU), which is derived from OCLC practice. This means that the charges incurred are all boiled down to the cost of an individual record from the data base. All the service and processing charges for the cooperative's role in the process are thereby charged

109

against intake and expected MARC coverage. LOCAS charges are levied on a cost-recovery basis and result in a complicated invoice identifying each task of their processing. For management the chief point is the question of organizing new funds or allocations in the estimates to cover likely costs. These costs can be worked out from the rate of intake, from estimates of cataloguing productivity and from the scales of charges levied by the agency and bureaux involved.

Various studies of the cost of cataloguing have been undertaken, and special attention has been paid to the methods so as to be able to compare the cost of manual systems with the cost of automated systems. Extensive comparisons were prepared by BLCMP for its founder members in 1970 and 1974. Even when the pressures and costs of manual systems were not the major impetus for the adoption of automation, libraries are nevertheless acutely aware of the costs of the new systems.

MARC-based cataloguing was conceived by libraries as an answer to the various needs and pressures described at the beginning of the article, and one can say that it has achieved most of its promise, albeit at a greater expense than expected. The benefits of automation are largely unquantifiable, and go beyond just cataloguing into reader services. Despite the argument over standards, excessive tinkering with MARC records and the wrangling that occurred at the time of the transfer of production of BNB cards from the British Library to BLCMP, the quality and the speed of cataloguing continue to improve. The point of automated systems is not just to make savings so much as to achieve more with the same effort as before.

CONCLUSION

The pattern of automated cataloguing systems that has taken shape during the last fifteen years is being changed by developments in on-line processes. On-line systems are vindicating the expense and effort of computerizing data files and housekeeping systems. Present automated systems have barely done more than to transfer manual systems to the machine. On-line activities, however, bring about a more positive use of computer capabilities, and they herald a dynamic development of catalogue files. As on-line files become more accessible, the present concentration on standards will give way to a concern over search techniques, borrowing some of them from the extensive work in information retrieval on the subject data bases.

While we may hope that the new cataloguing will come to be an integral part of everyday library operations, it is clear that it requires special knowledge and precise skills that tend to set staff, both managers and practitioners, apart in cataloguing as in other areas of automation.

The establishment of large data bases of cataloguing by the various cooperatives and the branches of the British Library, as well as the not insubstantial files of other libraries engaged in automated cataloguing, is of great relevance for the future. The prospect of merging at least some of these files, or of achieving access to them through networking arrangements is of great moment, for the release of a considerable volume of EMMA data may radically alter the balance of MARC production. The Cooperative Automation Group (CAG) is reviewing both the technical means and the bibliographic and formatting standards which would affect the establishment of a 'national data base'. Such a data base would be a national cataloguing resource and would constitute a major outcome of the first phase of MARC-based cataloguing.

An intrinsic part of automated cataloguing is its use in reader services, and one obvious use of these catalogues is as a tool for inter-library lending and requests. The British Library has set up a Working Party on Union Catalogues which is looking at the implications for the national interlending system of the wide availability of automated COM catalogues; their use in reader services may have a dramatic impact on inter-library lending. Catalogue managers will have to absorb these implications of automation, and they will have to be centrally involved in the integration of files in acquisitions and circulation systems, for these require a full bibliographic back-up to their library housekeeping functions. Where this has remained in an embryonic state in batch systems, the arrival of on-line systems will allow it to come to fruition.

BIBLIOGRAPHY

As this has been a general review of the administration of automated cataloguing references to particular developments have not been given in the text. A very large literature on the subject has now accumulated. The list below gives the sources used for this article, and is drawn mainly from the writings of the last few years.

Serials
Bath University Programme of Catalogue Research newsletter 1-   1978-
   BLAISE newsletter British Library, 1-   1977-
   Catalogue and index: periodical of the Library Association Cataloguing and Indexing Group 40-   Spring 1976-

Catalyst: information from the University of London Shared Cataloguing System 3- July 1981-

International cataloguing: quarterly bulletin of the IFLA International Office for UBC, 7- 1978-

Library technology reports American Library Association, 12- 1976-

MARC news British Library Bibliographic Services Division, 1- 1978-

Program Aslib 6- 1972-

SCOLCAP newsletter National Library of Scotland, 1- 1976-

SOUL automation projects University of Southampton Library, 1- 1970-

SWALCAP newsletter University of Bristol Library, 1- 1977-

Vine 1- 1974-

Books and reports

Abbott, G L *Card catalogs: alternative futures* Syracuse, New York, Information Yield, 1979.

Aschenborn, H J *Microfilming of library card catalogues* Hatfield, National Reprographic Centre for documentation, 1977.

Association of Research Libraries *Freezing card catalogs* Washington DC, Association of Research Libraries, 1978.

Bath University Comparative Catalogue Study *Final report* Bath, the University, 1975.

BLCMP costing catalogue systems Birmingham, BLCMP, 1971.

BLCMP final report London, British Library, 1976. (British Library Research and Development Department report no 5303.)

Boss, R W and Marcum, D B *The library catalog: COM and on-line options* Chicago, American Library Assocation, 1979. (*Library technology reports* vol 16 no 5.)

British Library *Specification for retrospective conversion of UK MARC files 1950-1980* and *Specification for conversion of LC MARC records to UK MARC* London, British Library Bibliographic Services Division, 1980.

Clements, F A, *MARC Users' Group: proceedings of a conference held at Plymouth, April 1975* Exeter, MARC Users' Group, 1975.

Gapen, D K and Juergens, B *Closing the catalog: proceedings of the 1978 and 1979 Library and Information Technology Institutes* London, Mansell, 1980.

Gore, D, Kimborough, J and Spyers-Duran, P *Requiem for the card catalog: management issues in automated cataloging* London, Aldwych Press, 1979.

Hunter, E J and Bakewell, K G B *Cataloguing* London, Bingley, 1979.

Irvine, R *Practical MARC cataloguing: proceedings of the second SCONUL seminar organized by the Universities of Southampton and Birmingham, and held at Southampton, September 1975* London, SCONUL, 1976.

Kaske, N K *A new catalog: some ideas on its purpose, form, cost and planning for it* Arlington, Virginia, ERIC, 1979. (ERIC report ED-176 728.)

Malinconico, S M and Fasana, P J *The future of the catalog: the library's choice* White Plains, New York, Knowledge Industry Publications, 1979.

Matthews, J R *The four online bibliographic utilities: a comparison* Chicago, American Library Association, 1979. (*Library technology reports* vol 15 no 6.)

Overton, C M and Seal, A *Cataloguing costs in the UK: an analysis of the market for automated cataloguing service* Bath, Bath University Library, 1980. (British Library Research and Development Department report no 5545.)

Reynolds, L and Spencer, H *Two experiments on the layout of information on computer-output microfilm* London, Royal College of Art, 1979. (British Library Research and Development Department report no 5480.)

Reynolds, L *Visual presentation of information in COM library catalogues* London, Royal College of Art, 1979. (British Library Research and Development Department report no 5472.)

Seal A *Automated cataloguing in the UK: a guide to services* Bath, Bath University Library, 1980. (British Library Research and Development Department report no 5545.)

Teague, S J *COM systems in libraries: current British practice* Guildford, Microfilms Association, 1978.

Wiederkuhr, R R V *Alternatives for future library catalogs: a cost model: final report of the Library Catalogs Costing Model Project* Rockville, Maryland, King Research, 1980.

Journal articles and papers
Bierman, K J 'Automated alternatives to card catalogs: the current state of planning and implementation' *Journal of library automation* 8 (4) December 1975, 277-298.

113

'BLAISE update' *Vine* 27 March 1979, 31-34.

Boaz, M 'Selections of bibliographic data bases: reasons for examining the design elements of various bibliographic systems before adopting one' *Journal of library automation* 12 (2) June 1979, 178-179.

'British Library Ad Hoc Working Party on Union Catalogues' *BLLD news sheet* 24 June 1981.

'A British OCLC network in 1981' *Vine* 33 May 1980, 16-20.

Bryant, P 'Progress in documentation: the catalogue' *Journal of documentation* 36 (2) June 1980, 133-163.

Butcher, R 'National data on microfiche: bibliographic and MARC based use of COM' *Reprographics quarterly* 9 (3) Summer 1976, 104-107.

Capewell, P 'The customer and the network: a customer's view of BLCMP' *Catalogue and index* 45 Summer 1977, 5-7.

'Cataloguing futures' *Cataloguing Australia* 5 (3) July-September 1979, 7-53.

'The cataloguing revolution' *Library Association record* 83 (5) May 1981, 235-244.

Cathro, W S 'The upheaval in bibliographic exchange standards, 1974-1984' *Australian library journal* 29 (2) May 1980, 59-68.

Curwen, A G 'Working to rule?' in *Seminar on AACR 2: proceedings of the Library Association Catalogue and Index Group held at Nottingham, April 1979*, edited by G Roe, London, Library Association, 1980, 60-75.

Davis, R J 'The availability of MARC records for cataloguing' *Aslib proceedings* 33(6) June 1981, 260-262.

De Gennaro, R 'Computer network systems: the impact of technology on cooperative lending in the USA' *Interlending review* 9 (2) April 1981, 39-43.

Dwyer, J R 'The effect of closed catalogs on public access' *Library resources and technical services* 25 (2) April-June 1981, 186-195.

Evans, M E 'University of York library automation project, 2: production of cards by computer terminal' *Program* 13 (2) April 1979, 96-100.

Fasana, P J '1981 and beyond: visions and decisions' *Journal of library automation* 13 (2) June 1980, 96-107.

Freedman, M J 'Automated network catalog products and services' *Journal of library automation* 9 (2) June 1976, 145-155.

Furlong, E J 'Index access to on-line records: an operational view' *Journal of library automation* 11 (3) September 1978, 223-228.

Gredley, E J 'Standardizing bibliographic data: AACR 2 and international change' *Journal of librarianship* 12 (2) April 1980, 84-101.

Grills, C M 'Videodisc: friend or foe?' *IMC journal* 17, (2) 1981, 6-12.

Hayes, R M 'On-line microfiche catalogs' *Journal of micrographics* 13 (4) March-April 1980, 15-63.

Hayes, R M and Borko, H 'Using an on-line microfiche catalog for technical service and retrieval of bibliographic data' *Information processing and management* 16 (6) December 1980, 277-289.

Hewitt, J A and Gleim, D E 'Adopting AACR 2: the case for not closing the catalog' *American libraries* 10 (3) March 1979, 118-121.

Hickey, D J 'The search for uniformity in cataloging: centralization and standardization' *Library trends* 25 (3) January 1977, 565-586.

Hoffman, H 'Cataloguing work performance' *Cataloguing Australia* 4 (3-4) July-December 1978, 40-45.

Horder, A 'The reproduction of card catalogues on roll microfilm and microfiche: choice of microform and format' *Reprographics quarterly* 13 (3) Summer 1980, 94-98.

Howarth, P 'Cataloguing work performance' *Cataloguing Australia* 4 (3-4) July-December 1978, 46-53.

Humphries, M N 'MARCfiche' *Catalogue and index* 48 Spring 1978, 7-8.

Jeffreys, A 'Management in cataloguing services' *Catalogue and index* 46 Autumn 1977, 2-4.

Jolliffe, J 'Retrospective bibliography: the needs of academic libraries' *Catalogue and index* 49 Summer 1978, 1-4.

'The library cooperatives and LOCAS: ten years of growth' *Vine* 28 May 1979, 37-48.

Lovecy, T 'What's in co-operatives for me?' *Catalogue and index* 61 Summer 1981, 1-6.

McElderry, S 'Alternatives to the conventional card catalog from the user point of view' *IFLA journal* 2 (4) 1976, 232-236.

McSean, T 'One library one catalogue' *Assistant librarian* 72 (4) April 1979, 56-60.

Malinconico, S M 'Technology and standards for bibliographic control' *Library quarterly* 47 (3) July 1977, 308-325.

Mullikin, A G 'The King Research Project: design for a library cost model' *Library resources and technical services* 25 (2) Spring 1981, 177-185.

115

Norie, E 'False economy; or, sabotage at the catalog!' *Library resources and technical services* 24 (1) Winter 1980, 69-70.

Ohmes, F and Jones, J F 'The other half of cataloging' *Library resources and technical services* 17 (3) Summer 1973, 320-329.

Royan, B 'Developing a standard for COM fiche library catalogues' *Microdoc* 18 (1) 1979.

Russon, D 'Union catalogues at the British Library Lending Division' *Interlending review* 8 (1) January 1980, 1-6.

Seal, A 'Estimating the market for automated cataloguing services in the UK' *Journal of librarianship* 12 (3) July 1980, 159-170.

Seal, A 'Monitoring UK MARC' *Vine* 38 April 1981, 32.

Sheridan, C and Butcher, P 'A comparison between the short and full entry catalogues at the City University Library *Catalogue and index* 53 Summer 1979, 3-5.

Stevens, N D 'The catalogs of the future: a speculative essay' *Journal of library automation* 13 (2) June 1980, 88-95.

Svenonius, E 'Direction for research in indexing, classification and cataloging' *Library resources and technical services* 25 (1) Winter 1981, 88-103.

Thomson, M 'The cataloguer in the network' *Cataloguing Australia* 4 (1-2) January-June 1978, 20-30.

Veaner, A B, 'Management and technology' *IFLA journal* 7 (1) 1981, 32-37.

Vervliet, H D L 'Alternative physical forms of catalogues in large research libraries' *International cataloguing* 6 (1) January-March 1977, 6-8.

Watson, P 'Converting a card catalogue to microfiche' *Australian academic and research libraries* 9 (3) September 1978, 164-167.

Whitehead, J and Frost, T 'The preparation of specifications for microfiche copies of card catalogs' *Microform review* 9 Spring 1980, 96-99.

Willers, J M 'A survey of retrospective conversion of existing catalogues' *Program* 15 (2) April 1981, 91-99.

Part two

Demonstrating library value: a report of a research investigation

CHRISTINE OLDMAN

The aim of this article is to report and reflect on, some years after its completion, a library management research investigation which was conducted at Cranfield School of Management between the years 1973 and 1977.

Much of the discussion will be concerned with reporting both the methodology and the substantive findings of the investigation. However, the opportunity to present conclusions some time after the completion of a project allows the researcher to consider the validity of both the research approach and its results when the dust, so to speak, has settled. In the conclusion of this article, therefore, I will consider both the state of the library evaluation art and the relevance of library management research in the early 1980s some four years, in fact, after the completion of the Cranfield research.

The background to the research

The Marketing and Logistics Group at Cranfield School of Management received a British Library Research and Development Department grant for a period of three years to undertake a longitudinal methodological study of the value of libraries. A further three months support was given until December 1976 for the exploration of the research conclusions. The BLRDD grant was titled 'A longitudinal study of the costs and benefits of selected library services'. The final output of the research was a report *The beneficial library*.[1] The research was confined to the methodological study of library value in two particular institutions, namely Cranfield Institute of Technology and Loughborough University of Technology. It looked at the delivery of library services to specific selected courses in both these institutes. I hope to show, however, that the insights derived from the study can be applied usefully to formal information systems other than those of technological universities. I myself was principal investigator on the project.

117

The impetus for the research lay in the threats facing library and information services which have been imposed, in the public sector at least, since the early 1970s. Academic libraries, and perhaps to a lesser extent public libraries, had managed to escape major financial cutbacks until this period. Industrial libraries, however, and others funded within the private sector, have never been considered an indispensable service. Increases in the rate of inflation over the last ten years or so have caused politicians to demand, increasingly, 'value for money' exercises in many spheres of 'economic' life. I feel it is important to identify the rationale behind any social research project, and my own Cranfield research project is no exception. The research had many well wishers at the onset, many of whom were bitterly disappointed when our research report was published. It was hoped, I think, that our research would provide a neat and easily applied management formula which could be applied to many library situations in order to demonstrate the worth or the viability of the service. Research funds have been provided for countless other economic studies of libraries; the rationale is similar — how can libraries save their jobs?

We began to argue, as the project developed, that such a search for the Holy Grail is misguided. Value for money exercises, cost-benefit or cost-effectiveness studies have their uses but too often they are politically naive. Studies of library value that are conducted in a 'saving our skins' spirit are likely to flounder. The starting point for such studies is the present situation, the status quo. The assumption that is usually, and most tendentiously, made is that the library or information service is providing a satisfactory service. The analysis, at worst, is an opportunity to collect data to support that assumption and at best is a systematic examination of the past. I hope to show in this article that by attempting to identify the impact of a library service by tackling head on the question of attitudes held by user, funder and librarian, we have made a contribution to library resource management insofar as we have confronted political realities.

Traditional research solutions to library management problems
In order to show why the research abandoned the hoped for (by others) specific cost-effective study of the library services of Cranfield and Loughborough Universities and concentrated on identifying a library's impact or benefits rather than on its output or effects I review below some favoured approaches to library resource management. This is not an attempt to review comprehensively the literature on the economic
118

evaluation of library and information services. This has been done by myself and many others. The most recent example is an excellent critique by Tom Whitehall.[2]

The criticisms that are offered below stem from a belief that university libraries, at least, have much to do with the transfer of knowledge. The library is a key instrument in the transfer of knowledge/information. So too is the formal lecture. Since a university is an information system containing formal and informal elements, some, like the library, consisting largely of documentary information and some, like the one to one tutorial consisting largely of verbal information, it seems fairly essential when discussing budgets to discover what contribution it is envisaged each element can best make to the overall transference of knowledge. Moreover, it does not seem that university libraries, simply because they are explicitly concerned with 'knowledge', are really intrinsically different from other formal information systems. In my library school days we had separate lectures on 'academic libraries', 'public libraries', and 'special libraries'. As far as resource allocation decisions are concerned certain elements exist in all three library situations. Namely, the library is *one* type of information system competing with, supplementing or complementing a whole variety of other methods of transferring what we will, for convenience sake at this stage of the argument, call 'information'.

Information is, traditionally, a free good even in the private sector where the information service may be chalked up as an overhead. The economic technique available for decision-making in public sector economics where the price mechanism is absent is cost-benefit analysis (CBA). I have just alluded to the fact that many library and information cost-benefit studies have been conducted. We were critical of CBA because it forced quantification where it could best be avoided. Moreover, although CBA of all types is beset with problems CBA applied to information seems particularly hazardous. Information defies definition. It is not so much information *per se* we should be interested in but what the information artefact-document, or whatever is being acquired *for*. Although the methodology of CBA seemed to us to be unsuitable, its underlying philosophy is extremely valuable for judging empirical studies. The essential question underlying a cost-benefit approach is 'How much good is X doing?' So applied to the question of library value answers are required to the question 'How much good is the library doing?' rather than 'How good is the library'. The distinction between the two formulations is important. The first implies a

119

concern with impact, with user benefit. The second approach may lead to libraries doing the wrong things, achieving erroneous goals *efficiently*. In the case of this particular research topic if we seek to identify how much good the library is doing then we may be in a better position to discuss what proportion of university income the library should receive. One popular category of effectiveness study aimed to help with library resource management has been *availability* studies. The Library Management Research Unit (now the Centre for Library and Information Management, CLAIM), perfected the technique. The hallmark of all availability studies is the measurement of the library's ability to react to users. The role of a library is assumed, not investigated. In other words, it is taken as given, for example, that the proper goals of a library are to maximize user satisfaction, to provide immediate availability. Such studies are not employing the cost-benefit stance, referred to earlier on, 'How much good is it doing to provide the instant book?', but rather they are answering the question 'How good is the library at providing the instant book?' Those studies which cost availability are therefore cost-effective studies not cost-benefit studies.

Another characteristic of availability studies and indeed of other types of library evalutaion economic or otherwise, is the isolation of the user from the library system. Availability surveys are carefully designed so as to show the incidence of both *reader failure* and *system failure*, to show, in other words, the distinction between genuine absence of the book from the shelf and the reader's ineptitude at finding the book. It is not unreasonable, however, to assume that a document was sought from a library *purposely* in order to help with some task. It seems more important to see if that purpose has been thwarted by the non-acquisition of the book rather than by sophisticated techniques for apportioning the blame. Managers often feel that reader failure is to be overcome by teaching the user the mysteries of librarianship. Some users do indeed become very sophisticated and take some pleasure in learning how to 'crack' the system. In the course of our research we developed the belief that system reform might be more effective than continually making distinctions between the two types of failure. Tearing the user from the system does disservice to good resource management.

A number of researchers have made the important point that use of a library is partly a function of what the user expects the library can do for them. Orr, for example, in his work on the economic evaluation of library was concerned to circumvent this 'problem' of users' expectations.
120

Orr argues that assessing a library in terms of a user's perceptions is essentially subjective. Orr used a document delivery test. Users' needs are simulated by the construction of a sample of publications. A library is rated according to its capability at delivering these publications.[3]

Various studies, English and American, have employed operations research techniques on the task of diagnosing the workings of a library system. The diagnostic characteristic of these system analyses certainly mark them out as a further category of effectiveness studies. The Lancaster University Library Research Unit, for example, has examined what they called the pathology of library provision. Their work demonstrates that a library is a system, a set of interrelated parts such that a change in one of these parts may affect one or more of the others. They show clearly, for instance, the inverse relationship between satisfaction level and collection bias, the higher the percentage of immediate availability the lower the percentage of browsing material, ie the range of material on the shelves will be limited. The Lancaster work demonstrates clearly the relationship between users' expectations and the ability of the library to react. The overall satisfaction level established in one investigation was thought to be low (60%). In order to improve it the library introduced a variable loan policy. The most popular 10% of the collection was made subject to a one week loan period and carefully monitored. This policy led to a massive increase in borrowing. Satisfaction level shot up but then returned to its former level. An improvement in the system's performance had the effect of releasing previously suppressed preferences. This process has brought into the vocabulary of librarianship the concept of the homeostatic library. Demand and supply will tend to find their own level. It is suggested that the level for academic libraries with open access is around 60%.[4]

In the discussion that follows this section I attempt to show how we at Cranfield developed the insights of the Lancaster work, namely that users learn to feel very happy with the library system they have, they learn to adjust. The Lancaster model of the library system is a behaviouristic rather than behavioural one. The library is depicted as an autonomous processing mechanism. Demand and supply will equate. We departed from this, to us, mechanistic, approach principally because the inevitablity of the homeostatic library has dismal implications for funding. I explore this observation later on.

Some, a notable example is the American library researcher Morris Hamburg, argue that utilization is a better overall measure of the performance of a library than availability since it covers both a library's

121

capability to *initiate* and *promote* as well as to *react.*[5] Hamburg's work is prefaced by a well-argued justification. He does not assume that a library's role is simply to react; A library's benefits are, rather, 'things' like increase in knowledge, creativity, motivation and confidence. Since, Hamburg argues, we cannot directly observe these effects in order to justify a library's worth we are forced to substitute a proxy measure – document exposure. Hamburg's approach was more attractive to us when we were designing our own research. We were concerned, however, to go beyond output measures towards measuring impact.

The final category of research solutions to library management problems I intend to discuss here are those which see evaluation research as *explicitly* an economic exercise. Two of the best known cost-benefit type studies applied to university libraries are those conducted by Raffel and Shishko and by Hawgood and Morley at Durham University.[6,7] Hamburg's study already mentioned is also in this category. Both Raffel and Shishko's MIT study and Hawgood and Morley's PEBUL study (Project for Evaluating the Benefits of University Libraries) by examining systematically the current resource mix in the libraries under study discovered the implicit values of those who had made the budgetary decisions. The benefit measures of these two studies are the budget allocations. These budget allocations are tangible evidence of the values held by those making resource decisions. The obvious importance of these two research investigations is that they make explicit the relative importance of library activities. The researchers are in a position to say for example to the library committee members, 'Did you realize that this is how you valued your library?' Equally importantly, the models are predictive. They say what will happen to the total library system if a resource is diverted. The principal criticism of these studies lies in their inability to say anything about the worth or value of a library. They are, rather, examination of past, resource, decisions. So despite employing cost-benefit techniques, the underlying philosophy of a cost-benefit analysis is missing, namely 'How much good is a library doing?' The scientific study of past decisions scarcely makes the original decision any more scientific.

Various passing comments have been offered on the contribution that these various categories of effectiveness study have been made to the resource allocation argument. It is now necessary to make some basic criticisms. This criticism applies to all the categories and involves identifying assertions common to them all. The criticsms are made in the firm belief that the benefits of a library are most convincingly

122

demonstrated by identifying its role in the organizational environment in which it is situated. This implies looking at the effect of use and non-use. It may he helpful to give just two specific examples of what is involved:

What good does it do a research student to use an on-line retrieval system?

Conversely, what harm is done if the student waits three months for a research report from an inter-library loan service?

The first assertion found in all the categories of studies is that use equals usefulness. Hamburg argues very persuasively in favour of using indirect measures or value utilization measures as surrogates for direct measures of value.[5] We must, he says, settle for indirect measures because the benefits of libraries such as creativity or self-improvement cannot be observed. It is very common in public sector evaluation to substitute output measures for impact measures. Moreover Hamburg's argument about the impossibility of finding a measure for the almost metaphysical effects of libraries are unassailable. However, there is another, albeit less than totally satisfactory, way forward. What we can do, and what we did do, is investigate the purposes for which information was sought or acquired. In the case of an information service it seems unhelpful to substitute output measures for impact measures. A library is, as has been asserted earlier, one part only of an information system serving the decision-making and/or knowledge acquisition of those in the wider organization. Information is not of much interest in itself. The demand for information is a derived demand; in other words it is acquired to solve a problem or aid a decision. When the argument about resources is taking place, we must show what contribution the university library, or any type of library for that matter, has made to the total amount of decision-making and/or knowledge acquisition in the university.

A second belief about performance measures to be found in all studies is that use must be maximized. It is a belief that follows on quite naturally from the mechanistic as opposed to creative view of academic librarianship implicit in the first assertion. The library is not necessarily proving its value either, if it demonstrates an increase in its users, or an increase of use amongst existing users. A library must be seen in its organizational, educational context. We must beware of assuming that information is good for people. There is plenty of evidence from the user behaviour studies we carried out, that acquisition of information can impede the task on hand. Evidence for this behavioural

123

supposition comes from many other sources. One of the respondents in the famous INFROSS investigation commented: 'The importance of information can be overrated. More information does not always result in increased knowledge and seldom produces increased wisdom'.[8]

The mechanistic view of academic librarianship held by the library research establishment assumes that the prevailing use of academic libraries is the known-item search. A library is, therefore, evaluated accordingly. How well does it react to user demands? There are some real problems here. Users' expectations are, I have argued, partly a function of their experience of contact with the library system. The Lancaster Library Research Unit work, referred to earlier, demonstrates the relationship between perceptions and satisfaction very clearly. Users will behave how the librarian wants them to behave. If a user perceives his library to be a repository for his known needs he will continue to use the library that way. This view is inherently conservative. It precludes almost any possibility of the library having any other role. Jones has written a polemic against the mechanistic school of library research: 'The quantitative approach emphasizes the service conception of librarianship as opposed to the synergetic. It emphasizes a stimulus-response system in which the users provide the stimulus and the library responds'.[9]

An obvious corollary to the mechanistic approach is the research technique which divorces the library from its organizational setting. All the studies that have been mentioned in this section are concerned only with the user's contact with the library system. The context in which information is sought and the context in which it is used are neglected. If library use is not put into the overall information/ educational context it is difficult to understand the library's role in the host organization. However, it must not be assumed as Brewer and Hills did in their discussion on library user education programmes that the moment the library is taken out of such a vacuum it automatically assumes increased importance.[10] It can be demonstrated that a careful scrutiny of a university's educational objectives can lead to a down-grading, not an up-grading, of the library function. It may be decided that the most effective way of producing good managers for tomorrow is to present each MSc in Business Studies student with a pack of most carefully selected and retrieved information and actively discourage him from casually gathering information from neighbourhood libraries.

These observations about the basic elements in traditional library evaluation are not separate and distinct from each other. The criticism

124

that the majority of studies see university libraries as document distribution centres or warehouses is intimately related to the other criticisms. No one would presumably deny that libraries are in the information business but a distinction can be made between the information contained in libraries and the communication artefacts which contain the information. A considerable number of studies concentrate on the logistics of supplying these communication artefacts. It will be obvious by now that I profoundly disagree with this view. Unless we can show how a library contributes or does not contribute, as the case may be, to the educational life of its market, the library manager is inevitably in a weak position vis-à-vis his academic colleagues. To reiterate, information is not of much interest in itself. 'Information derives its value from the effect it has on the behaviour of the organization.'[11]

The most fundamental criticism of all the categories of evaluation studies is deliberately left to the last. It concerns the basic philosophy which underpins these studies and therefore necessarily dictates their methodology. Put simply, the work that has been discussed in this section can be labelled quantitative and the research carried out for our research — qualitative. The two approaches come from two different epistemological traditions — the work discussed in this section employs a positivist method of enquiry. This positivist approach developed by Comte in the nineteenth century has served as the model for research in the social sciences. Its validity, however, has often been challenged. It purports to be value free. Time and time again in the literature of both librarianship and library research, concern is voiced for the objectivity of any evaluative activity. The predominance of this method of enquiry explains why only contacts with the library system are investigated and why use is assumed to equal value. It also explains the trend away from user studies. All else is subjective. Urquhart for one writes: 'The test of the adequacy of a library should be the actual needs of users, not what they thought they needed'.[12] Similarly, Menzel argues that valuable information may not be the information that users are aware of wanting, not even the information that would be good for them but instead the information that would be good for the progress of scientific research.[13] I believe that a contrary mode of enquiry, the phenomenological approach, is more suitable for tackling the problem posed, with which I was confronted. Namely, how is the library's value to be demonstrated? Gollop gives a very readable exposition on phenomenology and its application to librarianship.[14] It is sufficient to say for current purposes that such a methodology involves under-

125

standing and not simply describing user behaviour. It does not seek to discover absolutes such as 'the good library'.

Our point of departure at Cranfield, with the establishment research style prevailing at that time lay in the claim, or perhaps obsession, with objectivity. Surely, objectivity is ultimately an illusion? Menzel and Urquhart are two who believe that involving the user in designing an information system is basically unsound and unreliable. Does some *deus ex machina* rescue us from the problem of deciding what real information needs are? An act of use is objective in that it is observable — but it is only a manifestation of somebody's perceptions and expectations. To show what contribution a university library is or is not making to the organization it serves, we must understand acts of use.

Before concluding this section it may be useful to make one or two comments about the issues involved in identifying the costs of providing a library or information service. The preceding discussion has dwelt on the larger topics of evaluation, cost-effectiveness and cost-benefit.

Estimating the costs of an information service presents less formidable problems than measuring the benefits. However, the problems should not be minimized. In some way the cost problems are similar to the benefit problems and arise partly because it is difficult to define the nature of information. It perhaps should be clear by now that overall our investigation eschewed the notion of focusing on costs to the detriment of an all out attack on benefit analysis. Some very useful rule books and/or critiques on costing information exist,[15,16,17] though only Flowerdew and Whitehead's[16] comments are specifically made in the context of cost-benefit. The problem of costing library and information services they and others discuss can be ordered into a number of groups.

i Marron contends that traditional cost accounting techniques are not applicable to library services.[17] The output on information service cannot be categorized with precision or certainty. The use that will eventually be made of a document collection can only be guessed at in the vaguest terms. Moreover what is a user? Are all people who visit a library users?

ii The accountants' normal concept of depreciation may not fit the information model. It is not possible to talk about the depreciation of a document collection in the same way as that of machinery. The bibliometrician's work on obsolescence notwithstanding, information can still perhaps defy the laws of entropy.

126

iii One of the difficulties when putting a cost on to information is deciding a way of assigning input costs to output products and services. Data collection is by no means standardized, however much progress has been made by organizations such as Aslib on agreeing a list of output measurements. The treatment of overheads, the use of accounting costs instead of economic costs when decisions are being made about alternative procedures and the distinction between fixed and variable costs have all been subject to much examination.

iv The most difficult problem is the estimation of user costs. This is the problem that most concerned us in our research since it relates very much to the question of the value of information. Since the calculation of user costs is so very difficult, most studies are limited to producer costs. User costs involve tangibles such as frustration. For example, how are the costs of delay, of waiting for information, to be calculated? The user is usually ignorant of the usefulness of information until it is acquired. Effective resource management cannot ignore user costs since they are a fundamental determinant of the demand for any information service.

In conclusion, I have attempted in this section to show that critical scrutiny of the literature on library evaluation led us to reformulate our research brief. Originally we were to have embarked on a conventional cost-benefit, or more likely, cost-effectiveness study of the libraries of two higher education institutions. It became apparent, however, that the neglected research area was that of benefit or what I have referred to in this article as impact. Retaining the cost-benefit question 'How much good is a library doing?' we attempted to identify the value being derived from library services by post-graduate students of management studies and mechanical engineering at Cranfield and by both post-graduate and undergraduate studies in human sciences, management studies and electrical engineering.

A qualitative approach to library evaluation
I have endeavoured to show in the previous section that exposure to the literature of library evaluation resulted in a feeling of disquiet about using library utilization measures as a substitute for the value of a library. In the first year of the project we conducted qualitative pilot fieldwork which we believed to be necessary before we could embark on the main fieldwork. In this section I report on this first phase of empirical work that was carried out at Cranfield with two groups of post-graduate students from the schools of management and

127

mechanical engineering, and with their academic staff.

Certain beliefs shaped the research design. Evaluation was felt to be an effective concept. The process of evaluation is highly complex and subjective. It involves a combination of basic assumptions underlying the activities being evaluated and personal values on the part of both those whose activities are evaluated and those who are doing the evaluation. Evaluation is a continual social process, merely stopping to challenge these assumptions or to bring the values into the open. Finally, it was believed that users' perceptions are not irrelevant to the question of resource management.

The first phase of fieldwork was very much influenced by marketing ideas and was embarked upon in a fairly simplistic manner. It was quite clear that the benefits of university libraries had not been identified in others' research so an exercise in consumer research was planned in order to identify the dimensions by which people value libraries. Since consumer research of this type always seeks to explore the purchase context of the service rather than solely opinions about the service *per se*, it seemed appropriate to discuss with library customers the contextual notion of sources of information not simply the subject of libraries *per se*. If consumer research, for example, was being undertaken into the use of local sports centres, the investigation would explore the respondents' *total* leisure activities in order to assess the relative importance of sport in their lives. Consequently, the first stage of empirical work with students and staff at Cranfield discussed the sources of information used to pursue certain courses of study. The decision to widen the discussion rather than concentrate it on libraries was made because the investigation was seen as market research. It was only after the initial investigation that it was properly understood that a library is part of an information system which consists of both formal and informal elements and that exploration of the value of a university library must explore how all the elements interact.

Elicitation techniques were used. Unstructured interviews were held with students on Masters degree courses. The wording of introductory remarks in such interviews is important:

— 'We are carrying out a small study of the way in which students carry out their work . . .'

— 'I believe you are a . . . student in your . . . term. Thinking of the subjects you personally have been studying this term as part of your course, could you tell me from what sources you have gained information about these subjects?'

128

If necessary, a restatement of the above was used:

— 'You must have been gathering quite a lot of new information. People do when they study in a structured way. What I am interested in is where the information came from.'

— 'Try to think of all the sources you can of information you have gathered since the beginning of term which is relevant to your course.'

The respondents were then asked for their 'salient beliefs' about each source of information mentioned in the following way:

— 'Now I want you to think about these sources of information one by one. Take . . . for instance. Can you tell me what you think of . . . as a source of information relevant to your course?'

This sort of methodology was successful in that the salient beliefs that emerged were limited and most definitely manageable when a content analysis was performed on the interviews. Moreover an understanding was gained of the relative merits of each source of information and how each complement the other.

Group interviews are another technique applied in qualitative research of this type. The format we used in our sources of information group interviews was typically:

— 'Why do you want information for the MBA/MSc course? What are you trying to get out of the course?'

— 'How do you decide what information you need?'

— 'How do you go about getting information once you have decided what you want?'

A funnel technique was employed. The broad themes were discussed first and then the discussion was narrowed down to the subject of libraries. The following extract from a group interview with twelve Masters students demonstrates how sources of information interrelate:

— 'Ignorance gives one few options for information gathering; time is the constraint which decides relevance; information gives confidence but paradoxically can increase uncertainty; if one comes on a course to re-orientate there is more motivation to seek information; oral information transfer preferred to written — a good lecture better than five books; gambling process involved — would be more profitable to go to a tutorial or read a book . . .'

The second part of our qualitative research aimed to explore both in an individual and in a group setting one particular source of information discussed in the first part — namely 'libraries'.

— 'What do you feel is the purpose of an academic library?'

— 'How essential is the library for you?'

— 'How useful is the library for you (a) for the course generally (b) for your specialization?'
— 'How would you assess the stock and services offered?'
— 'Do you regard yourself as a user of libraries?'

The importance of this first phase of fieldwork was that it influenced the future development of the project quite fundamentally. It led to the use of methodologies which examined the user of information, not uses of information, and which explored the user's total information behaviour, not simply his library behaviour. The first phase of fieldwork was not conducted with any particular set of preconceived notions of a library in mind. What was elicited in the free response spontaneous fashion that has been described above was organized in the following way:

a It was obvious that our group of respondents saw their library as part of the complex intellectual apparatus available to them. The library would be mentioned as a source of information relevant to their course; they discussed it not in the mechanical terms used by library evaluators but in a creative sense. They discussed how they used library information and how such information related to other sources of information. An example of the vocabulary used is the following statement: 'The library is useful for temperature taking'.

b Library evaluators concentrate on the service aspect of information. Respondents talked in the same breath about the service aspect and about the actual value of the information contained in each source. Management Information System designers have recognized for some time that information is valued not only for the end-use consequences but also for its form, time, place and possession utilities. For example, if the language or format of an information product is not understood, if the product is received before the need is perceived, value will diminish or may not even exist.

c Any examination of the value of information runs into problems of definition. Information is not a concept people are familiar with. Our respondents talked about information vociferously but they did so unconsiously. Consciously they were talking about their educational activities. This led us to plan future fieldwork which would explore the totality of academic working life, not just their library seeking behaviour. Traditionally university managers operate as though education and information were distinct entities. Consequently when funding decisions are made about libraries, they are not seen as educational organizations. It seems far more advisable to manage as people actually

130

behave. In other words, when organizational information systems are being designed, the starting point should be the decisions people have to make, followed by the information inputs to those decisions, rather than starting with the informational 'inputs'.

d A relationship between educational style and library value began to emerge. A structured course implicitly precludes choice. The student delegates the task of deciding what information to use. Who the information decision maker is appears to become a crucial factor affecting the library. In any educational activity there is a continuum. At one end the student entirely delegates the task of deciding what information to use and at the other, as with a doctoral degree, the student must master most if not all of the decisions. The value being derived from a library in the case of these two extremes is entirely different. In other words, the style of a library is very much the result of the style of education.

The first phase of fieldwork produced findings which enabled a more positive criticism of library evaluation methods to be made. Since it was felt that the purpose of an investigation into a library's value is to inform the resource allocation decision, the live fieldwork was designed to show the library's contribution to the educational objectives of the organization. Two survey techniques were used. Firstly, students and staff's expectations towards the library and their use of the library were surveyed over time. Secondly, a sample of students logged over time their work behaviour and the associated information inputs. These techniques are discussed in the following section.

The research design for the main fieldwork
It was apparent from the qualitative phase of empirical work just asserted that the reasons behind any act of use and equally importantly any act of non-use are influential in a methodological investigation of the value of a library. Behind an act of use is an *expectation* of what the library can or cannot do. Expectations consist of two elements (a) a predisposition, favourable or unfavourable towards a library and (b) a behavioural intention, an intention to use or not to use a library. A group of students new to Cranfield were trailed information-wise for a complete academic year. On their first day at Cranfield they completed a questionnaire which asked them to react to some normative statements about post-graduate taught courses and about libraries serving courses of this type. Built into the questionnaire was the relationship between educational norms or philosophy and the style of

131

library that had been identified in the first phase of fieldwork. This questionnaire was called the Initial Expectation Study. It acted as a bench-mark for the five subsequent questionnaires. Each of these questionnaires contained questions on the use of the library since contact with or experience of the library system is obviously one continuing influence on expectations. Shifts in expectations were anticipated. Dissonance emerged. Some dissonance persisted and some dissonance evaporated. (Dissonance is defined as the library not delivering the expected or required value.)

The second main survey technique used in the live fieldwork was a student panel. Students were asked to log their educational tasks in diaries. They were asked to say what verbal or recorded information they used to tackle their tasks, the source of awareness of the pieces of information used, and the actual source of the piece of information. Moreover, they were asked to say what had been the intention of any library visit and whether they perceived that intention to have been achieved. As already noted, we were increasingly influenced by research conducted into Management Information Systems (MIS). Modern work on MIS is more concerned with information flows in an organization and less with the technology of information systems. The starting point of much MIS work is the decision-making process in an organization. The objection to applying the research framework of MIS work is that in organizational terms a university is a different entity from a business organization. It will be said it is impossible to talk of decision-making activities in a university. The goals of a university are notoriously and deliberately diffuse. Universities are composed of individuals who are deliberately employed to spend much of their time working quite separately and distinctly from each other in their respective educational pursuits, which makes universities very different from business organizations. However, the MIS emphasis can be usefully employed. What is at issue here is the definition of decision-making. If it is accepted that anybody in universities, the taught or the teacher, is decision-making in the sense of tackling an educational activity be it a small weekly essay or a large government research contract, then an MIS approach is valid.

It is important to dwell for a moment on the notion of expectation. The notion became one of the basic elements in the research design. We preferred the term to that of demand because it conveys a less purposive, less rational feeling than the concept of demand. Behind any act of use or non-use is an expectation of a library. In other words,

132

the expectation may be positive or negative. Demand is equivalent only to one of the two elements of expectation — behavioural intention. Expectation is an attitudinal construct.

We hypothesized that a student's or staff member's expectations of the library confronting them would be composed of four underlying factors.

i Psychological characteristics, ie those characteristics that are *predominantly* individualistic. We can suppose that some differences in information behaviour cannot be explained by reference to social or organizational factors but must be attributable to personality characteristics. Some people are more information-orientated than others.

ii Organizational characteristics. Most research on library use has neglected educational arrangements or mechanisms. If a course is project-based expectations of a library are likely to be different from a lecture-based course. We also included under this organizational heading the nature of the intellectual discipline being studied. We can suppose that the library expectations of a person whose information needs are technological will be different from those whose information needs are in the social sciences. This latter component of evaluation has been much researched by others.

iii Inter-personal characteristics. Expectations of a library will be influenced by the nature of communications between information seekers and information givers. The nature of this communication is, of course, partly determined by (i) and (ii) above. For example a member of academic staff will encourage library use only in certain educational circumstances.

iv Experience of the library system. As I have attempted to show above in the section entitled 'Traditional research solutions to library management problems', expectations of a library are influenced by previous experience of that library. The sorts of demands placed on the library will be affected by previous successes and failures of such demands.

Figure 1 summarizes the basis of argument from which the research design was drawn. We proposed that the value derived from a library service is a matter of individual subjective assessment. This subjective assessment is the difference between what was expected and what was perceived as happening once contact is made. A good library manager tries to understand how his users perceive success or failure, how their expectations are met or frustrated. The figure demonstrates the relationship between the educational organization of a university and its formal

133

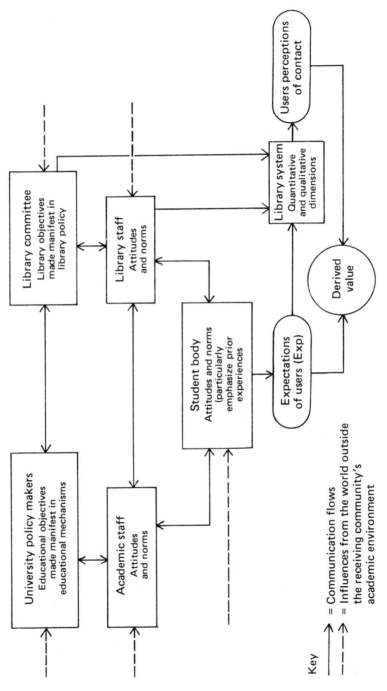

Key

⟶ = Communication flows

⤏ = Influences from the world outside the receiving community's academic environment

Figure 1 The derivation of value by students from a library system

information system — the library. The origins of expectations and consequences of the feedback between expectations and perceptions of contact with the system are shown. The figure demonstrates a communication flows network. The broken arrows indicate influence from the outside world, for example the effect of 'foreign' library backgrounds of users. The university power system is shown as the apex of the sequence. The expectations of staff, students and librarians are partly a consequence of that power system. Our emphasis on power systems explain our concern to make a distinction between attitude and norms. Norms in this instance refer to all those corporate beliefs about how education in our fieldwork institutions should be conducted.

The implications of the research findings

My purpose here is to discuss the implications of the Cranfield research rather than the research findings themselves. The project was a methodological rather than a substantive investigation. The final research report which presents the conclusions of the methodological investigation is *The beneficial library*. The detailed findings are presented in a Cranfield School of Management working paper.[18]

As a basis for discussing the implications of the research I present below a summary statement of the findings.

The more a library does for its users, the more critical they typically are of it. The less it does for its users, the less critical they are.

Accordingly, expectations adjust. A student or staff member of a university can possess expectations which are higher or lower than his perception of contact with the library system. The dissonance can disappear, however. There is then no impetus for change in the system.

Encouraging a student to see a library as a major source of ideas is a genuine educational alternative to that student being presented with packaged information by his tutor. A library need not be and is not always a supplement to a teaching programme. In certain circumstances, it can be and often is a rival educational process.

The purpose of the empirical research was to isolate the library's contribution to the lives of those whose information use at Loughborough and Cranfield was being investigated in order to say something about library value and subsequently library resource allocation. The most important single outcome of the fieldwork was the weight political and social factors played in determining how much money goes the way of the library. Economic analysis, such as a cost-benefit study will only give a partial picture of the value of a library.

135

At the time of the study Cranfield was spending considerably less on its library than most other British universities and certainly less than its fieldwork partner, Loughborough. The London Business School library was spending three times more per full-time equivalent student than was Cranfield School of Management. However, this fieldwork showed that very few of the potential market feel the pinch. The expectations study (the attitude surveys) showed that respondents did not feel the library was undervalued. The panel study (the behavioural work) showed that incidence of failure at Cranfield, that is the library not delivering the required item of information, was relatively low. The failure rate reported at Loughborough was higher. Two levels of satisfaction seemed to operate. At one level, what could be called the macro level, is the interface between the educational system and the library system. At the micro level there were ripples of dissatisfaction. The micro level is the interface between user and internal library system. Examples of dissatisfaction at this level are irritations with the classification system, with the lack of textbooks, with the tightness of the catalogue cards in their card drawers. However, neither educators nor librarians link up the macro and the micro. The dissatisfaction at the micro level is not seen in terms of the library's contribution to educational goals.

The message of our empirical exercise is that rigorous measurement of library value misses the point. By neglecting intangibles such as educational values it fails to understand the subjective process of resource allocation decision-making. The Cranfield situation at least was a self-perpetuating one. Very little activity was demonstrated by the library. Consequently, very little was required of it. Those who are most powerful in resource decision-making tend to be the non-users. Educational programmes have been designed at Cranfield which require very little of the library. One programme, the Master of Business Administration, is an extreme example of this. The course is a self-contained activity. The MSc in Mechanical Engineering required more of the library but course designers had not thought out what precisely the library's contribution was to be. Consequently, the style of library reflected the style of course. The providers and recipients of course seemed happy. There was no impetus, therefore, for change. Our expectations monitoring tools showed that expectations adjust over time. Those, for example, who came to Cranfield from a different library and educational environment were not always initially happy with the prevailing educational/information culture. One rather blatant

136

example of dissonance which was observed was one particular course preparation. A new member of staff on examining the library drastically altered his syllabus. Typically it is the style of education which shapes the style of the library. However, the direction can, as in this case, be the other way around.

The argument so far is not a polemic on behalf of distressed librarians. In other words, we did not argue from our findings that the libraries being studied, particularly that at Cranfield should receive increased financial support. It was simply an attempt to uncover value judgements. The value judgement that operated in Cranfield School of Management is that the deliberate confining of a students' information makes the best manager. Other educational arguments, of course, could be advanced. It could be said that a manager will, during his career, have to face many situations, when it will be unclear as to what and how much information will aid a decision. If he has not received training on how to select, he may not perform very effectively as a manager.

Our fieldwork, in fact, revealed that the majority of users are 'satisficers', they do the minimum to get by, their use of the library is minimal. A sizeable minority, however, we labelled the maximizers. They used the library more and in a different way to the satisficers. They tried to use the library as an alternative as well as an added dimension. In some instances, information was used from the library to challenge that provided from the information packages presented to students. Interestingly the maximizers were two types of person; the intellectually strong who wanted to challenge the orthodoxy or the intellectually weak who exhibit that very common phenomenon of collecting more information when uncertainty is felt. The others were low performers. They wanted to collect information to boost flagging confidence. The Cranfield maximizers, not the Loughborough ones, could not use the library very well as a source of information or ideas because it was not given the type of financial support that would make it a source of information.

The library budget at Cranfield could be said to be at a reasonable level given what those in that institution who made funding decisions had, almost unconsciously, asked the library to do. It could be argued, moreover, that at the time of the research there was slack in the system, unused capacity. For example the School of Management journal collection and inter-library services are little used.

The contribution a library does or does not make to the objectives of its parent organization to some extent revolves round the question

of the pattern of use made. It is often assumed by library evaluators tat major use of university libraries anyway is for the 'known item', the 'instant book'. Our explicit and positive evidence for asserting that a university library is used creatively comes from the users' answer to the following question:
– 'Tick the statement below which *most* describes your approach to the library'

	Managers	Mechanical engineers
	%	%
'I looked for a specific book or journal, ie an item I knew about already. The title or author was known.'	17	12
'I looked for anything that might be useful for a particular task I had.'	37	26
Both approaches.	36	61
'I did not use the library in either of the above ways.'	6	2
No response	0	3

Such evidence as the above is not conclusive. There are enormous methodological difficulties in establishing type of use. However, there would seem to be from our research some strong indicators that the potential for a library to be more than just a document storehouse is there.

I will conclude this section by returning to the finding from the research which presents a paradox; that the more a library does for its users, the more critical they typically are of it – the less it does for its users, the less critical they are. I have observed that many commentators dislike user research because its inherent subjectivity does nothing to demonstrate a library's worth or value. We would argue along contrary lines. Instead of regarding users' perceptions as a factor inhibiting attempts to establish an absolute norm – the good library – the dynamic of user satisfaction should be understood and managed. There is, inevitablity implicit, in homeostatic library theory that demand and supply will equate and satisfaction level will eventually settle at 60% which has dismal implications for funding. Our own work
138

shows that this approach can be demoralizing and can lead to a self-perpetuating situation. Expectations were modified by contact with the system. Users learnt to feel happy with the system they had. They may have had expectations originally which were in excess of what was perceived as being delivered but they learnt and they adjusted. Such satisfied expectations, such little scope for dissonance were virtually certain to ensure that a given level of funding persisted and at Cranfield that stood at 50% of the British university average per student and as a proportion of gross income.

This bland 'settling for the library system' you have got is a pattern to be found in other library and information situations. Blagden writes that his evaluation of the information service for the GLC's Department of Architecture and Civic Design rated very highly on the measures of availability. However, *penetration*, his measure of the success the library had at reaching its target audience, was poor. The relationship between the service and its users had stabilized. 'The stabilizing process has the effect of reducing the quality of feedback to the point where user and library are so isolated that the library is forced to use the arid, albeit apparently precise, statistics provided by user rates.[19]

The stabilizing phenomenon was more evident in one fieldwork location that at the other. Loughborough University Library with more items per capita than Cranfield and with an active user education programme released previously unexpected preferences. For instance more library 'failures' were reported in the Loughborough panel diaries than in those from Cranfield. The fieldwork in both locations did throw some light on the relationship between the manifestations of educational norms, that is the methods used to transfer information and library use. Expectations are, as we and countless others have shown, modified as a consequence of contact with a library system. The biggest single influence on library expectations, however, are what we have labelled educational norms.

The implication, therefore, of the research is that the librarian managing in recessionary times cannot simply rely on use statistics, that is, indirect measures of value in order even to maintain the current level of funding let alone avoid a cutback in real terms. To paraphrase a marketing theorist, Theodore Levitt, librarians should see themselves as being in the communications industry not the book supply industry.[20] This means identifying by means of user research the library's impact and contribution to educational goals. It also means that the librarian has to be prepared to adopt a proselytizing role in order to break out of

139

the dismal stabilizing phenomenon just referred to. Demonstrating library value, arguing for financial support, has to mean the ability to identify, understand and, hopefully, manipulate attitudes — attitudes of both those who hold the purse strings and those who could, if things work out, be counted on as allies — the ordinary library users.

Some years on
Without conducting a review of the literature of the library evaluation I feel reasonably confident concerning the following comments. The debate still rages concerning cost-benefit and cost-effectiveness. No major empirical study has been conducted since *The beneficial library* was completed. However, there is still a concern to seek objective measures of the value of a library; the search for the Holy Grail which I identified at the start of this article is still on.[2]

The Atkinson report was published at the end of the research period of the Cranfield report.[21] We welcomed some of its assumptions and disliked others. The Atkinson committee had been charged with the task of plotting the future of university libraries in a no-growth era. We agreed with its view that size of library collections does not necessarily confer value but on the other hand we were disappointed that it shared with many other approaches, some of which I have discussed in an earlier section of this chapter, a mechanistic view of libraries. Libraries are seen as document distribution centres rather than part of the intellectual apparatus of a university.

Since the publication of the Atkinson report in 1976 things have gone from bad to worse for librarians and for that matter most other people particularly those defending their pitch in the public sector. Pointing, as librarians are wont to do, to use statistics does little good. We argued in *The beneficial library* that librarians in order to cope with these changing circumstances might have to be more willing to take part in the political process. This article has discussed the process of value being derived from university libraries. However, its insights and the implications of the research have relevance for all library and information situations. The research's conclusion that libraries should be concerned with information itself and not only with information artefacts in order to demonstrate the library's contribution to the working lives of its clients can, of course, have interesting repercussions. It might well be as John Blagden[22] has recently argued, that such efforts to understand the library's role will show that the library has no role; that it is, relative to other systems of information transfer, inefficient.
140

An aggressive approach borrowing from the ideas of marketing may help the librarian. A marketing approach means not making, as libraries often do, a distinction between needs and wants; it means being user orientated not 'product' orientated. Librarians often think they are user orientated; they have been running extensive user education programmes for years. The mere phrase 'user education', however, smacks of a product orientation. What perhaps should be developed is librarians' education programmes not user education programmes.

The criticism that is often made of marketing's refusal to make a distinction between needs and wants is that that is not applicable to 'free' service. It is argued that library users are not consumers in the true sense of the word and, moreover, it would be impossible to plan a service based on user preferences since their demands would be massive. But information is not free except, sometimes, in a monetary sense. It takes time to find it, often perseverance. There are considerable acquisition costs on the user. Any choice situation requiring a decision between acquiring information from a library, or from a colleague, or doing without it altogether is open to managerial influence. Furthermore, it is only too obvious from our research and that of many others that users' expectations are very modest, far too modest, of most library systems.

I have said that little has changed since the completion of the Cranfield research in the resource allocation debate. The assumptions, such that value is objective, which I identified in the second section of this report are still widely held. However, interesting changes have taken place in library research and in library practice. The qualitative methodology of *The beneficial library* was treated with some suspicion. However, many developments have taken place. Colin Harris[23] and David Streatfield,[24] for example, writing a few years ago argue for research that is concerned to demonstrate impact or value and not research that simply measures acts of use. Tom Wilson at Sheffield Postgraduate School of Librarianship has launched a journal which devotes itself to the social scientific study of information and three years ago the British Sociological Association set up a new section — Libraries and Information. So changes are taking place in the way information is viewed and researched. Sadly so far these ideas have not been particularly applied to resource management.

141

References

1 Willis, G S C and Oldman, C H *The beneficial library: a methodological investigation to identify ways of measuring the benefits provided by libraries* Cranfield, Beds, Cranfield School of Management, 1977.

2 Whitehall, T 'User valuations and resource management for information services' *Aslib proceedings* 32 (2) 1980, 87-105.

3 Orr, R H and others 'Development of methodological tools for planning and managing library services: measuring a library's capability for providing documents' *Bulletin of the Medical Library Association* 56 1968, 241-267.

4 Buckland, M *Book availability and the library user* Oxford, Pergamon, 1975.

5 Hamburg, M and others *Library planning and decision-making systems* Cambridge, Massachusetts, MIT Press, 1974.

6 Raffel, J A and Shishko, R *Systematic analysis of university libraries: an application of cost-benefit analysis to the MIT libraries* Cambridge, Massachusetts, MIT Press, 1969.

7 Project for Evaluating the Benefits from University Libraries *Final report* Durham, University of Durham, 1979.

8 Bath University *Investigation into information requirements of researchers in the social sciences*, 2 vols, Bath, University of Bath, 1971.

9 Jones, K H 'Creative library management: part one, the limiting factors' *Assistant librarian* 66 (10) October 1973, 158-165.

10 Brewer, J G and Hills, P J 'Central to every facet of university life' *Times higher education supplement* 30 January 1976.

11 Emery, J C *Organisational planning and control systems* London, Macmillan, 1969.

12 Urquhart, D 'The Urquhart report' in *The future of library collections* edited by T W Blackwood, Loughborough, Library Management Research Unit, 1977.

13 Menzel, H 'Can science information needs be ascertained empirically?' in *Communication, concepts and perspectives* edited by L Thayer, Washington, DC, Spartan Books, 1967.

14 Gollop, M 'Sociological ideas and librarianship' *New library world* 79 (932) 1978, 25-28.

15 Armstrong, A 'Analysing industrial information service costs: a simple check list' *Aslib proceedings* 24 (2) 1972, 635-639.

16 Flowerdew, A D J and Whitehead, C *Cost effectiveness and cost benefit analysis in information science* London, London School of Economics, 1974.

17 Marron, H 'On costing information sciences' *Proceedings of the American Society for Information Science Conference*, 6, 1969, 519-520.

18 Oldman, C M *The role of library services at Cranfield Institute of Technology and Loughborough Institute of Technology: an exploration of findings of a measuring exercise* Cranfield, Beds, Cranfield School of Management, 1978.

19 Blagden, J and Rose, J *How good is your library: a new approach to benefit* London, Greater London Council, Department of Architecture and Civic Design, 1977.

20 Levitt, T 'Marketing myopia' *Harvard business review* 38 (4) 1960, 45-46.

21 University Grants Committee *Capital provision for university libraries* London, HMSO, 1976 (Atkinson report).

22 Blagden, J *Do we really need libraries?* London, Bingley, 1980.

23 Harris, C 'Illuminative evaluation of user education programmes' *Aslib proceedings* 29 (10) 1977, 348-362.

24 Streatfield, D 'Information services in local authority social service departments: preliminary review' *Journal of librarianship* 10 (1) 1978, 1-18.

New technology in academic libraries
NEIL MCLEAN

The prospect of rapid change through the application of new technology is shared by many sectors of industrialized societies. The ability of librarians to make the best use of this new technology remains an open question both in terms of management skills and the ability of individuals to adopt changing roles. There has been an increasing awareness which is now reflected in the professional literature that the ability to control change may have as much to do with the attitudes of librarians as the new technology itself. With this in mind I intend to explore some of the key issues associated with the introduction of new technology in academic libraries. The gap between what we do in libraries and what we think we should be doing is always considerable; the gap between what we regard as traditional library services and those promised in the electronic age is even wider. I write as a manager in an academic library faced with the prospect of clarifying these issues prior to formulating longer term strategies.

THE PROSPECT OF CHANGE
Any attempt to isolate attidues to new technology from general attitudes to the organization and the management of libraries would be unwise because general attitudes are bound to influence the approach to new technology. It would also be a mistake to think that libraries are static organizations bound in their own particular brand of inertia by their sheer size and traditions. Both in the United States and the UK organizational and management trends come and go and there is considerable diversity at any one time between institutions within each country. The pendulum swings between centralization and decentralization of the various processes and functions and because libraries like any other organization are essentially dynamic entities there is a constant element of self-correction. It is often difficult to write with any certainty on the rationale behind organizational principles knowing personalities

144

often play a crucial role in the formulation of management strategies. So generalizations will never be complete but they are necessary in order to understand the principles governing the potential rate of change.

By surveying the literature it is possible to grasp the main strands of thinking influencing potential management strategies, but as I have already stated the gap in most libraries between what we say we intend to do, and what we actually do, is often considerable. Library managers, particularly in the UK, are remarkably reticent when it comes to analysing their broad management strategies. This is partly a matter of style but it may also be a reflection on the absence of any broad strategy. It is even more difficult to assess grass-roots reaction because the evidence is invariably sparse, but at this level the gap between theory and practice appears to be even more substantial. For any significant change to occur there has to be a narrowing of the gap but the present lack of a consistent focus makes this a formidable proposition. It is therefore not just a matter of understanding the implications of the new technology but understanding how and why librarians at the various levels react in the way they do to these new factors.

New technology as a catalyst

The new technology itself covers a wide range of activity. This means that neither librarians nor managers know precisely what it is that they are responding to, and the lack of a clear perception lies at the root of the problem. In technological terms the rate of change is self-evident: the rapid expansion in memory capacity, the growth of intelligent terminal devices to facilitate user interaction and the move to distributive processing all appear to have ready application to library problems. As Earl Joseph says 'Computer evolution is increasing ten-fold every decade, chip technology at one hundred times per decade while innovation is going at one thousand times per decade'.[1] He goes on to say '. . . breakthroughs in mass storage technology in this decade will see the creation of very large computer-stored data bases economically feasible for even small organizations — orders of magnitude larger in capacity, and at least an order of magnitude less costly. There is no doubt that an order to two orders drop in mass storage costs will have profound business and societal effects: quicker movements into the information society, higher economic productivity, massive jumps into the paperless future-office-of-the-future, real-time and lifelong educational systems, knowledge (instead of data) based computer systems;

145

and much more, including business and social infrastructure changes'.[2]
There are equally disturbing predictions for libraries. At the most extreme viewpoint the paperless society will remove the need for libraries completely and everyone sits at home or at their desk with a terminal calling up the information as required. This vision may be simplistic in that it ignores a whole host of probelms inherent in organizing knowledge and it is too generous in the estimate of people's ability to know what they require in the way of information. But because it is simplistic it is a powerful vision and leads to a variety of reactions, from vague panic amongst some librarians to bland disdain amongst others. Because it still seems far from the reality of everyday life in most academic libraries it is difficult to anticipate the rate of change that is either possible or desirable over the next few years.

Whilst predictions concerning the rate of change in the technological field have in general been fairly accurate there has been far less success in predicting software development and practical applications. This is inevitably linked to the amount of human resources available to program the machines and to the resistance of change within society as a whole. Libraries have had limited success in software development and in the mid-seventies it was common to assume that the complexities of libraries were rather unique and in this sense librarians accepted limited goals. But banks and other institutions operating large data bases have been enormously successful in computerizing their operations because they devoted considerable financial and human resources to the task. Society has not yet decided to invest large-scale resources in the information industry to bring about a comparable change because it is not yet seen to be sufficiently important. In so far as libraries are but one strand of the so-called 'information industry' it is important to realize that the rate of change will not simply be dependent on the initiative of librarians but on the pressures within the academic institution and the society which it serves. Having said that, librarians increasingly feel obliged to respond constructively to these pressures. There are, however, a large number of factors militating against them at the beginning of the 1980s.

COMPUTERIZATION OF HOUSEKEEPING SYSTEMS
Computerization during the 1970s has brought mixed blessing to academic libraries in that the failures in many cases outweigh the successes. This has hardened attitudes at all levels and in some respects may slow further attempts to change systems in the 1980s. There are a number

146

of reasons for this which are worth noting. Many academic libraries gained their initial experience in computerization through a link up with their in-house computer centre. There was a tendency to concentrate upon particular aspects of housekeeping operations such as issue systems, periodical lists or subject indexes and in a few cases cataloguing. The reasons for a number of unhappy experiences are now much clearer. The computer centres themselves were basically geared to teaching requirements and not to the sort of data processing loads involved in library operations. Programmers were unaware of library systems and constantly underestimated the complexity of development effort required; librarians were unskilled at analysing their own systems and this meant that in most cases they attempted to computerize the existing manual systems without analysing the strengths and weaknesses of the particular systems. Because these systems were being operated in-house there was little attempt to cost them, indeed there was no need to cost them, as the services offered by the computer centre were supposedly free. The resulting systems showed all the signs of pioneering effort and whilst some have lasted remarkably well many collapsed as the computer centres found themselves unable to sustain regular data processing of an increasing magnitude.

Politics and resources
The reaction of both library managers and library staff to this phase was varied as one might expect. Because the systems had been developed in-house at relatively low cost the political loss of face for library managers was not all that significant and their political masters were not aware of the implications for the library at the technical level. These systems were developed by very small groups of staff often including the senior library managers and they tended to become alienated from the library staff as a whole because there was little attempt to communicate at the systems level and almost no attempt to communicate at the technical level. At the same time library staff were often involved in a lot of boring clerical work preparing data for conversion to machine-readable form. This was done without question in many cases but it diverted a lot of energy from normal services. There is no doubt that it brought with it a certain cynicism because the systems seldom produced the anticipated benefits and this was primarily because they were mostly based on existing manual systems. This disenchantment has probably had a significant impact on future developments because staff are understandably reluctant to face the prospect

147

of yet more data conversion and moreover they are suspicious of the promised benefits of computerization. It has been exacerbated by the fact that library managers often persisted with misplaced confidence in getting deeper and deeper into commitments which could not be justified either in terms of cost or improved services. This must be seen in the context of what I call 'the management of growth' syndrome which dominated most management strategies during the 1970s. Libraries expanded on the principle that new activity could be paid for out of an increased budget. This meant that new layers of costs were added to existing costs without the need for any significant rationalization. Whilst cost-effectiveness became a fashionable concept, its impact has only begun to take effect now that resources are actually diminishing. This earlier phase took place in a climate where a conscious choice of priorities for development purposes was a somewhat academic exercise. As a result the attitude of staff to these partially successful computerized systems was acquiescence, particularly if there was no direct interference with their own sphere of activity.

Because of the relatively passive acceptance of computerization, library managers were not challenged as they turned their attentions to the use of cooperative services, a movement which dominated the second half of the decade. With hindsight it is easy to be over-critical of this new phase in that most libraries joined up without any substantial analysis of existing systems or any real assessment of the benefits to be derived from the increased costs. In general it was felt to be a safer approach and resource-sharing had become the revered concept on which management strategies could be safely justified when asking for yet more money to invest in computerization. Is there ever a right time to embark on such projects? It is a question which most library managers ask themselves and so far there is no meaningful answer. Certainly the evidence suggests that the original justification of increased efficiency and labour saving has been challenged often enough to raise doubts on the subject. But the fact remains that automation can only develop over a long period and it may be entirely justifiable to bear increased costs and even a loss of productivity if the basis is being laid for a period when the technology and the software can produce more tangible benefits. It is, however, this credibility gap which still leaves rank and file librarians doubtful and often somewhat indifferent to future outcomes.

The problem is made worse as resources diminish because there is, as Harrison Bryan says, '. . . a mismatch between the demand for services and the resources to supply them'[3] and this mismatch is largely to do with human resources. I suspect that the first phase of this problem leads most librarians to take a more conservative view of their operations. They attempt to tighten up existing practices by refining loan systems, streamlining selection policy and cutting down on the so-called frills such as current awareness services and, more recently, user education. In this context it seems incongruous to many librarians to be investing in new computer projects which, if past performance is a guide, will not ease the resources dilemma.

Management techniques

Part of this drive to increased efficiency has been the belief that if only librarians could manage and administer more effectively the end result would be better. It is all part of what Adrian Mole has called the 'technocratic' approach.[4] Librarians looked at the high street supermarkets and believed that this particular supply/demand practice could be emulated in libraries. As a result there has been a change in emphasis in management techniques in most libraries which is partly attributable to the size and complexities of libraries and partly to librarians adopting a role which they perceive as favourable in this age of systems and scarce resources. Computerization has added another layer to this syndrome in that it supposedly requires logical, well-organized librarians to manage computer systems. Librarians cannot be blamed for this trend because it is clear that progress in the profession has come most easily to those either with technical expertise or those with so-called administrative flair. The end result of this movement has been a decided shift away from the idea of the librarian as an intermediary with the user, and so self-service tends to become an end in itself. Thankfully there is a self-corrective mechanism at work in that those library staff who are in constant contact with the users know the limitations of this approach and they continue to raise the most awkward questions for library managers. Ironically it is very often non-professional librarians working on issue counters who carry the brunt of daily contact with readers; professional librarians favour enquiry work in theory but it is not quite so evident in practice.

It is interesting also to reflect on the influence of new technology in the participative management trend that has become popular in recent years. The growth of this style of management probably owes more to social pressures within society than to factors inherent in libraries. Library managers do not want to be seen as autocratic even though actual decision-making may well be as autocratic as ever. But while wider consultation has probably had beneficial results in terms of readjusting internal routines and assessing priorities in terms of reader services, the size and complexity of decisions surrounding computerization often reveal the weaknesses of collective management. Overall strategic decisions on one system as against another and the development of technical systems are not areas which easily lend themselves to participative management. But there is a difference between consultation and decision-making and line managers at least are beginning to be more involved in the consultative process even if the decision-making is still left with the specialists or senior management. This failure to embrace effectively new technology as part of the general movement towards participative management is a matter for concern in that it potentially breeds further alienation amongst staff at lower levels.

Functional processes
At the functional level the new technology has brought shifts in the way processes are organized but there is no consistency in their pattern, primarily because there is still a vast variety of organizational frameworks in academic libraries. As Michael Gorman says: '. . . the distinction between technical services and public or reader services in individual libraries is based on custom and tradition arising out of incidental circumstances rather than any fundamental principle'.[5] Harrison Bryan observes that subject specialization meaning total functional integration within a particular area was abandoned in the US in the early seventies[6] just at a time when it came into vogue in the UK particularly in many of the newly established polytechnic libraries. This constant shift represents the inability of academic libraries to reconcile the two activities as they are currently understood into a compatible whole. Cataloguing, particularly, and sometimes classification are regarded as technical services and as such require specialist knowledge and constant practice. Before the computerization of cataloguing attempts to combine both functions often failed because librarians favoured one or other activity according to their personal talents and outlook, and thereby an imbalance occurred in the efficiency of a particular subject area. Whilst many large academic libraries already had centralized cataloguing and acquisition systems many other library services with multi-site or departmental libraries decided to centralize these processes with the advent of batch mode computer produced catalogues. This need for centralization eased one dilemma but produced another.
150

The creation of central units, often achieved by taking staff from reader services areas caused tension in that the communication gap widened, the speed of throughput often slowed up and catalogues were not only produced irregularly but had more visible faults than conventional card catalogues.

Technical services

Within technical services departments reactions have been mixed. Again there is a wide range of organizational frameworks, many of them being replicas of older manual systems, and quite often systems have been built up as an additional layer on top of existing systems. It quickly became evident that the quality of data bases which were the source of the new age of cataloguing were inferior and the level of manual intervention required sometimes exceeded the time of original cataloguing. Classification too was a problem in that the national classification by BNB or LC seemed inadequate to deal with the existing shelf order requirements so the amount of checking and changes proved substantial. Many cataloguers began to feel that their roles were being eroded as a large number of new clerical routines were introduced and this uncertainty still persists. Computerization also raised fundamental questions about the nature of the record needed in catalogues and the fashionable view in many quarters that an abbreviated record is just as effective as a finding tool has further eroded the confidence of cataloguers who of necessity are having to produce a higher standard of work to meet MARC requirements. Computerized catalogues have undoubtedly produced additional benefits in terms of union catalogues and multiple microform copies but it is not always acknowledged that these benefits have only been achieved through increased human and financial resources.

Reader services

Those on the reader services side watch these developments with interest, if not with a great deal of sympathy. But they are not immune from the effects because issue systems impinge directly on their affairs and the use of computerized information data bases falls directly in their path. Computerized circulation systems fall into an uneasy area of responsibility in many libraries, particularly where they have been organized on subject function lines. Because of this uncertainty the development of computerized circulation systems has often relied on individual initiative from staff in either technical services or reader

151

services. This may well explain the lack of any coherent pattern in the development of cataloguing and circulation systems. In some libraries circulation was developed first, presumably because it was perceived as the most important area of labour saving, and in other libraries cataloguing has come first and this invariably stemmed from a technical services librarian with a natural aptitude for systems development. In retrospect most librarians would agree that the development of a cataloguing system from which a stock file could be derived for the circulation system is the best approach but this was not as clear when these systems were originally conceived. As a result there are many libraries which require the creation of two records independently for the respective systems. The development of circulation systems did demand a rethink of loan policy and issuing procedures. The energy devoted to this exercise may have reinforced the supermarket philosophy in that many librarians felt that if only they could get it right the persistent problem of matching supply and demand would diminish. But of course the interesting fact is that loan policies and circulation procedures did not radically change and the so-called management information which is now a by-product of the more sophisticated systems is rarely used to adjust the supply/demand ratio. The reluctance of librarians to analyse this particular aspect of their activity is interesting given the fashionable emphasis on optimizing the use of existing resources. It could be that those librarians capable of applying their minds to this particular problem see their role as something other than a manager of a book warehouse.

Growth of systems thinking

The meeting of cataloguing and circulation systems in the need for a record that would serve both systems led to the idea that integrated systems were necessary. The term has a variety of connotations because integration can be achieved at a number of levels and the present limits of software development means that integration is of necessity restricted. The term, however, has an importance far beyond its technical implications because it symbolizes a new approach to library organization. The awareness that systems do interact means that library managers can no longer ignore the 'ripple'[7] effects of systems development. It means that any system is now likely to affect all staff and therefore their requirements and reactions have to be taken into account. It is more difficult to assess the reaction of staff to this trend but in general I think it has led to a breaking down of traditional institutional barriers.
152

In most respects librarians are remarkably passive in their acceptance of systems changes of this magnitude. They protest at length about details but seldom challenge the overall strategy. This may indicate a reversion to the acceptance of more autocratic decision-making process but it may be more attributable to the fact that it is not fashionable to question the need for automation. There is the additional point that most librarians have insufficient grasp of the technical background to mount such a challenge. It is also true that those who take the trouble to learn the detail do so because they want to be involved in these new ventures so they are unlikely to question the basic strategies. But for the bulk of librarians outside technical services computerization has yet to challenge their perceived role so there is unlikely to be any major resistance to the introduction of new systems.

Library cooperatives
The previous paragraph assumes that there is some scope for deciding between one major strategy and another but there is little evidence from past experience that this is so. After the series of failures of in-house systems the rise of the cooperatives and their relative success is not surprising. But in the British scene the reasons for managers deciding to join one or other of the major cooperatives offering centralized services are often based more on an act of faith than any hard facts. I say this not as a harsh criticism because the methodology and knowledge to make such major decisions are still underdeveloped. Most libraries taking this particular path did so because it was felt to be safe; systems development and the operational matters were taken care of by experts. There was also a strong feeling that cooperation in creating and sharing data bases must be a good cause and that a cooperative provided the best means of creating such a data base. The limitations of particular shared data bases are now becoming evident but out of these early ventures in cooperation has emerged the concept of a national data base and discussions are currently in progress between the relevant bodies in the UK on the feasibility of producing such a data base. But it must be recognized that the safe approach in joining a cooperative has been an important phase both in practical and psychological terms. Whilst the costs may have escalated there was little possibility of a major systems disaster and as such the rank and file accepted the change with a certain amount of relief. From time to time there has been speculation on the loss of autonomy in joining the cooperatives. I doubt that the loss is significant because the approach to systems development

has been conservative and there have been limited gains for limited input. In order to accommodate these new systems most libraries have not had to change their organization radically apart from centralizing technical services. There is a growing body of opinion that sees these cooperatives in their present form as merely a phase in development filling a gap between crude in-house systems based on mainframes and a new era of cheaper hardware and sophisticated software producing stand-alone in-house systems. But they have provided managers with a safe strategy and this should not be underestimated in reviewing the first decade of library automation.

On-line: a panacea?

The stand-alone era has already begun with the advent of turnkey issue systems which seem to be highly successful in performing their basic purposes. It still leaves the cataloguing and the maintenance of large files as a real problem but with systems such as GEAC the integrated in-house approach seems feasible. There is no doubt that this trend will increase and with it there will be functional realignment in libraries as on-line catalogues become a reality rather than on-line input which is the limitation of present cooperative systems. It again raises the question as to when library managers should consider entering into these new ventures. To take on an untested system is a high risk in itself and some of the problems of the initial development period may reassert themselves at least temporarily. On the other hand the servicing back-up from the firms selling these new systems will be critical and if sufficient back-up is available the major pitfalls of the past may be avoided.

The chief drive in all these developments is towards on-line catalogues; they are considered by some to be the panacea for all the deficiencies of the present systems. Given that it is seen in this light a certain amount of debunking is necessary and this has already started. In the main this criticism is more concerned with the pace of the change rather than with the concept itself. At the moment the storage is a basic limitation but it is conceivable that this will be overcome in the next few years. More importantly as stated in a timely article by Fasana: 'It is critical to keep clearly in mind the distinction between a file of records that can be rapidly and mechanically addressed by a computer and an online catalog wherein the computer is used to maintain the integrity of a file by ensuring and maintaining consistency among records. An online file of records is, in terms of technical requirements a trivial accomplishment. An online catalog is far more

154

complex and difficult to achieve. We are still technically years away from achieving this vision'.[8] Apart from the inherent technical limitations there are those who maintain that a microform catalogue is a far more acceptable form of searching for a book than an on-line catalogue. But assertions such as this assume that systems will go on as they are when the odds are that they will change dramatically as the decade progresses. The immediate danger is that versions of on-line catalogues will be introduced which will be both costly and ineffective.

CONCEPTS OF INFORMATION PROVISION

The predominant emphasis in the last decade has been upon computerized housekeeping systems. This preoccupation has tended to overshadow the importance of providing information for users. The term 'information' evokes a wide range of responses simply because there is no consistent agreement amongst librarians in academic libraries as to what the provision of information means. Concepts of information provision also appear to be in a constant state of flux within libraries and it may be that they mirror the pendulum effect that is evident in organizational change. Generalizations are difficult in this area because librarians have a remarkable capacity to gear their concept of service to their own particular strengths. The traditional concept where the library was seen to be the collector and guardian of knowledge gave ample potential for those preferring a passive approach as opposed to one based on interaction with users. It was possible to be a scholar, to be steeped in the knowledge of a particular area, and to see tangible rewards for effort in the sheer size of the collections acquired. This concept was challenged in newer universities and certainly in the new polytechnic libraries in the UK as they did not have large collections and in the initial phase there was a more dynamic approach to reader service. This new movement in its most pure form saw the librarian as an information officer who actually distilled raw information in the interests of the user. The librarian not only interacted with users but had a say in the type of information being passed on to the reader. This unleashed a new phase of activity which alas did not survive in the pure form outlined above. There were insufficient resources available to support such time-consuming activity and it was also realized that interpreting users' needs was a complex task. The technocratic supermarket approach came into vogue and it contrasted sharply with this earlier high-minded vision of service. Energies were directed into making it easier for the user to find the information but this is not to say that

155

librarians became completely passive once again. They redirected energy into extensive user education programmes aimed at assisting users to make better use of the resources in the library. This has proved an interesting blend of the factory approach and the interactive approach. Many librarians felt that in this new educative role they were more part of the academic community and hence higher in status. But the whole movement was based on the premise that users could be taught how to manage the keys to information and this is now being challenged. There are signs of a widespread reaction, particularly in the light of diminishing resources, to this movement of the 1970s and many library managers suspect that it has not proved to be a very productive exercise.

On-line information data bases

Whilst this phase was in full swing the seeds of the next phase were being sown. As computerized data bases began to grow, particularly in the science and technology areas, small groups of librarians took the initiative and trained themselves in these new techniques. The growth of use has not yet matched the growth of the data bases themselves and this is largely due to the high costs of telecommunications and computer connect time. Most libraries still only have a small number of highly trained staff but the impact is being felt far and beyond the degree of use. Librarians are once again having to become intermediaries, they have to define a search strategy in consultation with a user and to provide the information for the user. This calls upon skills which have to a certain extent gone out of fashion and in some libraries have never existed. It also calls for more generalist techniques in terms of search strategy. The conventional idea of subject expertise built up around a collection of material which could be actively searched on site will no longer suffice. The discipline of this intensive interaction with the reader may require many of the skills of the good old fashioned reference librarian but it is alien to a large number of young academic librarians. Most libraries have yet to show any basic change in emphasis in this field as it is only a few enthusiasts who have been encouraged to take the initiative in the early phase of on-line information retrieval.

It is also interesting to observe the effect of introducing charges into a previously free service environment. Whilst the current necessity to pass on some of the costs to the user may only be a temporary phenomenon, the entrepreneurial spririt is certain to leave its mark as many librarians find themselves becoming aware for the first time of

156

the value of information, and it is ironic that it is librarians who are often surprised when users actually pay up willingly for the results of a computer search. It may be that the performance of librarians in this more rigorous environment will improve enormously but as mentioned earlier only a small number of librarians are involved at present.

There is little evidence as yet that this kind of activity has had any effect on the way in which libraries organize themselves. This is because the time devoted to it has not upset the balance of the functional processes. Moreover, it is relatively easy for librarians to retain the status quo by simply not promoting these new services in an active manner. In one sense they have again become the guardians of information, albeit remote information and the initiative for the time being lies firmly in their control. This is already exposing the weakness of the traditional librarian who relied on providing hard copy information for all to use. In general the idea that 'if it is not in my library the best I can do is get it on interlibrary loan' still predominates. There is considerable reluctance for instance actually to use a telephone to ask for information. This almost total dependence on document provision may spell trouble in attempting to mould a new environment.

STRATEGIES

Having analysed the significant strands of the past decade there is some evidence of a positive response to the potential of new technology but the broad strategies are fragile and there is a need for a more concerned vision of how libraries are to respond to these considerable external pressures. It is a matter of bridging the gap between the more extreme forecasts for the electronic age and the far more mundane situation in which most academic libraries find themselves. Without a consistent sense of purpose it is unlikely that librarians will be motivated to accelerate the rate of change.

One of the most immediate problems in facing up to these issues is the fact that the experts who are conversant with the technical aspects of the electronic age are inclined to emphasize the inevitability of these changes in a manner which makes debate about the transition to this new age seem slightly futile. Moreover this approach tends to provoke exaggerated reactions ranging from the conservative view that the threatened revolution will never happen 'and anyway we'll always need books' to the opposite view that 'if it is going to happen then it will happen anyway'. There is little in the way of constructive debate

157

mainly because it is difficult to find an appropriate framework in which to discuss the central issues.

The 'de-institutionalized' library

Lancaster, whose views of the electronic age I admire, does tend to stress the inevitability of this process. In translating the electronic age into the library context he says, 'Beginning in the early 1980s, academic and many special libraries have followed a familiar pattern of development:

1 An increasing portion of the budget allocated to the purchase of on-line access to information sources when needed at the expense of outright purchase: . . .

2 Drastic curtailment of physical growth: . . .

3 Staff reductions accompanied by reductions in the size of the library: . . .

4 Departmental libraries in academic institutions begin to disappear: . . .

5 A partial dichotomy between those librarians that handle electronic information and those dealing with print and microform material: . . .

6 Members of professional staff of academic libraries as well as public and school libraries tend to be generalists rather than specialists: . . .'[9]

But the question remains as to how we cope with these changes even if the Lancaster premises are valid. In his own terms there has to be a process of 'deinstitutionalization'[10] before the new age appears. This immediately raises the question as to whether this process will happen irrespective of what librarians may think and do or whether there can be an active role for library managers in controlling both the nature and rate of change in achieving the transition.

Information technology: a convergence of thinking

A fundamental problem in confronting the challenge is the fact that there is no general agreement as to what we mean by the new 'information technology'. There are now articles in a wide range of disciplines referring to the implications of new technology, its likely effect on the availability of information, and its consequences for the social political and economic well being of the world. The most noticeable feature is the lack of any consistent conceptual framework in discussing the new developments. Information is used in a vast number of

158

differing contexts ranging from being a basic right of every citizen, to being a commodity to be bought at a price by those who can afford it. As yet we do not know what we mean by the information society; all we do know is that the potential of the electronic age to provide access to information is of a magnitude comparable with that introduced with the age of print. Libraries can ill afford to be isolated from this broader debate. It will be necessary to understand the nature of this argument and to assess the shift in attitudes to the whole question of access to information prior to formulating a professional response. This may seem self-evident but we as practising librarians have a remarkable capacity to grapple with our problems as though they were unique in their own right. Any renewed philosophy of librarianship suitable for the rest of this decade will depend on a broad appreciation of the role of information in society at large.

The process of self-examination

Having said that, it is essential that the process of self-examination within our academic institutions should be renewed. Most academic libraries are learning to live with diminished resources and this is a painful process. As I have already mentioned libraries along with many other organizations tend to tighten their belts in the most conservative fashion in the initial phases of economic restraint. 'A little less of everything' is the approach most often adopted as this seems the best way of alleviating the worst effects of cutbacks. Whilst noting in the earlier analysis that a surprising amount of development work has taken place in these allegedly straitened circumstances it could be that this particular path of development is now coming to an end. Most of these developments were achieved within existing organizational frameworks by adding a new layer of resources either in computer costs or technical staff. Librarians now have to face the prospect of substantial change at a time when they feel they can least afford to take advantage of it. This is most visible in the approach to computerized information services which are still seen by many as a luxury to be provided in better times. It is a dilemma common to many academic libraries and as yet is unresolved.

It seems to me that we must revert to a re-examination of some long established principles on the role of a library in an academic institution and apply these to the potential advantages of the electronic age. As intermediaries in providing information there is the dual role of providing information and educating the academic community in

159

finding information for themselves. We are ill equipped to reassess these two principal roles since both have received a setback in recent years. Librarians provide less information in the active sense partly because of inadequate human resources and partly because user education was supposed to teach people to be self-sufficient in finding information for themselves. But such programmes have been of limited success and I have already referred to the widespread reaction to deploying further resources in user education. Having first abandoned the role of actually providing the information and now abandoning the hope that users can be effectively taught to find information for themselves, academic librarianship begins to look somewhat threadbare. If my analysis is correct then it is time we reassessed the role of the library irrespective of new technology. But one looks in vain for inspiration in terms of our traditional concepts of library provision. I am not suggesting that we abandon the past in favour of a new-fangled futuristic library, but that any major reassessment must be made not only in the light of our knowledge of technological change but in terms of basic traditional concepts of service.

INSTITUTIONAL CONSIDERATIONS

It is already evident that computer technology is having a wide impact on a large number of teaching departments in academic institutions. With the introduction of interactive mainframes serving the whole community and microprocessors operating at the local level the emphasis in teaching method is changing. This in turn means that telecommunication networks and processing facilities are developing across institutions as a whole. Whilst clearly the applications will vary enormously the seeds of the electronic institution are already evident and this in itself should be a warning to librarians that a new approach in terms of integrating the library physically into the academic environment is now necessary.

Beyond this there is a growing capability to access information outside the library that has not previously existed in the formal sense. The present complexities of accessing bibliographic data bases tend to make some librarians complacent about this wider threat simply because they think librarians will always remain the guardians in accessing information. But as 'user-friendly' software develops, the current difficulties will recede so there is little scope for complacency. It is also evident that most librarians are bibliographically minded but display little or no interest in data banks which are growing even more

160

rapidly than bibliographic data bases. Access to these data banks through specialized software designed to manipulate the data will become commonplace and librarians have to consider whether they are to have any role in this development.

I can foresee the time when teaching institutions will become large information networks in which the library is but one component. Given this possibility the library has the challenge of becoming active again as a partner in the learning process. There is nothing new about this concept. It became highly developed as an aim in the sixties and seventies in terms of the role of traditional library services but in spite of the continuing spate of literature on the subject the outcomes of this partnership have often been disappointing in reality. As noted earlier formal user education is on the wane; it is spasmodically integrated into the curriculum and the role of the librarian as a teacher has receded somewhat. Equally, the idea of educational technology becoming central to library provision, with the library acting as a learning laboratory has had only limited success in higher education with the exception perhaps of teacher education. But there appears to be much more ground for optimism in considering information technology because the principles underlying the development are firmly based in the professional training of librarians.

It is this question of basic approach that will be fundamental to the development of library services in the next decade. To be seen to be assuming an active role again at a time when we are on the defensive in the traditional sense may seem contradictory both to librarians and to outside observers but that is often a characteristic of new developments in any organization. It is bound to heighten tension between various competing demands within the library service both in terms of allocation of resources and the changing role for key professional staff.

Growing in a 'no-growth' environment
Central to this struggle for resources, and indeed to the role of librarians, is the longheld view of the library as an autonomous organization with a tangible rate of growth measured basically by the growth in book-stock. In many academic institutions it took years to establish the library as an important physical entity capable of directing resources in its own right. Librarians in their professional exchanges are almost always impressed by the size of bookstock irrespective of its relevance and it is now difficult to escape the influence of this concept. The transition will almost certainly demand a reduction in the physical

161

growth of bookstock as resources are redirected to computerized information services. This is not to say that books will become irrelevant in the near future because it is clear that for educational purposes the demand for basic books will continue to be strong for many years to come. But information requirements for the educational process are likely to change as the potential both for the access and manipulation of information increases and it is this area that will be developed quite rapidly.

After a decade of some growth, even if it was illusory growth resulting from inflation, library managers now accept no growth as a reality and this means that new developments must be at the expense of existing services or physical resources. So a key consideration is to decide on the rate of change required to achieve success and to then assess whether resources are available to support this planned rate of change. There are three important aspects to this problem. In the first place there is the hardware to set up systems. For most academic institutions this is regarded as a capital investment and it is surprising how often capital is found when recurrent funds for maintenance and other support are notably absent. It is also true that hardware costs are falling rapidly and so the capital investment need not be all that extensive, particularly if there is investment in an information network within the institution as a whole. Because computers are often regarded by those controlling resources as being 'different' libraries have an opportunity to compete for resources that were traditionally reserved for equipment based teaching departments.

Recurrent financial support for information retrieval or housekeeping systems is more difficult. The problem is often exaggerated, however, because the thought of paying money to receive information down a computer or telephone line always seems more extravagant than maintaining expensive abstract services year after year. Very few institutions actually devote a significant proportion of their finances to information retrieval at present. But increasing the cash resource often means cancelling other hard copy services and the confidence actually to take this step is yet to be established in most libraries. If a more active strategy is adopted in collaboration with teaching departments there is a strong likelihood of resources being made available from outside traditional library sources. This seems an important strategy and it could provide the required impetus in the key development phase.

The perceived role of the librarian

By far the biggest outlay in achieving a change in direction will be human resources. Whilst it is difficult to redirect financial resources in times of scarcity it is even more difficult to redirect human resources because a shift in attitudes is required. At a time when most librarians see the gap between the demands of the users and what they can provide in reality widening it will be exceedingly difficult both for line managers and individual staff members to realign their priorities. Hence the importance of reverting to first principles concerning the role of information services which have been relegated in the priority list over recent years. Academic libraries have various ways of organizing their reader services activities and I do not wish to analyse these differences at this stage but irrespective of how staff are organized there will need to be a rethinking of the role of professional staff in relation to academic staff. To readopt a more active role in seeking an integrated approach to information technology will probably require a certain degree of technical skill which has traditionally been the province of technical services personnel together with all the flair and imagination of those who have been involved in subject liaison work. But ultimately success or failure will depend on the restoration of a more comprehensive view of the librarian's role.

Most librarians are faced with a major challenge to their professional role. At the broadest level it is likely that just as the physical autonomy of the library will be challenged so the librarian will be working in a much more nebulous environment where many users will now have similar skills in manipulating information and the ability to access information without approaching the library staff. This is bound to cause anxiety because most professions build their status and prestige on skills which are unique to their particular profession. The interaction with the users will take on a new importance but the emphasis is likely to be different. Lancaster[11] predicts that librarians dealing with electronic information are likely to be generalists rather than specialists which I assume means that subject knowledge will be of less importance than the technical knowledge of data bases and the manipulation of the data bases. This implies of course that subject specialists dominate academic libraries at the moment when this may not be so. The best librarians are probably generalists in the traditional sense in that their active response to a wide range of users' needs demands a broader approach.

There are signs in many libraries of a generation gap developing over

163

this matter. It is perhaps more difficult for the majority of librarians occupying line managerial posts to come to terms with the prospect of change simply because their own experience of computers is limited and the fear of coping with keyboards and VDUs is a reality. Personal fears can be partly translated into management objectives which strengthens the traditional practices at the expense of change. Frustrations then develop amongst younger staff who see the potential of the electronic age both in terms of the users and their own career development. With many traditional information services it has been possible to give enthusiastic staff a fair degree of latitude because the activity generated could be accommodated within the existing framework. However, any substantial involvement in computerized information services is likely to demand a reallocation of resources of sufficient magnitude to challenge traditional beliefs on the importance of collection building and on the manner in which staff resources should be deployed.

High density storage
The major catalyst in producing change may be the introduction of the optical digital disc with its ability to store high density information very cheaply and at the same time allow easy access. This will strike at the heart of the traditional library in its most basic role of storing books. When this becomes a reality it will be impossible to ignore the economies it potentially offers both in terms of the cost of acquiring the information and the cost of the space it occupies. In some respects this development may be accepted more easily by librarians because full text retrieval is a concept readily understood whereas computerized bibliographic searches or data bank manipulation often appear more complicated and require more active intervention by librarians.

Laws of supply and demand
It will not be easy for individual librarians to readjust their thinking and to acquire new techniques. Most librarians are cautious in adopting new methods. It is sometimes inferred that this reflects the type of personalities within the profession but it is more to do with the fact that traditional library systems have considerable inbuilt resistance to change and therefore the expectations of librarians are influenced by their environment. Being an open ended public service the rewards for human endeavour are often short lived because success breeds a level of demand that frequently outstrips the ability of librarians to
164

satisfy effectively the increased demand. There are many unwritten laws governing supply and demand in libraries and it is a subject requiring more attention in the near future.

Trade unions
In the UK some of these tensions show signs of becoming institutionalized through trade union activity and librarians are exploring new tactics which may have an impact on the rate of change. I am not suggesting that this is primarily a negative process. Many of the more talented younger librarians are in the vanguard of this movement and it must be acknowledged that there is considerable scope for improvement in areas such as conditions of service, performance appraisal and health and safety. There are, however, inherent dangers. In polytechnics, for instance, librarians find themselves aligned with administrative and clerical staff who often have entirely different objectives both in their work and in what they expect of their union. This is exemplified in the attitudes to new technology. There is a prevalent feeling amongst clerical staff that new technology will reduce job opportunities and affect the quality of working conditions. Whilst librarians share some of these fears they generally appear more willing to embrace the benefits of new technology. The effects on professional librarians will probably differ considerably from those experienced by clerical staff and this will lead to diverse expectations. Librarians may find therefore that they have formed an uneasy alliance which could produce some problems in redefining their professional role and it will require careful consultation between managers, unions and librarians to avoid negative responses.

Staff development
There has been considerable interest in staff training and staff development in academic libraries over recent years but it has been spasmodic in approach and lacking in overall purpose. Staff training was seen largely in terms of improving skills in existing jobs. Staff development has been regarded predominantly as a matter for individual initiative being mainly directed towards acquiring better academic qualifications. In the future staff development may have to be seen more as an agent of change. This idea often brings adverse reactions because it is regarded as 'social engineering' and contrary to professional ethics. This reaction can only be overcome by having a concerted sense of purpose which gives staff some firm insight into the impli-

165

cations of technological change. It will require a significant investment in staff development programmes and this will be yet another strain on resources.

CONCLUSION

In exploring the various aspects of the effects of new technology on academic libraries the recurring theme is the attitudes of librarians as they face the prospect of change. There can be no substantial revision of attitudes without a consistent view of the basic aims of a library service and I am advocating a thorough re-examination of more traditional concepts prior to any radical implementation of new technology. That the new technology will force changes in our concepts and practices is certain. What is less certain as yet is how rapidly we can adapt our thinking to make the most of the technical advances.

References
1 Joseph, E 'The 80s and 90s' *Computer age* 16, March 1981, 5.
2 *Ibid.*, 6.
3 Bryan, H 'Trends in staff organization in large academic libraries' in *Studies in library management* Vol. 5, edited by A Vaughan, London, Bingley, 1979, 43.
4 Mole A 'A critical view of librarianship and library management' in *Studies in library management* edited by A Vaughan, *op. cit.*, 144-145.
5 Gorman, M 'Technical services in an automated library' in *Clinic on library applications of data processing* Vol. 16, edited by F W Lancaster, Urbana, Illinois, University of Illinois, 1979, 49.
6 Bryan, H *op. cit.*, 53.
7 Montague, E 'Automation and the library administrator' *Journal of library automation* 11 (4) December 1978, 313-323.
8 Fasana, P J '1981 and beyond: visions and decisions' *Journal of library automation* 13 (2) June 1980, 103.
9 Lancaster, F W and others 'The role of the library in an electronic age' in *Clinic on library applications of data processing*, edited by F W Lancaster, *op. cit.*, 182.
10 Lancaster, F W and others 'The changing face of the library: a look at libraries and librarians in the year 2001' *Collection management* 3 (1), Spring 1979, 55-77.
11 Lancaster, F W and others 'The role of the library in an electronic age' *op. cit.*

Part three

The incorporation of the British Museum Library into the British Library

ALEXANDER WILSON

The author is the Director General of the British Library Reference Division but the article represents a personal view of the topic.

The British Museum Library inheritance

This is a brief account of management changes in the British Library Reference Division since 1973, with a look into the eighties. However, it is necessary to gain some understanding of the history and latter-day problems of the library departments of the British Museum (BML) to put the story in perspective. The reader is referred particularly to Edward Miller's standard history, *That noble cabinet.*[1] Because of the great collections of books, manuscripts, maps and other materials inherited from the British Museum (BM) which comprise in size one of the world's greatest libraries, but in quality without peer, the Reference Division (RD) forms the central and major component of the British Library (BL) (see statistical summary appended). Its incorporation therein commenced the second of two great reforming periods since the Museum was founded in 1753; the other being the making of an eighteenth century institution into the first great modern library by Sir Anthony Panizzi, chiefly in the years of his period of office as Keeper of Printed Books (1837-56), although carried on for some years later both by him (as Principal Librarian) and his lieutenants, particularly J Winter Jones and Thomas Watts. During his time, Panizzi laid down objectives which are broadly fulfilled today, obtained the necessary accommodation for readers and the rapidly expanding book stock, achieved his £10,000 annual book fund (a fabulous sum at the time), made legal deposit work in England, fought successfully for a rational staff structure and decent conditions of employment and laid down procedures which with little modification were still in use in the 1960s, although the systems had for long been strained by the presence of a rate of accessions which even 'the Prince of Librarians' could scarcely

167

have envisaged. Book stock in 1837 was a quarter of a million volumes, 1872 1.1 million, pre-1914 3 million, 1968 6 million and in 1980 8.6 million (Department of Printed Books (DPB) only). The Director General today sits under the eye of the great man, in a striking early portrait by Spiridioni Gambardella, and must continually reflect on Panizzi's management skill which devised systems for a library whose stock was then about half a million volumes but somehow coped with over eight million printed books by the end of the BM days.

But if the collections had by the late 1960s outgrown their accommodation and by sheer volume gone far to outmode the systems designed for their organization, the strength of the library and its attraction to scholars remained. This appeal rests on two grounds: the richness of the older materials and the universality of the modern publications. The rare and early books and manuscripts are in very heavy demand, whilst amongst modern books the average publication date of books in use in the reading rooms at Bloomsbury is about 50 years ago. It follows that the reputation of the library today derives considerably from the selection decisions of several generations ago and so the policy makers and selectors of so great a library must always take the long view, considering usage at the present day as but a passing phase of an overall utility that will be proved over the centuries rather than decades. Unfortunately, the concept of a library in perpetuity is out of harmony with the struggle of public institutions to prove their contemporary relevance to those who hold the purse strings of an increasingly meagre bag of gold.

Underlying the many excellent proposals in the Dainton Report (1969) is the idea that the primary change in the BML should be to make its collections more accessible.[2] However, the subsequent record of the BL Board will show that the need to accommodate both the needs of present-day users and the claims of posterity, requires vast expenditure upon conservation, and this has been one of their main priorities.

The Dainton/Eccles reforms, 1969-
An essay by Samuel describes the Library about 1968.[3] He is candid about the strain on the Panizzian systems, due to a phenomenal growth of users as well as collections and makes clear that the BM Trustees, well aware of the deficiencies, have been labouring for many years under Treasury restrictions on the budget. The Trustees' report for 1969/72 relates that by the end of 1971 half the General Catalogue was

168

up to date and the other half five years in arrears, but had been fifteen years in arrears only twelve months before. A new building for the Library had been sought for at least twenty years without success.

Various institutions had come into being since the end of the Second World War which would be brought together in the future British Library, of which one can here notice only the National Reference Library of Science and Invention (NRLSI) based on the former Patent Office Library. The case for associating NRLSI with the BML was partly economic – the acquisition of scientific and technical literature received by legal deposit – and partly in order to achieve the unification of the scientific collections. The DPB would add older literature no longer needed by NRLSI for the use of historians of science. This latter proposal has not yet been implemented, because of the incompatible catalogue records of the two departments so that industrial archaeologists and other students of the past still use the Science Reference Library (as the NRLSI is now entitled). The NRLSI became part of the British Museum in 1960 and was formally constituted part of the DPB in 1966. However, the management of this new science and technology library developed on different lines from that of the BM library and it is not surprising that the Dainton Committee eventually recommended that the NRLSI should be constituted as a separate part of the new national library as the Central Science and Patent Collection. This has not proved to be the policy of the BL Board.

The NRLSI was allowed to increase its resources and to develop its own classification and cataloguing systems, staff structure, objectives and programme. These differences made for considerable difficulty in assimilating the library as a department of the future Reference Division.

The second period of reform owes much to Viscount Eccles, as the Minister in charge of the preparations leading up to the formation of the BL, who became first Chairman of the British Library Board, and his successor in that office, Sir Frederick Dainton (1978-), who also chaired the National Libraries Committee whose report (1969) was a a major factor in the creation of the BL. Much is to be learned of the BM and its problems in the report of the ADP study commissioned by the Department of Education and Science and used as input to the Organizing Committee for the BL particularly the report on processing in the DPB by SCICON.[4] This stated that machine-based systems were essential for book processing, but first a 'fundamental rethink' was needed leading to a complete redesign of systems. The recommendations of the ADP study contained the following important points bearing on the future management of the Reference Division:

– There should be coordination of cataloguing practices between the BM Library, the NRLSI and the proposed bibliographic services unit (the future BSD) in order to eliminate duplicate cataloguing, speed up the process and facilitate joint outputs.

– If the AACR cataloguing code was adopted and a standard subject indexing scheme (the BNB-invented PRECIS was recommended) then this would have the great advantage of compatibility with outside libraries.

– ADP should be used throughout the British Library.

– A 'placing and streaming unit' should be set up using a 'master administrative record' to achieve control over material in processing – as many as 25,000 to 50,000 items at one time – which would enable one to trace wanted items and to spot bottle-necks. The existing system was endearingly described by a member of the BM staff as one of 'gravity feed'.

Other recommendations in the ADP study were: an integrated BL serials file, a careful study of alternative catalogue formats such as COM, a computerized system for the listing of books absent from the shelves – it had been pointed out that an applicant waited just as long to be told that an item was not available as he did for the delivery if more fortunate – and the loan of non-legal deposit books from the Reference Division as a back-up to the future lending function of the British Library.

The museum at this time employed few professionally qualified librarians. A university degree was regarded as the basic qualification for senior staff but librarianship training was not regarded as essential. (The BL changed this policy and by 1981 about 15% of the officers in professional posts held library qualifications.) Few of the senior staff had experience in any other institution: they therefore tended to cope with change by commonsense adaptation of traditional procedures, although it must always be remembered that these officers and their predecessors had established this great asset and had preserved and enhanced its scholarly reputation throughout the world.

Figure 1 shows the final departmental structure under the BM, whose Director spent about equal parts of his time on library and museum matters. This was appropriate since the staff of the library departments accounted for about half the total staff of the museum. The Board of Trustees exercised its responsibilities in part through
170

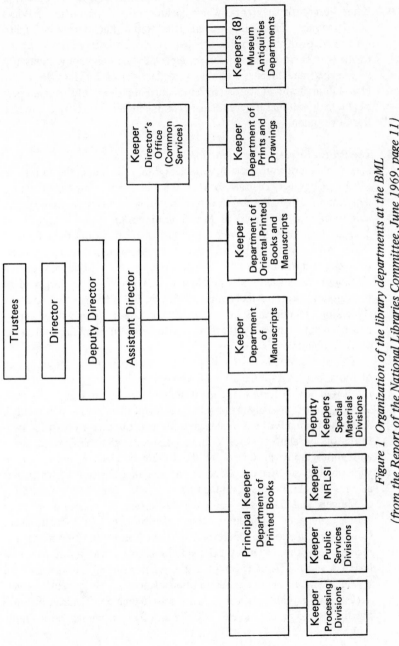

Figure 1 Organization of the library departments at the BML
(from the Report of the National Libraries Committee, June 1969, page 11)

sub-committees, of which one looked after the DPB and another the other library departments, which included the Department of Prints and Drawings. The Dainton Committee found that there were significant overlaps of use between this department and other library departments (the Department of Manuscripts (MSS) contains some thousands of drawings and there are significant collections of drawings also in the Map Library) and therefore recommended that it should become part of the new national library. This recommendation was not adopted by the Government.

The British Library at its formation
A general description of the new British Library, including the formation of the Reference Division out of the old British Museum's library departments (including the National Reference Library for Science and Invention) can be found in *British librarianship today*.[5] Significant changes from BM days were the transfer of the Copyright Receipt Office to the Bibliographic Services Division, which thereupon undertook the cataloguing for DPB of books received by legal deposit, as well as English language books purchased from overseas; the Department of Prints and Drawings had remained with the BM, although the Philatelic Collections remained as part of DPB; the Library Association library had been taken over by the Division to serve BL staff as well as its previous clientele.

The BL was divided into bibliographic services, lending and reference divisions but these designations oversimplify the real position. In fact, the Reference Division is the greatest producer of catalogue records — about 100,000 annually in many languages and all degrees of complexity. Also, the demands of external users and other libraries account for two-thirds of the almost eleven million frames of microfilm, reprography and photography produced by the Reference Division each year, in some analogy to the functions of the Lending Division to which RD also provides limited back-up facilities.

Mergers and take-overs cause serious stresses in organizations as in people, and good leadership is essential if morale is to be maintained. It is most unfortunate, therefore, that the former BM library departments were without a Director General for almost a year before Donovan Richnell took office. During the interregnum the situation was saved by the highly autonomous nature of departmental management. Nevertheless, this gap at a critical juncture was to create difficulties in forming the new division. The SCICON study had recommended a simple
172

functional organization for the Department of Printed Books but the new Director General had to recognize that the situation was complicated by the different techniques required for the many types of special materials handled and by the subject content and the linguistic and cultural features of the collections. A functional reorganization would have caused further upheaval for the staff and in any case, some cross-functional groupings would have had to be created analogous to the existing structure. This is not to suggest that the existing structure was entirely logical. Over a long period, departments and branches had been created *ad hoc* on different bases of language, subject, physical format and function, but within the concept of one universal library. For instance, Gaur has written a case study of the way in which material of interest to orientalists can be found throughout the division.[6] Such an arrangement calls for the duplication of skills; thus we find specialists in Slavonic and oriental languages in the Science Reference Library (SRL), specialists in maps and music in the Manuscripts Department and so on.

During the years preceding the creation of the British Library, changes had been taking place in the acquisitions pattern of departments for which their traditional procedures were sometimes inappropriate. The Oriental Manuscripts and Printed Books Department (OMPB), once dedicated to the study of the classifical cultures of its regions, had to cope with the rapid growth of modern publications from Japan and the Middle East (including under the BL responsibility for the large intake by official exchange), which demanded different treatment and were of interest to different publics. The Manuscripts Department was receiving large collections of family and private papers for which the summary techniques of a record office seemed more apt than the exhaustive description normally accorded to individual manuscripts. The Newspaper Library at Colindale had steadily evolved over the years from a storehouse to a branch with its own reading rooms and microfilming studio and having a growing need for professional skills. The Official Publications Library was groaning under the weight of paper resulting from the world-wide spread of bureaucracy and was very much under-used in proportion to the size of its collections, largely because of the inadequate bibliographical information provided by government and other official bodies, to whom the needs of libraries and scholars were not an important consideration. The astonishing growth of annual intake from 18,000 items in 1938 to 218,000 in 1980/81 is partly due to a more systematic pursuit of official publications.

173

Despite severe rationing of admission passes, the principal department (DPB) was suffering from overcrowding in the reading rooms, brought about by the post-war spread of higher education coupled with the cheapness of modern air travel. There was increasing concern about the wear and tear on certain sections of the book stock, most significantly the eighteenth century and older books, of which the Library has the world's finest collections – perhaps 80% of all extant eighteenth century titles in English and 50% of all known incunable titles.

Only a small proportion of resources was occupied by Public Service (about 20% today), for the development of the collections through selection, acquisitions and technical processes was much the major cost. An important source of acquisitions was the role of the Division as government agent, both for official exchanges and as a depository in respect of patents, official publications, Ordnance Survey maps and postage stamps. The DPB had lost about 250,000 volumes due to enemy action in the Second World War, about half of which have since been replaced, whilst Colindale lost a large number of British provincial newspapers.

As to its users, in the words of the BM Trustees this was 'simultaneously a library of last resort and a library of first instance . . .' Academics of the University of London looked on it as part of their normal resources, as was true to a lesser extent of Oxford and Cambridge dons.

The administration of world-wide acquisitions by legal deposit, purchase, exchange, gift or barter is a complex task, involving hundreds of sources, some of which have had so long and friendly a relationship with the library that they hoarded wartime publications during the Second World War, for later transmission to the British Museum.

The objectives which guided the first Director General in drawing up his plans for the new division are to be found in *British librarianship today* together with a key section from the British Library Act (1972) that 'the Board shall make the services of the British Library available in particular to institutions of education and learning, libraries and industry . . .' The last few years have seen a greater emphasis on objectives such as preservation of the national heritage of manuscript and printed material, developing a museum of the book and book arts, and strengthening the UK information network. Essentially the Bloomsbury part of the Reference Division constitutes a free public reference and research library in the humanities and social sciences, open on a restricted basis to readers and to remote users world-wide, whilst the

174

SRL, mainly serving industrial users, is open without restriction but draws it readers mainly from London and South-East England.

The pressures for change were many. It was essential to create an office for the new Reference Division. This was done by taking over the departmental office of Printed Books, although this had the regrettable effect of leaving the administrative sections of other departments *in situ*, and thus creating a three-tier structure of central, divisional and departmental administration. Secondly, it was necessary to replace the common services which had been withdrawn by the BM at handover day or later: photographic services, exhibition design, education and works planning. Through the creation of a divisional office, providing administration and these common services, to which would be added a publications office and a conservation branch, the reality of the Refernce Division began to be apparent. Although at first the autonomy of departments was gently encroached upon by managing most of the cross-divisional functions through advisory committees of departmental representatives, these were in due course to become subordinate to line managers with their own budgets, responsible to a Director of Divisional Administration. The policy themes of the BL Board, in such areas as conservation, rationalization both within the division and between the various parts of the BL, and the desire to make the national library the 'hub' of a wider library community, were reflected in a growing centralization of control.

The ADP study had pointed the way to new systems using the computer, but these were rather slow to come about, due to the struggles which the Bibliographic Services Division (BSD) was having in its own formation. The DPB general catalogue changed over to microfiche for new additions during 1975. One welcome change brought about by the new BL was a rate of acquisitions grant generous by any previous standard but since staff numbers did not increase to anything like the same extent, and automation was both slow to arrive and did not reduce the intellectual content of cataloguing, the flood of new books, serials and manuscripts steadily exceeded the ability of the library to handle them. Nevertheless, the arrears were much less serious than in earlier years: during 1972 the average processing time had been two and a half years, which had shrunk to between two months and one year by 1980 except in certain areas.

The problems of achieving change
Lack of accommodation was and remains the prime difficulty facing the Board. The division is split among many buildings in central

175

London, with its major pemises at the BM and Holborn suffering from gross overcrowding, the collections incurring environmental deterioration and a seemingly endless chain of removal being caused by the unstable tenancy of certain buildings. The SRL has been the prime victim of accommodation shortages, having been split into various buildings since its inception.

Within the British Museum building, cost and time penalties are exacted for such pervasive services as books supplied to the reading rooms and the photographic service, which concerns considerable numbers of staff in all grades working throughout the building. A number of suggestions for change of the DPB would involve different presentation, but it is impossible to contemplate new subject departments or other facilities except of a very modest nature.

The inflexibility of the staff structure is another major problem. The staff are divided into separate streams of the old museum curatorial grades, scientific grades, the typical Civil Service administrative, executive and clerical grades, technician grades and industrial grades. There are five separate trade unions, their membership dividing interests both vertically and horizontally. The high degree of specialization amongst the staff inhibits career development by level transfer or internal promotion; few officers in middle and senior posts are management-trained. The Board's desire to create a unified grading system for the BL yet remains unfulfilled, although the designation of some new posts as open posts for which any appropriately graded person can apply helps to open up the structure somewhat.

The next major problem to be mentioned is the conflict between present-day service and preservation of the invaluable collections. One of the early acts of the new Board was to commission a consultant to report on the conservation problem. His report confirmed their worst fears. Between 700/800,000 books were in urgent need of binding and other forms of conservation, environmental conditions were totally unsatisfactory and could only be remedied by the new building, many years away. Even if the vast sums of money could be found to tackle these binding arrears there was not the technical capacity within the BL dedicated binderies or elsewhere in the country to cope with so enormous a problem which later estimates calculated was growing by perhaps 40,000 volumes yearly plus the need for first binding of about 100,000 volumes of annual intake. Beyond the well-tried crafts of binding lay the technical problems of how to arrest the chemical deterioration of paper or to strengthen it mechanically.

The sheer size and complexity of the library's collections and the records thereof made a gargantuan job of redesigning and implementing new systems. For example, cataloguers were found to spend 80% of their time checking existing catalogues for authorities and precedents. The complex procedures designed over centuries for controlling these collections called for caution if they were to be radically altered without damage to the service.

Another long-standing problem was the inability of the photographic service to cope with the rapidly growing tide of orders as well as the library's own photographic needs for research and conservation purposes. Incidentally, this growth was a prime indicator of the increasing demand for remote use of the collections, another underlying pressure for change.

The merger of record creation for the British National Bibliography and the UK MARC data base with English cataloguing for the Reference Division, including not only the material received by legal deposit but that purchased widely from overseas, together with the development of computerized systems for RD cataloguing out of those designed to serve external customers of BSD, must be admitted to have caused serious problems and bottle-necks in the early years of the new national library. A prime example is the decision, recommended in the ADP study, to adopt the PRECIS subject indexing scheme for all purposes. This proved very much more costly than traditional methods in manpower terms, until in 1981 a simpler version of PRECIS was devised for internal purposes. The Reference Division was also unable to derive records and index entries from LC MARC, as recommended in the ADP study. The three-tier administration of the new division involved duplication of effort and is currently under review. There was also a difficult marriage of incoming procedures, based on Civil Service practice, with the inherited procedures of the Museum, yet further complicated by a move towards a more managerial style, to which the growing economic recession gave impetus. These are typical examples of reorganization of a 'living' institution under stress, and without major new investment.

Finally, in this list of problems, one should not underestimate those of running a large organization in central London with all of its environmental difficulties for employees and managers alike.

The first years in the Reference Division
Figure 2 shows the divisional structure as it is today.

In his article already cited, Richnell has described the steady but

177

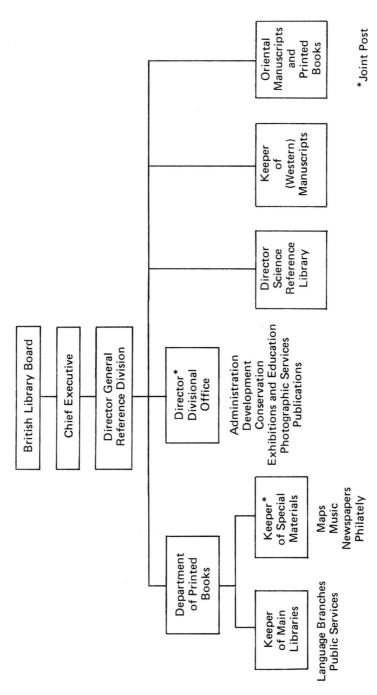

Figure 2 *The Reference Division Structure in 1981*

British Library Board

Chief Executive

Director General Reference Division

Director* Divisional Office

Administration
Development
Conservation
Exhibitions and Education
Photographic Services
Publications

Director Science Reference Library

Keeper of (Western) Manuscripts

Oriental Manuscripts and Printed Books

Department of Printed Books

Keeper of Main Libraries

Language Branches
Public Services

Keeper* of Special Materials

Maps
Music
Newspapers
Philately

*Joint Post

cautious approach which he took to strengthen overall control and give leadership, moves which gradually restored confidence and morale, although there would always be those who looked back with nostalgia to less changeable times under the former administration, confusing the painful cure with the chronic disease. As the years went by, it became possible to strengthen the corporate direction of the Division by appointing specialists as line managers of the common services. The staff at divisional level now number 250.

Further change was taking place within departments. In DPB there had been a principal keeper over two keepers, responsible for processing and public services, respectively, and a number of heads of special materials branches (maps, music, newspapers and philately). Somewhat contrary to the recommendation in the SCICON Report that this arrangement should be changed to a functional division of responsibilities, the processing part of the department was reorganized in 1976 into a series of language branches each responsible for selection, acquisitions (including official publications), cataloguing and other processing. It was believed that this would create work teams of reasonable size and give job satisfaction to the junior curatorial staff, formerly employed in routine cataloguing, as they could involve themselves in the study of languages and cultures for which they had relevant academic backgrounds. The model was that of the special materials branches; which latter were brought together under a keeper also having responsibility for divisional administration and common services. Shedding its acquisition role to the language branches of the Departments of Printed Books and of Oriental Manuscripts and Printed Books the Official Publications Library took on responsibility for the social sciences, beginning modestly with a reference collection. In 1980, the residual parts of DPB were brought together as a public services branch under a deputy keeper. The organization of the Science Reference Library has remained largely unaltered from NRLSI days, being based on premises at Holborn, specializing in patents and related literature, and the physical sciences and engineering, while the life sciences were housed until recently at Bayswater; however, the organizational structure crosses this divide as the deputy keepers are responsible for public services and processing across the department. The exigencies of accommodation cause functional splits between the processes, so that staff are constantly involved in movement between buildings some miles apart. In 1981 the life sciences branch was separated into three premises, with a public reading room at Aldwych only, with the saving grace that the branch is now more closely located to the rest of the library. The Manuscripts Department responded to the change in the pattern of its acquisitions by creating a large collections group in which a team approach is taken to the organization of such collections as the Blenheim Papers, amounting in the end to over 600 bound and indexed volumes. In other respects, this department remains most typical of the former BM Library. The mainstream grade of assistant keepers mostly work independently of the three deputy keepers and are supported by a small number of curatorial staff in the lower grades.

The scholarship of the staff has always been one of the great assets of the library and was mentioned as such in the Dainton Report. Consequently, promotion to deputy keeper rank would often be on grounds of scholarly merit and the individual would not be expected to undertake a heavy administrative burden, certainly not such as to inhibit his or her ability to maintain and develop scholarly achievement. Such an arrangement may have been appropriate in decades when the ratio of staff to acquisitions was adequate, but it has created severe difficulties in trying to reorganize the curatorial staff to select and process the vastly increased volume of acquisitions. Some senior staff find themselves forced into demanding managerial roles for which they have not been trained and which may not be congenial to them, whilst the mainstream of curatorial staff, particularly in DPB, find themselves with little time to undertake research. This is, of course, a generalization, for there are many parts of the library where the work simply cannot be done other than in the mode of scholarly investigation, eg rare books, maps and, for the most part, manuscripts. Nor does the managerial load inhibit exceptional individuals from continuing to undertake scholarly projects.

Specialization presents the most intransigent problems in the Department of Oriental Manuscripts and Printed Books (OMPB), whose staff command between them about 200 languages and other expertise in cultures stretching from North Africa to the Middle East and across the whole of Asia and the Western Pacific. They must also be deeply knowledgeable in the great religions which have moulded the cultures of these regions. The normal practice, therefore, is for small language sections, perhaps consisting of one person, to undertake the selection, acquisition and control of material, maintaining relations with the countries of origin, advising visiting scholars and compiling catalogues and bibliographies which become standards in the particular disciplines.

180

As some safeguard against gaps in expertise which might result if declining budgets force a reduction of staff numbers, OMPB has recently been reorganized into appropriate language groups, a number of which groups is supervised by each of the two deputy keepers, whilst the keeper remains responsible for departmental administration and relations with common services.

Quite recently the status of the head of the Newspaper Library has been upgraded to take account of the growing responsibilities, both managerial and professional, resulting from the world-wide spread of interest in newspapers as important source material and a study in themselves.

Corporate relationships
At the divisional level, the arrival of a new Director General in 1980 has given a stronger impetus to centralization and a corporate approach. The four directors and keepers meet weekly as the executive committee which takes decisions on short-term matters, and monthly as the planning group, concerned with budget forecasts, corporate policy and such major planning decisions as preparation for the new building at Euston Road. A small development office has been created under a deputy director to support the planning group and to bring together advice from various standing and *ad hoc* groups of experts relating to resource control, new technology, systematization and automation. The division is geared to the overall policy and planning process of the British Library through the Director General's membership of SPARC, a committee of the chief officers of the BL under the Chief Executive. Like the latter and the other two Directors General, the DG is a full-time voting member of the BL Board, a most unusual feature for British public institutions and one which works very well in practice.

SPARC has spawned various standing or *ad hoc* working groups and increasingly the divisions themselves have built bridges at different levels for groups of experts. Such links were essential due to the functional interrelation of RD and BSD, but they are also beginning to appear between the Reference and Lending Divisions, especially with SRL. The proposals for national science libraries for lending and for reference both emanated from the Advisory Committee for Scientific Policy. The Dainton Committee saw more in common in this last relationship than between SRL and the BM library proper. Central Administration specialists in personnel work, finance, accommodation planning and other functions attend the Executive Committee of the Reference

Division regularly to ensure coordination of effort.

Staff are entitled to apply for any vacancies within the BL. The appointment system is based on civil service practice and it is normal for appointing boards to be constituted from various divisions and departments at appropriate levels. Problems of distance and the cost of housing in London inhibit cross-flow between the Lending and Reference Divisions, but there are increasing numbers of staff with experience in more than one of the component parts of the BL, which must make for improved understanding and better communication.

A pattern of joint consultative committees exists to manage the relationship between RD and the three dedicated HMSO binderies, HMSO also placing the substantial amount of work put out to private contractors. Another part of the administrative environment is that the BL relies upon the Property Services Agency (PSA) of the Department of the Environment to maintain its buildings so that a chain of relationships exists with PSA at different levels. Planning for the Euston building is becoming significant for senior management and specialists in the BL.

The position is complicated at Bloomsbury where the BL is in a position of being a tenant to the British Museum, which provides security and maintenance on an agency basis. Security of the collections, which are invaluable in any sense of the word, is an increasing concern, when one combines the factor of rising prices with the trend in the crime rate. Both institutions recognize that the other has severe accommodation problems and that their operations are interdependent so far as the general public are concerned. Therefore, another series of links exists between the division and the BM.

One could go on describing the threads of the complex administrative web of which the division forms a part, such as relations with the Patent Office and the Ordnance Survey.

The international and national library communities
However, we proceed to place the division within the international and British Library communities and in the scholarly world. As one of the greatest national libraries the library has long played a leading part in setting standards and developing cooperative ventures with the other major research libraries of the world. Possessing as it does the world's largest collection of early books, the library has been particularly active in the retrospective union cataloguing of pre-nineteenth century publications. The independent efforts of Pollard and Redgrave for the period

182

1475-1640 and Wing for the years 1641-1700 have been followed under the BL administration by a much more ambitious project to list and locate copies of all material published in English during the eighteenth century plus foreign material published in England in that period — the Eighteenth Century Short Title Catalogue or ESTC. This is mainly an Anglo-American project, with participation of various Commonwealth and European countries, the editor in chief being Dr R C Alston at the BL. The ESTC techniques are now being used successfully with incunabula.

The curatorial staff of the many specialist sections within the division maintain correspondence with a small but world-wide fraternity and they undertake extensive foreign travel, combining the maintenance of these scholarly links and the exchange of technical expertise with the development of book supply and awareness of recent development in the countries and cultures in which they specialize. Within the UK staff are expected to participate fully in the activities of learned societies and institutions as well as in the affairs of the various professional library organizations.

To these personal and professional links has recently been added a deliberate campaign to strengthen understanding with external libraries of particular relevance to the division. Open days have been held for groups of chief librarians from universities, public libraries and various national bodies. Tours of the division on a group and individual basis are a daily occurrence. The division is now prominently featured at professional library and information science conferences. The external relations section of the Science Reference Library is adopting very positive methods including commercial advertisement in order to reach management in small to medium sized businesses and industrial firms, particularly in the provinces. This is part of a new strategy to create an infrastructure for reference and information services paralleling the networks created by the Lending Division. As with that division, the approach is a pragmatic one, rejecting what Jefferson has described as '... the old regional reference libraries concept, grant-aided and linked together, and with the British Reference Library [sic] ...' in favour of a multiplicity of open systems where an end user can apply direct to an RD service, or use it indirectly by various routes. At the same time, RD services are being developed on a selective basis determined as far as possible by what users say they need. The thorough reform of the system of distributing patents was preceded by a long period of consultation. A working party on access to newspapers, now in fact a standing advisory committee, provided a useful model for consultation, consisting as it does of a mixed body of external and BL experts who can both advise on proposed developments within the division and stimulate external cooperation.

Next came a working party on business information, this time including representatives from the Lending Division. The main recommendation of this working party, for the setting up of a business information referral centre within RD, was very quickly implemented. At the time of writing, a working party on provision for law is in session, comprising both academic lawyers and law librarians; there is also an advisory committee supervising a year's experiment in running a national register of printed ephemera and local publications in which BL staff come from all divisions and the Research and Development department. This experiment responds to the recommendations of several research projects commissioned by the R & D department, a welcome precedent since such reports have often recommended initiatives which could only be undertaken by parts of the national library and it is desirable that there should be close liaison as such proposals begin to firm up. Another precedent is that the Business Centre and the Ephemeral Register are regarded as action research projects sponsored by RD, whose management will not hesitate to curtail or close them down if experience does not confirm the usefulness urged by researchers and advisers. These moves towards the networking of information and co-ordination of collection policy are not just indications of an intention to make RD resources more widely available, although that is the primary purpose. But the BL also needs the formal cooperation of other libraries in order to carry out its own unique responsibilities; for example, the objective of forming the national printed archive involves a cooperative effort to ensure the capture and bibliographic description of the great number of minor publications which escape legal deposit. Again, RD has not the space to house all versions of provincial newspapers and must rely on the cooperation of public and university libraries.

Seen from inside, the organization of the division is complex; from outside it may be quite baffling, unless the approach of the potential user follows one of the typical streams such as long-term academic research or patent searching. Even in these cases, self-service is the rule and this requires a degree of familiarity with cataloguing and indexing systems. It is not too difficult for the academic worker to make good use of the Science Reference Library although it is mainly organized

184

for other purposes. But a subject specialist in the humanities, the arts and social sciences may find obstacles in the organization of the Library unless he is fortunate enough to be studying in one of the areas, like maps or music, where a special branch exists. The universality of the collections, which constitutes the great strength of the division, thus has its disadvantages. In their plans for a new library, the BM Trustees were hoping to overcome this problem by having a cluster of reading rooms devoted to particular subject interests and staffed by specialists, surrounding the general reading rooms. As an interim substitute, various tactics are being adopted to try to make the library more 'user friendly', to borrow a term from the new technology. This is a main reason for having formed a public services branch. There is closer liaison with major public and specialist libraries in London, reading room staff are encouraged to draw more upon the skills of specialists behind the scenes (although there must be severe limitations to the time they can spare), whilst the business information referral centre is an attempt to create an application point through which materials scattered throughout the departments and branches can be brought together to aid enquiries from external library and information services. If successful, other foci could be established, under the general coordination of the public services branch. Whether it will be possible in this way to extend coverage so as to exploit the Bloomsbury departments more fully for information purposes remains to be seen. Even if the business referral centre is successful, the development of further public services of this kind must be at the expense of existing activities because there is every possibility that the staff numbers will decline rather than increase in the next few years. Already it is clear that the relationship between the SRL and DPB needs to be more carefully defined. The Map Library and the Music Library both show what is possible, since they serve various professional and business clienteles without neglect of scholarly users.

To change priorities and develop new services at a time of cutback in resources is to demand a corporate loyalty of staff in the various component departments and divisions, since some diminution of existing services and standards is implicit as it is optimistic to assume that better organization and the use of technology will make the transition painless.

This is one aspect of the fundamental conflict between service to the present day and the building and conservation of the collections for service to future generations of users, that cuts across all RD policy: in more practical terms this means the division of resources between public

185

services on the one hand and acquisitions and conservation on the other. The very existence of the vast collections of the Reference Division as a 'library in being', a library of last resort, is a prime asset to the library and information community of this country and of all countries, on which they must increasingly depend as they have to take hard decisions locally at this time of economic difficulty. Typically, the university or public librarian will preserve services at the expense of acquisitions which makes it all the more important to maintain the range of RD acquisitions in compensation. Yet the BL must also endeavour to support other libraries by maintaining its services to them. That is the dilemma of the eighties.

Early successes
It was stated earlier that the library has been going through a second great 'centennial' reform since 1973. What successes can be claimed and what lessons can be learned from these first few years? Internally, many of the systems have been modernized, most cataloguing has been automated and there has been a great expansion of the photographic and reprographic services. Managerial control has been improved, most notably through the introduction of a system of cost accounting which has identified cost centres on which responsible management can be based. Book supply to the reading rooms has greatly improved whilst a much larger volume of acquisitions has been handled with relatively small increases of staff. The great expansion of binding output has been a major success and it is now finance rather than technical capacity that will determine the library's ability to overcome the great arrears of neglect which it inherited.

The division has successfully established its own publishing office which currently offers a list of over 170 titles comprising indispensable scholarly catalogues and bibliographies, publications aimed at the general public and additionally many leaflets, postcards and facsimile reproductions. The library has associated itself with commercial publishers, especially microform publishers, and this is likely to increase rapidly. A substantial programme of temporary exhibitions is mounted for the three and a half million visitors to the BM each year, whilst a good deal of time is spent in lending important treasures to exhibitions in other countries.

Although it would be wiser at present to claim significant improvement rather than total success for the photographic service, which has come under criticism for a number of years, its administration has been tightened up, a head of service appointed and both delivery times and revenue have improved considerably. The photographic and reprographic services are most complicated to administer, depending as they do on a complex network of about 200 staff, technical, administrative, curatorial and industrial, and ranging across the entire division. Many orders for photography are disguised enquiries requiring the assistance of a specialist.

Moving one stage out to see how far the former BM library departments have been integrated into a truly national library service, genuine improvements can be claimed in the integration of English language cataloguing, music cataloguing and the automation of other cataloguing originating in RD, although the resolution of the varying purposes of BSD and RD has had its difficulties. There has been relatively little operational connection with the Lending Division although the rationalization of holdings of low-use serials has accelerated recently. The recommendation in the ADP study that there should be lending of non-legal deposit material from the RD has only been implemented in a very marginal way by the loan of books in non-Western languages from SRL and to a small extent OMPB and also some loans from the Library Association library. However, there is much more provision of photocopies as a back up to LD, whilst some two-thirds of the annual output of almost eleven million frames of photographic and reprographic material from RD itself are supplied to order from outside libraries and individuals. It would be controversial for RD to extend its lending function substantially but this is one of several challenging precedents which may have to be faced, as the Board's broad strategy of first integrating its initial components and then being the 'hub' of the national library and information system develops to the extent of questioning the traditional policy assumptions of the great BM library, whose staff and collections comprise most of the resources of the BL.

The creation of a compatible bibliographic record system across the BL is a pre-condition for further integration of stock and services, so that the recent inauguration of a combined list of *Serials in the British Library* is a good augury for future cooperation. Experience in harmonizing the requirements of the BNB with English book cataloguing for RD has shown that although the result must necessarily be sub-optimal for both parties, a reasonable compromise can be reached which is in the end economic for the library world as a whole.

Planning ahead

A recent development in divisional management is the preparation of a five-year plan, two years firm and three years in outline, based on the 44 cost centres for which financial information is now available. Apart from the factors already mentioned, these plans are influenced by recent developments, most notably the government decision at the end of 1980 to approve the first stage of the new building at Euston. Although occupation only commences in 1988, advance planning for the building is already forcing imperatives into short to medium term planning: equally, any important change of divisional policy must be considered against the Euston assumptions. One example is the project for the control of book requests by computer. In the present building this is not economic but because it is essential that such a system be designed and fully tested for Euston a start should be made within the next two or three years. Other influences on divisional planning will be familiar to library professionals: the impact of the new technology, economic recession, and the strengthening of inter-library cooperation being among them.

In assessing priorities one has to put the plans on several pairs of scales – the balance between the archival and the service roles, the balance between service to academics and other legitimate users of the national reference libraries, the balance of acquisitions funds as between the active antiquarian market for rare books and manuscripts and the still growing volume of significant publishing world-wide, especially from Third World countries. Most vexing of all, perhaps is the balance between serving the unique purposes of the national library (the maintenance of the national printed archive, international activity in such fields as official exchange, standardization and retrospective union cataloguing) against the growing need to support the library system of the UK.

One cannot help thinking that Panizzi would have thoroughly enjoyed this decade of reform which has been as fundamental as were his reforms of the 1840s. The library is larger in scale and complexity than he could have imagined whilst the power of decision over its future is shared by various interests: government, the Board, corporate influences, the trade unions and the not inconsiderable collective force of the readership being the most direct of these influences.

Although it would have been far more comfortable to make the major adjustments which are necessary in a period of financial expansion, the opposite condition of economic recession may prove to be a greater stimulus to fresh thinking. The formalized discussion of policies and programmes against budget forecasts, coupled with an attempt to

188

create an open debate at all levels, contrast with the traditional modification of practice by incremental change and very limited participation in policy making. The new systems approach and computing applications have succeeded due to the willing take-up of these techniques and approaches by staff specialists and by middle and senior managers in the curatorial grades.

The unique strength and virtue of the Reference Division rests on its two great centuries of history, first the riches of the foundation collections, then the Panizzi reforms which carried it forward with the expansion of recorded knowledge so that only the Library of Congress and the Lenin State Library exceed it in sheer size. The reforms of the 1970s have created a third generation national library which grafted on other functions and now has the ability to use the new technology to lead such great international projects as the ESTC and play its full part in all major projects devised by the international library community.

The future of this powerful library complex is secure against the inroads of information technology; indeed in the short-term a wider awareness of its resources through the new technology will accentuate demands from remote users, whilst the division is as free as any other library to use the new methods so as to become an information switching centre. Some interdependence with external libraries will become necessary but RD must retain its essential autonomy to fulfil the unique objectives of the national library; also, service to its direct users must not be neglected. The maintenance and development of the collections inherited from the BM must remain a priority.

References

1 Miller, E J *That noble cabinet* London, Deutsch, 1973.

2 Great Britain, Department of Education and Science *Report of the National Libraries Committee* London, HMSO, 1969 (Dainton Report).

3 Samuel, E *See how they run* London, Woburn Press, 1976.

4 Great Britain, Department of Education and Science *The scope for automatic data processing in the British Library* 2 vols, London, HMSO, 1972. The SCICON studies (investigations by Scientific Control Systems Ltd) are summarized in Annex B of the report.

5 Saunders, W L *British librarianship today* London, Library Association, 1976.

6 Gaur, A 'Oriental material in the Reference Division of the British Library' *British Library journal* 2 (2), Autumn 1976.

APPENDIX – BRITISH LIBRARY REFERENCE DIVISION

SUMMARY STATISTICS 1980/81

Total staff   1,158 (350)

Earnings   £1,093,000

Holdings   About 10,200,000 (see under Departments)

Acquisitions   In 1980/81 about 2,000,000 items were registered. (A registered item may compirse, for example, a single issue of a serial or a single patent. The figure quoted above may be taken to represent about 230,000 volumes.)

DIVISIONAL SERVICES

Total staff   250 (38)

Department of Printed Books

Total staff   453 (156)

Holdings   About 8,600,000 volumes

Acquisitions   672,800 items ie books, serial and newspaper parts, atlases and map sheets, and printed music scores. See note under Reference Division acquisitions.

Readers   15,350 new and renewed admission passes issued, 795 seats (412 in the main Reading Room).

Issues   625,800 book application tickets issued

Newspaper Library (part of the Department of Printed Books)

Holdings   522,700 volumes and parcels, 153,700 microfilm reels.

Acquisitions   3,000 current titles, 16,800 microfilm reels

Readers   20,900 visits, 80 seats

Department of Manuscripts

Total staff	62 (34)
Holdings	83,300 volumes of manuscripts
Readers	16,900 visits, 60 seats

Department of Oriental Manuscripts and Printed Books

Total staff	65 (34)
Holdings	438,000 monographs, 37,200 volumes of manuscripts, about 19,000 manuscript fragments
Acquisitions	69 manuscripts, 13,800 monographs, 99,000 serial and newspaper parts
Readers	8,800 visits, 26 seats

Science Reference Library

Total staff	328 (88)
Holdings	168,400 monographs (excluding leaflets), 21.2 million patent specifications, 32,300 current serial titles, about 1,900,000 microforms (mainly microfiche and aperture cards)
Readers	129,500 visits, 204 seats
Computer search service	1,532 searches

The above shows the (full-time) equivalent numbers of staff in post at 31 March 1981. The figures in round brackets are the numbers of staff in managerial grades, which include academic and professional staff.

Collective management in the public library: a study of collective management in Denmark with illustrations from two Danish libraries

POUL ANDERSEN AND BØRGE SØRENSEN

The purpose of this article is to examine the notion of 'collective management', whereby all members of an organization make decisions collectively. It will discuss the possibilities and limitations of its being introduced in a country like Denmark, and review in some detail two approaches to collective management in two Danish public libraries.[1]

All Danish public libraries are run by the municipalities. In relation to other municipal services, however, libraries have a rather special position, partly because they normally have their own buildings, quite separate from the town hall or council offices, and partly because the library staff have not generally received the traditional education and training for local government administration. The chief librarian always has professional training in librarianship, but does not normally have any specific training in administrative law or personnel administration.

As a result the chief librarian has traditionally been given a rather free hand, and so in times when authority was more generally accepted than it is today, a strong chief librarian could generally limit the participation of his staff in decision-making to a minimum, if he so wanted. Until the beginning of the 1960s it may reasonably be asserted that management in most public libraries was strongly influenced by an authoritarian attitude, one that did not leave much room for experiments with democracy.

In the mid-1960s, however, librarians began to discuss seriously the 'democratization' of the management structure in Danish public libraries. In the beginning these discussions centred round an important, but narrowly professional subject, namely the participation of all librarians in book selection. After a fairly short time the principle of this change was accepted, primarily as a result of a new library act of 1964, which in principle gave all librarians in a library the right to participate in book selection.

The first step to democratization, then, was something that concerned the work of professional librarians. Other staff, such as the non-professional staff, were not involved in the discussions. One concrete result of this first phase of discussion was a suggestion that there should be established in libraries a management body to be called the 'librarians' council'. But, out of consideration for the other categories of staff, this idea was soon abandoned.

At the end of the 1960s there was much social and political discussion, stimulated by the radical actions of young people, about ways of spreading power in society. In particular, outspoken and politically active groups in the radical youth movement turned against any form of authority, and sought instead to develop forms of management based on collective groups comprising all members of the community. These ideas gradually found their way into the educational system, and had a strong impact on the discussions taking place about the best form of public library management.

Discussion quickly centred around the somewhat vague notion of 'collective management'. This idea is defined as a management system which gives all staff members the right and the obligation to participate in the management of their workplace. The phrase itself, 'collective management', is sufficiently suitable and precise when it is used to mean the spread of management authority to all members of the collective group. But in other ways the phrase is not so well chosen for it represents an idea far removed from the practical experience of most members of the library staff, and was felt to be by some completely utopian. It often became used as a catchword, devoid of any real content, and the idea treated as a fad, or considered as something totally unrealistic which could not seriously be attempted.

However, as a preliminary result of the many discussions among librarians a report on collective management in public libraries was produced. It came about on the initiative of the Bibliotekarforbundet (Union of Danish Librarians) and in cooperation with a number of other staff associations and interest groups. Using this report library staff have taken up the discussion on management structures, and have compared the present management system in libraries with new forms that have been developed. As a result it has been possible to develop a fairly high degree of democratic decision-making in some libraries within the limits of the ruling system.

NEW FORMS OF MANAGEMENT

A common characteristic of many of the new forms of management that have been developed within the last fifteen to twenty years, particularly in private industry, is that they have included a certain degree of democratization of working life. They are all based on the increasingly accepted fact that people work better, and get more personal satisfaction from work, the more they have a genuine control over what they do at work. For an employer or a manager this democratizing style is primarily a matter of obtaining a better qualified and more committed work force, which results in higher productivity. As soon as democratization gets close to the limit where the actual prerogatives of management are being infringed, the employer will call a halt. Other factors, like the question of private ownership, will then be decisive.

Resulting from these experiments the private sector has developed new organizational theories. Most of them accept a fairly high degree of participatory management of some parts of the work process. Ideas like 'self-governing groups' and 'overlapping groups' gave the workers a right to self-government within certain narrow limits, while the establishment of staff councils and the right of the workers to be represented on the board of industrial corporations also gave a fairly limited form of influence.

It is obvious that new forms of management will by nature have to be confined within the framework of the ruling economic and social system. In the private sector the new arrangements did not shake the employers' unlimited prerogatives of management, and in public institutions they did not to any extent affect the traditional hierarchical system. They may soften the practice, but they do not change fundamental principles in a capitalist social system.

A genuine collective form of management, in other words a form of management that gives all the employees the right and the obligation to participate in the management of their organization, cannot be established in a capitalist system. The task, therefore, is to develop a form of management which is acceptable to the ruling economic and social system, and which at the same time contains as many of the ingredients as possible of true collective management. It is a task which is certainly a lot easier to do in a publicly owned institution than in a private company, because the concept of private ownership is not blocking the way, even if the forms of management to be found in public institutions are also heavily influenced by the leading principles of the capitalist system.

194

However, if one wishes to develop even a modified version of collective management in an economic and social system like that found in Denmark, a number of legal and practical problems arise. Some of these problems will be treated in greater detail below.

The present system of management in Danish public libraries

Before looking at collective management in libraries it is desirable to describe the traditional system of management in the Danish public library. As in all municipal institutions management takes place at two levels, namely, a superior political authority, and an internal professional authority. The political authority is represented by the elected representatives on the city council. This council, in accordance with library legislation and with the general provisions governing the powers of local authorities, defines the general policy of the library. The day-to-day management of the library is then taken care of on the basis of these policy guidelines.

It is the daily, internal management of the library that can be made more democratic. In principle the internal management is in the hands of the chief librarian who cooperates more or less closely with the city councillors representing the political authority. This interaction between the political and the executive level is not based on any specific regulation, but has developed largely as a matter of common practice, so that it can vary from one local authority to the next. Normally, however, this cooperation is based on the principle of *delegation*, which means that most of the authority of the chief librarian is delegated from the political level, and can therefore always be revoked. The authority possessed by a chief librarian is not, therefore, something eternal. It cannot be transferred by right to, say, a collective body. Since the power of a chief librarian derives from the political authority, any system of collective management which seeks to take over this power can only do so with the agreement of the political representatives.

The internal management of a public library is concerned with three main tasks:

organizational and financial planning of the library service;

establishing policies for the day-to-day operations of the library;

handling relations with the outside world, including the political authority.

These main tasks are then dealt with by the chief librarian in more or less close cooperation with the other staff. This cooperation takes

195

the form of a series of meetings of all kinds: staff meetings, industrial councils, heads of department meetings, and so on. In many cases these meetings are looked upon by the participants as pseudo-democratic events, because the educational and social differences among the staff block any sensible discussion, and because the amount of information possessed varies widely among the participants.

From the above it might look as if the management structure in most Danish public libraries today is well defined. This is far from being the case. In the majority of public libraries the greater part of the staff would be hard pressed to define exactly what the management of their library does. The functions of the management are often thought of with an almost mystical respect if for no other reason because they seem so comprehensive and so vitally important.

Further, there is confusion between management functions and administrative functions. Purely administrative decisions often undergo a lengthy and elaborate process of decision-making, while fundamental decisions of an economic or professional nature that have important implications for the whole library staff are not the subject of any broad process of decision-making. If democratic management systems are to get a chance to work, then it will be necessary to separate managerial matters from purely administrative matters much more clearly than they are today.

Official regulations concerning staff participation

Since 1967 in Denmark there has been in existence a set of recommended regulations concerning staff meetings in public libraries. The recommendations have been agreed upon by the Bibliotekarforbundet and the employers in the Danish Library Association. The regulations establish the right of staff to make proposals and statements directly to the political authorities. The existence of this right, including cases where members of staff disagree with the chief librarian, must be considered to be vitally important in the effort of staff to obtain genuine participation.

All essential questions about the library service, its organization, the budget, and so on can, in principle, be discussed at staff meetings. In smaller libraries especially, such meetings can be a suitable instrument to increase staff participation in the making of decisions. In larger libraries, on the other hand, where one may find seventy or a hundred people present, the large numbers hamper the talkativeness of the not so vocal and the more outspoken alike, and the staff meetings
196

may be reduced to an empty formalism or will discuss only petty trifles.

We should, finally, note that these regulations are only intended as a guide, so that before they can be implemented by an individual library they must be approved by the city councillors at the political level, at least as far as the right of access by the staff to the political authority is concerned. It is a matter of speculation to decide how far this right to make statements is actually being used, and hence a matter of speculation too, to estimate the real importance of these regulations about staff meetings in public libraries.

The regulations just discussed apply only to public libraries. But in many other libraries there has been a move in recent years to establish 'staff councils' as the supreme body of participation.[2] Such councils were set up in accordance with regulations which were negotiated in 1970 between the Kommunernes Landsforening (the association of municipal councils) and all staff associations in the country; they apply, therefore, to staff in all public institutions.

The regulations on staff councils are more in the way of a welfare measure than a method of obtaining genuine influence over work. The clauses in the regulations setting out the objectives of the councils state that their purpose is to involve the greatest number of employees in cooperative measures. The councils are supposed to establish good, stable working conditions which will increase the security and well-being of the employees, promote their interest in the development of the institution's activities, and so improve its effectiveness and competitive ability.

The staff council consists of an equal number of representatives from the management and from other staff. In a library the representatives of the 'management' will typically be the chief librarian, the deputy librarian and a number of heads of departments, while the staff side will be represented by the shop stewards of the various categories of employees together with a number of staff representatives elected in the various departments of the library.

The council can participate in making decisions; it can be consulted, and it can receive information. The right to participate in decisions concerns mainly working conditions, such as the organization of work schedules, matters affecting the job environment, welfare measures and staff conditions. It can also participate in staff matters like appointments, dismissals and staff education programmes. It should be noted, however, that the right to participate concerns principles, and not

197

specific cases. The council's right to be consulted is in the field of economic matters, like budgets and accounts.

In public libraries the staff councils are viewed with considerable scepticism. On paper the regulations concerning these councils give staff only a rather modest amount of real influence. In addition the regulations are subject to varying interpretations, notably in their distinction between what is a matter of principle and what is practice, thus leading to tedious procedural discussions and red tape. On the other hand the very ambiguities of the regulations enable the staff (if both staff and management sides agree) to exert a good deal more influence than perhaps the regulations actually intended. In some places staff councils have been established where the management has only two or three representatives, while the staff side has perhaps ten or twelve. Even so, there is still a long way to go from these officially recognized and limited forms of participation to real collective management.

Collective management
The essential point about collective management is that everybody must be able to participate in the decisions of all matters of a managerial nature. In practice, however, such an arrangement is only possible in those places of work where the staff have simple tasks understood by all. Certain administrative tasks in public libraries are of this nature, but mostly the work is more specialized, requiring specialized knowledge which is not directly possessed by all members of the staff.

In such cases it is therefore important to decide at what points in the decision-making processes the collective management procedure should enter the scene. Following generally recognized management theories, we can say that the process of making decisions can be divided into four stages:

the formulation or delimitation of the problem;
suggested solutions, with alternatives;
comparison of the solutions and their consequences;
taking the decision.

The latter two steps, together with the formulation of the problem itself, are clearly matters which can be done collectively, while the task of finding suggested solutions with their alternatives is not necessarily a matter which can be considered collectively.

By definition all employees take part in collective management. The organization must be built up around a meeting that summons all staff

198

so that the collective management function can be properly carried out. But in practice this is impossible if an institution employs a large number of people. It has been said that if one wishes to set up collective management in its pure form, the maximum number of employees is twenty-five. Beyond that figure, and therefore in the case of most public libraries, it will be necessary for the staff to elect *representatives*. When this happens the core of the collective management arrangement will still be an assembly consisting of all employees, but the daily management tasks have to be entrusted to a smaller number of staff, elected, however, by the staff as a whole. This means a move away from the ideal of collective management, so it is essential to establish that the elected representatives in the management are elected for a limited timespan, and that the elected management is responsible to all employees.

One pre-condition for the effective participation of all staff members in the making of decisions is that a system of meetings and channels of information has been established in the library. A further prerequisite is that among the participating staff there is some measure of agreement on the decisions that have to be made. There must be a reasonable consensus of opinion on the purpose and the essential functions of the institution, so that disputes about fundamental principles do not prevent decisions being reached. This means that in principle the regular method of making decisions should not be by a vote. For a collective management system to work properly it is essential that all participants acknowledge and accept a common set of values, but at the same time it is highly likely that establishing this common set of values will be a difficult and cumbersome process, putting strains on the collective management system, especially in the early years of its existence.

The daily allocation of work in the library will not differ in principle from what it is today, except that managing a library by collective management will mean the participation of all staff, and will not be something solely in the hands of professional librarians. Collective management does not necessarily introduce a new division of labour in the library as a whole. Nor does the internal organization of the library need to undergo great changes. The usual functional divisions, or the combination of functional division with departments based on geographical areas can continue to exist. But each department or branch in the library will be linked through a collective management arrangement, which will add up to a collective management system for the library as a whole.

199

Legal problems

It is the sharing of the management process, and the ensuing shared responsibility which present the greatest legal problem for collective management. According to Danish law and custom it has been established that a collective management body can be made legally responsible in the same way that an individual can. This is true both for the criminal code, and also, and this is more relevant in our case, for the civil service regulations. In connection with these regulations we must not forget the basic fact of library management, namely that it is based upon a delegation of authority from the political level of municipal councillors etc. All decisions, even day-to-day decisions, made by the internal management processes of the library, whether collectively organized or not, can be set aside by the municipal councillors, unless library legislation prevents it. The power and responsibilities of the political authority cannot therefore be challenged, even by collective management within the library. Workers' participation in publicly owned institutions or industries is therefore limited by the right of the general public, through its elected representatives, to exercise the ultimate powers of decision-making.

The question then arises, can the political body delegate this authority to anything other than an individual? Can it, for example, delegate it to a collective body? The regulations governing the administration of municipalities do not prevent the delegation of responsibility to a collective. In fact the whole question of delegation within the municipal administration is not covered by any law or regulations, so it is up to each municipal council to decide whether it will accept a collective management arrangement or not.

As for library legislation, there are no provisions that would exclude collective management from a library. True, the library act does contain a provision which states that the head of a library must be a trained librarian. This could be interpreted to mean that there has to be just one responsible chief librarian. However, this particular provision has been re-interpreted by a later revision of the library act, where it states that the existence of a chief librarian does not prevent experiments with various forms of management, and the revision committee actually recommends that experiments of this kind should be started as soon as possible.

To conclude, then. The establishment of a collective management system in a public library requires the approval of the municipal council. But once such approval has been given, there is nothing in any of the

200

own department. Matters of a more general nature that are going to be discussed in the coordination group will therefore often get a rather hasty and superficial analysis in the department. And if, in addition, the motivation of the staff to participate in the general decision-making is lacking, it may be that only a few staff members in a department, or at worst only the departmental representative on the coordination group actually has an informed and serious view on each of these general matters. It is often the case, as staff members say themselves, that a department is not itself able to submit a recommendation on a specific issue.

From the point of view of the traditional managers, that is to say, from the point of view of the chief librarian and deputy librarian, things of course look different. The matters that come before the coordination group are matters requiring a solution — which will be found by the management if by no one else. Therefore the managers are in all circumstances forced to give each matter a thorough review, and to submit a recommendation to the coordination group. This is the natural task for senior managers; that is what they have been appointed for, and that is what is expected of them.

When a particular matter comes up for discussion and decision at the coordination group, the outcome, therefore, is often that the recommendation for action proposed by the senior managers is the only one there is, or at least the only proposal which has been thoroughly presented. This recommendation is then discussed at the meeting, generally without any alternatives, adopted with perhaps some minor amendments, and the senior managers thereby have their decision confirmed by the coordination group.

It would be an exaggeration to assert that this is precisely the intention of the coordination agreement. And, we might add, this state of affairs is not necessarily all bad. A well-qualified management, one which acknowledges the necessity of staff participation, will not deliberately submit proposals that are against the interests of the staff if that can be avoided.

Obviously it cannot always be avoided. A fundamental condition for this kind of worker's participation is that the ultimate control of the library remains in the hand of the political authority. Besides this there are a number of constraints — budgetary, legal, political — that cannot be changed by even the most effective work-place democracy. If the chief librarian is asked by his political superiors to cut down the acquisitions budget by, say, a million kroner, something that both he

laws or regulations relating to local government or libraries which prevents a collective management system from functioning.

Practical problems

The legal problems relating to collective management can be resolved, as we have seen, without too much difficulty. However, there remain a number of practical problems of a fairly complicated nature. It is, for example, a practical problem to establish and operate a system of efficiently run meetings, and it is difficult to ensure that each single staff member has the same amount of information available to him. And there are practical problems in separating managerial and administrative tasks.

We can only mention a few of these problems in this paper. We shall look briefly at the problem arising from differences in the educational backgrounds of the staff, and at the effects on the salary and staff structure which collective management brings about.

In principle all employees in a collective management system have the same right to influence decisions, and the influence of all staff members has the same value. In real life, however, it will be found that the influence of some staff is limited, because they feel that their relative lack of education or training is a drawback, and so do not wish to participate on equal terms. This feeling will very likely be most pronounced among non-professional staff and among recently engaged staff. The problem is that the management of a library has traditionally been entirely in the hands of senior professional staff, and that to manage a library may be seen by others as something strange and perhaps also a little frightening.

This problem can be solved only by a change of attitudes. All activities in a library are essential to the service provided, and should therefore be considered to be equally important. Further, for collective management to function properly, everyone must recognize that everyone can contribute to the system because everyone has experience and expertise in one or other task. Regular attendance in the decision-making processes will give to the newly arrived and the timid a better insight into the work of the library and a better capacity to solve the problems. This probably means that all staff members have to acquire some basic knowledge of library problems and of the legal and economic framework of the library, if collective management is to work properly.

The introduction of collective management will soon lead to changes in the status and methods of work for those employees that at the present time manage the library. They will still have management functions, but they will in future be exercising them in cooperation with other staff members. This will influence the salary structure, which is traditionally partly based on the education and training of the various categories of staff, and partly on the amount of personal responsibility attached to each individual post. The notion of sole responsibility will immediately be called into question by collective management, and this will bring about a harmonization of salaries within each single staff category. Eventually changes in the value accorded to library work will imply that equal salaries for all employees will seem natural.

All this is a very slow process, and the general rule must be that changes in salary structures must follow changes in cooperation and management relations. It is difficult to conceive of a radically new salary system being introduced in order to impose a collective form of management, though, we may add, there are strong arguments for the harmonization of salaries in libraries, quite apart from those arising from the establishment of collective management.

APPROACHES TO COLLECTIVE MANAGEMENT IN PRACTICE

Influenced by the theories which have been discussed above, a number of Danish libraries have introduced some kind of democratization of their management structure. It has obviously not been possible to establish a true collective management system, but we have chosen to give an account of two libraries that have moved significantly in this direction. The libraries in question are two medium-sized public libraries in Nykøbing Falster and Skive.

Nykøbing Falster

The library in the municipality of Nykøbing is the county library for all the libraries in Storstrøms Amt, which has a total population of 260,000, and at the same time is the local public library for the people of the town of Nykøbing, with a population of over 40,000.[3] In 1980 the library employed the equivalent of sixty full-time staff, of which twenty-one are librarians and twenty clerical workers. The annual budget for 1980 totalled 15,312,000 Danish kroner (about £1,150,000), of which 7,848,000 kroner (£590,000) were for salaries and 3,415,000 kroner (£257,000) for materials.

In Nykøbing municipality there has been in existence for five years (the first two years on an experimental basis), a cooperation agreement

which in a number of important ways is more extensive traditional agreements for staff councils mentioned earlier. The agreement covers all the departments and services of the mu and was created as a result of a political initiative. It was planned in cooperation with the planning department of the of municipalities (Kommunernes Landsforening).

While the general agreement on staff councils gives possibilities for participation, the Nykøbing agreement al real participation in management. The agreement substan the power of the chief librarian, by allowing votes to management issues, thereby in effect eliminating the veto chief. It also largely eliminates the possibility of the directly talking to the councillors without the consent ation group, the group around which the new manag is centred. Finally, it allows the staff to participate in ing working and staff conditions and, unlike the staff discussion is allowed only of the general principles, the ment allows participation in particular cases of wor ditions.

However, what is probably the most important the agreement involves politicians (local councillo staff members and is considered to be an important municipal structure. The coordination group ca as a true coordinating and executive management b

The library at Nykøbing has a fairly long trad pation in management. Before the adoption of force they had already, during the preceding five ment where the traditional heads of departme replaced by a coordinating body consisting par ment and partly of representatives elected in the

How decisions are made at Nykøbing

As mentioned, the coordination group diff staff council by having a decisive group a fields. But how does the group actually mak sentatives both of the staff and the managen a crucial problem. Does the coordinatio tend to become a body which only con management? The staff in the various de engaged in the normal job routines and i

laws or regulations relating to local government or libraries which prevents a collective management system from functioning.

Practical problems
The legal problems relating to collective management can be resolved, as we have seen, without too much difficulty. However, there remain a number of practical problems of a fairly complicated nature. It is, for example, a practical problem to establish and operate a system of efficiently run meetings, and it is difficult to ensure that each single staff member has the same amount of information available to him. And there are practical problems in separating managerial and administrative tasks.

We can only mention a few of these problems in this paper. We shall look briefly at the problem arising from differences in the educational backgrounds of the staff, and at the effects on the salary and staff structure which collective management brings about.

In principle all employees in a collective management system have the same right to influence decisions, and the influence of all staff members has the same value. In real life, however, it will be found that the influence of some staff is limited, because they feel that their relative lack of education or training is a drawback, and so do not wish to participate on equal terms. This feeling will very likely be most pronounced among non-professional staff and among recently engaged staff. The problem is that the management of a library has traditionally been entirely in the hands of senior professional staff, and that to manage a library may be seen by others as something strange and perhaps also a little frightening.

This problem can be solved only by a change of attitudes. All activities in a library are essential to the service provided, and should therefore be considered to be equally important. Further, for collective management to function properly, everyone must recognize that everyone can contribute to the system because everyone has experience and expertise in one or other task. Regular attendance in the decision-making processes will give to the newly arrived and the timid a better insight into the work of the library and a better capacity to solve the problems. This probably means that all staff members have to acquire some basic knowledge of library problems and of the legal and economic framework of the library, if collective management is to work properly.

The introduction of collective management will soon lead to changes
201

in the status and methods of work for those employees that at the present time manage the library. They will still have management functions, but they will in future be exercising them in cooperation with other staff members. This will influence the salary structure, which is traditionally partly based on the education and training of the various categories of staff, and partly on the amount of personal responsibility attached to each individual post. The notion of sole responsibility will immediately be called into question by collective management, and this will bring about a harmonization of salaries within each single staff category. Eventually changes in the value accorded to library work will imply that equal salaries for all employees will seem natural.

All this is a very slow process, and the general rule must be that changes in salary structures must follow changes in cooperation and management relations. It is difficult to conceive of a radically new salary system being introduced in order to impose a collective form of management, though, we may add, there are strong arguments for the harmonization of salaries in libraries, quite apart from those arising from the establishment of collective management.

APPROACHES TO COLLECTIVE MANAGEMENT IN PRACTICE
Influenced by the theories which have been discussed above, a number of Danish libraries have introduced some kind of democratization of their management structure. It has obviously not been possible to establish a true collective management system, but we have chosen to give an account of two libraries that have moved significantly in this direction. The libraries in question are two medium-sized public libraries in Nykøbing Falster and Skive.

Nykøbing Falster
The library in the municipality of Nykøbing is the county library for all the libraries in Storstrøms Amt, which has a total population of 260,000, and at the same time is the local public library for the people of the town of Nykøbing, with a population of over 40,000.[3] In 1980 the library employed the equivalent of sixty full-time staff, of which twenty-one are librarians and twenty clerical workers. The annual budget for 1980 totalled 15,312,000 Danish kroner (about £1,150,000), of which 7,848,000 kroner (£590,000) were for salaries and 3,415,000 kroner (£257,000) for materials.

In Nykøbing municipality there has been in existence for five years (the first two years on an experimental basis), a cooperation agreement
202

which in a number of important ways is more extensive than the traditional agreements for staff councils mentioned earlier. The Nykøbing agreement covers all the departments and services of the municipality, and was created as a result of a political initiative. It was originally planned in cooperation with the planning department of the association of municipalities (Kommunernes Landsforening).

While the general agreement on staff councils gives only limited possibilities for participation, the Nykøbing agreement allows a more real participation in management. The agreement substantially reduces the power of the chief librarian, by allowing votes to be taken on management issues, thereby in effect eliminating the veto power of the chief. It also largely eliminates the possibility of the chief librarian directly talking to the councillors without the consent of the coordination group, the group around which the new management structure is centred. Finally, it allows the staff to participate in matters concerning working and staff conditions and, unlike the staff councils, where discussion is allowed only of the general principles, the Nykøbing agreement allows participation in particular cases of working or staff conditions.

However, what is probably the most important point of all is that the agreement involves politicians (local councillors), managers, and staff members and is considered to be an important aspect of the whole municipal structure. The coordination group can actually function as a true coordinating and executive management body.

The library at Nykøbing has a fairly long tradition of staff participation in management. Before the adoption of the agreement now in force they had already, during the preceding five years, had an arrangement where the traditional heads of departments meeting had been replaced by a coordinating body consisting partly of heads of department and partly of representatives elected in the departments.

How decisions are made at Nykøbing

As mentioned, the coordination group differs from the traditional staff council by having a decisive group authority in a number of fields. But how does the group actually make its decisions? The representatives both of the staff and the management understand that this is a crucial problem. Does the coordination group in actual practice tend to become a body which only confirms the decisions of the management? The staff in the various departments of the library are engaged in the normal job routines and in planning the work of their

203

own department. Matters of a more general nature that are going to be discussed in the coordination group will therefore often get a rather hasty and superficial analysis in the department. And if, in addition, the motivation of the staff to participate in the general decision-making is lacking, it may be that only a few staff members in a department, or at worst only the departmental representative on the coordination group actually has an informed and serious view on each of these general matters. It is often the case, as staff members say themselves, that a department is not itself able to submit a recommendation on a specific issue.

From the point of view of the traditional managers, that is to say, from the point of view of the chief librarian and deputy librarian, things of course look different. The matters that come before the coordination group are matters requiring a solution — which will be found by the management if by no one else. Therefore the managers are in all circumstances forced to give each matter a thorough review, and to submit a recommendation to the coordination group. This is the natural task for senior managers; that is what they have been appointed for, and that is what is expected of them.

When a particular matter comes up for discussion and decision at the coordination group, the outcome, therefore, is often that the recommendation for action proposed by the senior managers is the only one there is, or at least the only proposal which has been thoroughly prepared. This recommendation is then discussed at the meeting, generally without any alternatives, adopted with perhaps some minor amendments, and the senior managers thereby have their decision confirmed by the coordination group.

It would be an exaggeration to assert that this is precisely the intention of the coordination agreement. And, we might add, this state of affairs is not necessarily all bad. A well-qualified management, one which acknowledges the necessity of staff participation, will not deliberately submit proposals that are against the interests of the staff — it if can be avoided.

Obviously it cannot always be avoided. A fundamental condition of this kind of worker's participation is that the ultimate control of the library remains in the hand of the political authority. Besides this there are a number of constraints — budgetary, legal, political — that cannot be changed by even the most effective work-place democracy. If the chief librarian is asked by his political superiors to cut down the acquisitions budget by, say, a million kroner, something that both he
204

and the library staff will of course object to vehemently, then the coordination group has to accept this decision and has to try to carry it out once its professional arguments against such a cutback have been rejected by the political authority.

A chief without veto power
One of the fundamental differences between the Nykøbing agreement and the general agreement on staff councils is that the political authority must have a recommendation from the coordination group on all library matters. This obviously reduces the role of the chief compared to his traditional role where his authority to make recommendations to the political level is unquestioned.

In Nykøbing, with its long-standing tradition of staff participation, the reduced role of the chief has not caused many problems. However, it is important to make clear that the chief librarian is still the only librarian who may communicate directly with the municipal councillors. He alone presents library issues to the political authority, and this in itself, of course, is enough to give the chief a special position in relation to the coordination group.

Another important aspect of the Nykøbing agreement is that votes may be taken in the coordination group. That this possibility is hardly ever used is probably due to the excellent climate of cooperation in the library. But the agreement does provide that in principle the majority of the staff may reject the recommendation of the chief librarian, and if this happens the chief cannot use his veto power to overrule the group's decision.

Heads of departments
Effective democracy at the work-place must also affect the authority of heads of departments. In Nykøbing half the representatives of the staff on the coordination group must be heads of departments. They are considered as part of the management side in the coordination group. But as they do not have any particular management prerogatives in their departments, the question arises: on what side are the heads of departments actually to be found?

The evidence indicates that department heads think of themselves as representatives of the department, and not of the management. This has the advantage that the coordination group can function as a coordinating body where the management and the various departments are represented. Neither the senior managers nor the other

205

staff conceal the fact, however, that this democratic state of affairs has created problems for some of the older heads of departments that have been used to working in more traditional, hierarchical systems.

Skive

Skive municipal library is an example of an organization where a high degree of staff participation has developed without any formal acceptance by the political authority, and without any parallel development occurring in other branches of the municipal administration. Compared with Nykøbing, however, where the arrangement was formally accepted by the political authority, Skive has gone equally far towards internal democracy and has just as much genuine staff participation in the making of decisions.

Skive municipality has about 27,000 inhabitants. The library has the equivalent of forty-one full time staff, of whom fifteen are librarians. The library's annual budget for 1980 amounted to 8,461,000 Danish kroner (about £636,000) of which 4,609,000 kroner (£347,000) went on staff salaries and 2,035,000 kroner (£153,000) on library materials. About ten years ago, following some years of *de facto* work-place democracy, a set of regulations were made to formalize the arrangement. The regulations were submitted to the political authority of the library for approval. The politicians greeted this initiative without much enthusiasm, but also without a flat rejection. They found the regulations to be so much more detailed than the general regulations concerning municipal administration and administrative practice that they wanted to ask the association of municipalities (the Kommunernes Landsforening) for their advice and consent.

Since then nothing further has happened concerning approval by the political authority of the library's proposals for running its affairs. In the library this has been taken to mean that the politicians have accepted this state of affairs. Externally the chief librarian makes his recommendations to his superiors in a nice and decent way. Internally (within the library) each department manages its own affairs, the staff participates in the making of all decisions, and the chief librarian, as well as other staff, states that it is out of the question that the chief would go to the politicians with a recommendation that is strongly opposed by the staff as a whole.

Worker participation in Skive library is based on regulations that have been established jointly by the staff and the management. The basis of organization is the department, all of which operate as self-
206

governing groups. Each group has the following tasks:

1 To plan and coordinate work within its own field, and to decide on methods of work.

2 To allocate work to members of the group according to their own choice.

3 To submit plans, proposals, changes etc that influence or relate to other areas, to the coordinating committee or to the staff meeting.

4 To assist other groups when these need manpower to any large extent, and to receive help from other groups in periods with a heavy work load, or when it is necessary for the holding of group meetings.

5 To prepare budgets for its department.

6 To submit requests to the coordination committee and staff meeting for equipment and furniture for the department's premises.

7 To evaluate the need for staff in the department, and to submit recommendations to the staff meeting.

8 To review applications for posts within the department, to talk to the applicants and to submit recommendations to the coordinating committee concerning the filling of the vacant positions.

9 To submit recommendations to the coordination committee about dismissals, transfers, reallocations etc of the staff in the department.

10 To keep track of extra leave and of overtime within the department.

11 To elect for a half-year period a representative to the coordinating committee and to report to the coordinating committee on its group meetings.

In each department a person is employed as head of the department. The regulations do not specify any particular tasks or responsibilities for this person. Indeed where in traditional administrative procedures the role of the head of department is spelt out, at Skive all such activities are the responsibility of the group. However, heads of departments are entitled to appear before the coordinating committee meetings, with the right to speak but not to vote. This special privilege for departmental heads was introduced because the municipal councillors had expressed concern over the reduced influence of heads of department. Many of the library staff find such an arrangement inappropriate and would like to see it abolished.

It is obvious that this form of worker's democracy requires a great deal of commitment and mutual solidarity from the employees. These qualities will never be found in all staff members to the same extent.

207

There will always be someone to say — though perhaps not out loud — 'I'm appointed to do the circulation routines at the issue desk, and not to allocate and manage the work in the whole department, let alone the whole library'. It therefore seems a bit presumptuous to expect that the groups can suggest colleagues for dismissal, assist other departments in cases of heavy workloads, and themselves keep track of overtime, additional leave etc. In no circumstances could this be done without problems, and particularly not at a time when resources are scarce both of staff and materials in most public libraries. However, it seems that the democratic system handles these touchy questions in a fairly reasonable way, and one hears remarkably positive opinions from both management and other staff when this form of self-government for the departmental groups is discussed.

The coordinating committee

The next level in the internal management of the Skive library is the coordinating committee. This committee meets weekly, and consists of the chief librarian and a representative from each of the library's five departments, elected for six months at a time. As already mentioned the departmental heads can also appear before the committee with the right to speak but not to vote. It is part of the unwritten rules of the library that heads of departments, like all other staff members, are loyal to the proposals put forward by the groups which they belong to.

However, it is precisely this group loyalty, on which the structure is very largely based, which can present some problems in the case of decisions of a more general nature. It is of course never an easy task to reconcile conflicting interests among groups. In Skive decisions are arrived at through discussion, and votes are the exception. Often it is the general unifying viewpoint of the chief librarian, perhaps based on unavoidable political and economic facts, that influences the decisions that are made.

The work of the coordinating committee can be summarized as follows:

1 Allocation of the daily post.

2 Receiving reports of the weekly meetings of the groups from their representatives.

3 Submissions to the cultural committee of the municipal council on the appointment of regular staff based on recommendations from the groups.

4 Appointment of temporary staff and staff paid by the hour,

ble as a conclusion to sum up the main experiences of Danish
ibraries in relation to collective management. First, partic-
lemocracy means a better and much improved decision-making
 an organization that actively involves its staff in the making of
s is fundamentally better equipped to make correct decisions
 organization that is managed from the top. Second, partici-
lemocracy creates for the individual staff member an under-
 and knowledge of the total framework that the library operates
makes her, or him better equipped to do the job: this is true
respect of the librarian's primary purpose, to serve the public,
the secondary one of functioning as an active member of the
ion.

 are, then, enough professional — and also, as a matter of fact,
burely political — arguments to try to defend the ground that
 conquered, and, in spite of the recession, to argue for new
nts with the forms of management in public libraries. This
re that the set of praiseworthy ideals that have influenced the
 objectives and the external activities of public libraries, can
 their internal organization.

lective management (in Danish: kollektiv ledelse) is stronger
 ticipative management', and has a somewhat more precise
han a term such as 'industrial democracy'.

 Danish word 'samarbejdudvalg' has been translated as 'staff
 Staff councils resemble similar bodies established by law in
 stern European countries which give workers a statutory right
 esented on certain decision-making bodies in many different
rganization.

'amt' is a territorial division somewhat similar to a county.

based on recommendations from the groups.

5 Termination of temporary staff and hourly paid staff, based on
recommendations from the groups.

6 Transfers or reallocation of staff, based on recommendations
from the groups.

7 Approval of work schedules and holiday arrangements.

8 Organization of the training of library trainees and of probationary
clerical staff.

9 Organization of seminars on how to conduct meetings.

10 Coordination of plans from the groups regarding the layout of
the premises.

11 Approval of the choice of equipment, machines etc made by the
groups.

12 Coordination of public relations activities.

13 Practical administration of book selection, preservation and withdrawal.

These tasks will in more traditional organizations be part of the
administrative hierarchy in the library. It may seem odd that the
coordinating committee has the task of allocating the incoming mail.
What happens is that the chief librarian and some of the staff representatives, if the mail contains something that can be referred to one or
other committee, decides on how and when to discuss these matters.

In staff matters it should be noted that the recommendation from
the group involved is normally accepted, unless very special circumstances occur. When positions like deputy librarian or head of the
children's department are to be filled, it is common to appoint a committee across the groups to make a recommendation to the coordinating committee.

Staff meetings

The staff meeting, where all employees are assembled, is in practice the
supreme internal authority of the library. First and foremost the
meeting discusses recommendations to be made to the political authority, more often on the basis of recommendations made by *ad hoc*
committees than from the management. The recommendation on
which an agreement has been reached is then submitted to the political
authority with the signature of the chief librarian.

The tasks of the staff meeting can be outlined as follows:

1 Objectives of the library.

2 Rules and regulations.

3   The future development of the library.
4   The setting up of project groups.
5   Organizational planning.
6   General changes in the allocation of tasks.
7   Guidelines for the budget and accounts.
8   Budget proposals.
9   Guidelines for staff policy and staff administration.
10   Organizing internal meetings.
11   Examining local plans devised by the groups.
12   Selection of equipment, office machinery etc.
13   Planning and coordination of public relations for the library.

There is only one example of a case where the disagreement among the participants at the staff meeting was so great that two different recommendations on the matter were submitted to the political authority. It was in a case where the chief strongly disagreed with the majority of the staff. The two recommendations were not accepted, but the politicians asked for the chief librarian's recommendation alone. After this the matter was discussed at a staff meeting again, where both parties gave in a little and a compromise was found.

It is a fact, nevertheless, that the formal veto power of the chief librarian remains untouched. It has, however, been used only once, about ten years ago, right at the beginning of the democratic management system, and this can be taken as a sign that both management and staff acknowledge that they have common interests, and that they are ready to accept the rules of the game.

CONCLUSION

In this paper we have given a short description of the way two municipal library systems have been able to establish an extensive form of participatory democracy. In one case this has been achieved by means of regulations that have been formally approved by the political authority, while in the other case it is based just on internal rules and agreements. There are other ways of achieving the same ends, and there are in Denmark several other libraries where similar developments have occurred.

Genuine participation in Danish public libraries, where it exists, is based on self-governing groups and a coordinating decision-making body. The possibility — both formally and in practice — of accomplishing some sort of participatory power depends on the size of the library. Normally the degree of bureaucratization will increase with the size of

210

the library, and this is accompanied by a
pation. In very large libraries one will c
and manuals and a degree of rigid , hiera
all of which makes it extremely difficult
in management into practice. Frequently
middle-sized libraries that participatory d

As could be expected, the trend to
gathered momentum concurrently with
whole in the late 1960s and early 1970s
now in the 1980s, when Denmark, like
affected by a deep political, economic a
that this crisis creates strong pressures
by the desires of right-wing politicians
social and cultural benefits. The exte
goodwill which was associated with p
often replaced by a yearning for the
helm and bring the nation safely throug

Among library staff it is also possib
level a degree of doubt concerning the
Specifically this is revealed in the fa
Bibliotekarforbundet are ostensibly no
the responsibility' for the budget cu
brought about in their libraries. These
their place in the system, so that the
can take over full responsibility for
task of finding out how the cuts can
way. The chief librarian, even in org
pated in the management of the li
responsible for the cuts ordered by
course, a mental short-circuit of a
the more dogmatic left wing.

On the one hand, then, you can
in a rather tortured way, by referr
other hand you can find a number
that are only too happy to use th
democracy in times like this must
the precious working hours must
for meetings!

This is not the place to try and
reason are sceptical about partici

reasona
public
patory
process
decision
than an
patory
standing
in, and
both in
and for
organiza

There
enough
has been
experime
will ensu
aims and
also mark

Notes

1   Co
than 'pa
meaning

2   The
council'.
several we
to be repr
types of o

3   The

based on recommendations from the groups.

5 Termination of temporary staff and hourly paid staff, based on recommendations from the groups.

6 Transfers or reallocation of staff, based on recommendations from the groups.

7 Approval of work schedules and holiday arrangements.

8 Organization of the training of library trainees and of probationary clerical staff.

9 Organization of seminars on how to conduct meetings.

10 Coordination of plans from the groups regarding the layout of the premises.

11 Approval of the choice of equipment, machines etc made by the groups.

12 Coordination of public relations activities.

13 Practical administration of book selection, preservation and withdrawal.

These tasks will in more traditional organizations be part of the administrative hierarchy in the library. It may seem odd that the coordinating committee has the task of allocating the incoming mail. What happens is that the chief librarian and some of the staff representatives, if the mail contains something that can be referred to one or other committee, decides on how and when to discuss these matters.

In staff matters it should be noted that the recommendation from the group involved is normally accepted, unless very special circumstances occur. When positions like deputy librarian or head of the children's department are to be filled, it is common to appoint a committee across the groups to make a recommendation to the coordinating committee.

Staff meetings

The staff meeting, where all employees are assembled, is in practice the supreme internal authority of the library. First and foremost the meeting discusses recommendations to be made to the political authority, more often on the basis of recommendations made by *ad hoc* committees than from the management. The recommendation on which an agreement has been reached is then submitted to the political authority with the signature of the chief librarian.

The tasks of the staff meeting can be outlined as follows:

1 Objectives of the library.

2 Rules and regulations.

3 The future development of the library.
4 The setting up of project groups.
5 Organizational planning.
6 General changes in the allocation of tasks.
7 Guidelines for the budget and accounts.
8 Budget proposals.
9 Guidelines for staff policy and staff administration.
10 Organizing internal meetings.
11 Examining local plans devised by the groups.
12 Selection of equipment, office machinery etc.
13 Planning and coordination of public relations for the library.

There is only one example of a case where the disagreement among the participants at the staff meeting was so great that two different recommendations on the matter were submitted to the political authority. It was in a case where the chief strongly disagreed with the majority of the staff. The two recommendations were not accepted, but the politicians asked for the chief librarian's recommendation alone. After this the matter was discussed at a staff meeting again, where both parties gave in a little and a compromise was found.

It is a fact, nevertheless, that the formal veto power of the chief librarian remains untouched. It has, however, been used only once, about ten years ago, right at the beginning of the democratic management system, and this can be taken as a sign that both management and staff acknowledge that they have common interests, and that they are ready to accept the rules of the game.

CONCLUSION

In this paper we have given a short description of the way two municipal library systems have been able to establish an extensive form of participatory democracy. In one case this has been achieved by means of regulations that have been formally approved by the political authority, while in the other case it is based just on internal rules and agreements. There are other ways of achieving the same ends, and there are in Denmark several other libraries where similar developments have occurred.

Genuine participation in Danish public libraries, where it exists, is based on self-governing groups and a coordinating decision-making body. The possibility − both formally and in practice − of accomplishing some sort of participatory power depends on the size of the library. Normally the degree of bureaucratization will increase with the size of the library, and this is accompanied by a lessening of genuine participation. In very large libraries one will often find organization charts and manuals and a degree of rigid , hierarchical channels of command, all of which makes it extremely difficult to put workers' participation in management into practice. Frequently, therefore, it is in small and middle-sized libraries that participatory democracy thrives.

As could be expected, the trend to democracy in Danish libraries gathered momentum concurrently with similar trends in society as a whole in the late 1960s and early 1970s. But what about the situation now in the 1980s, when Denmark, like so many affluent countries, is affected by a deep political, economic and social recession? It is clear that this crisis creates strong pressures on the public sector, nourished by the desires of right-wing politicians to bring about drastic cuts in social and cultural benefits. The extensive rhetoric and pronounced goodwill which was associated with participatory democracy is now often replaced by a yearning for the strong man that can take the helm and bring the nation safely through the crisis.

Among library staff it is also possible to trace at the organizational level a degree of doubt concerning the blessings of participatory power. Specifically this is revealed in the fact that influential groups in the Bibliotekarforbundet are ostensibly no longer willing to 'participate in the responsibility' for the budget cuts that the economic crisis has brought about in their libraries. These groups prefer everybody to keep their place in the system, so that the traditional library managements can take over full responsibility for the undesirable and unpleasant task of finding out how the cuts can be managed in the least damaging way. The chief librarian, even in organizations where the staff participated in the management of the library, is in this way made solely responsible for the cuts ordered by the political authority, and is, of course, a mental short-circuit of a kind that is not uncommon within the more dogmatic left wing.

On the one hand, then, you can reject workers' participation, albeit in a rather tortured way, by referring to the economic crisis. On the other hand you can find a number of politicians and library directors that are only too happy to use the crisis to argue that participatory democracy in times like this must be limited to an absolute minimum: the precious working hours must now be used for hard work and not for meetings!

This is not the place to try and persuade those that for one or other reason are sceptical about participatory democracy. But it would be

211

reasonable as a conclusion to sum up the main experiences of Danish public libraries in relation to collective management. First, participatory democracy means a better and much improved decision-making process: an organization that actively involves its staff in the making of decisions is fundamentally better equipped to make correct decisions than an organization that is managed from the top. Second, participatory democracy creates for the individual staff member an understanding and knowledge of the total framework that the library operates in, and makes her, or him better equipped to do the job: this is true both in respect of the librarian's primary purpose, to serve the public, and for the secondary one of functioning as an active member of the organization.

There are, then, enough professional — and also, as a matter of fact, enough purely political — arguments to try to defend the ground that has been conquered, and, in spite of the recession, to argue for new experiments with the forms of management in public libraries. This will ensure that the set of praiseworthy ideals that have influenced the aims and objectives and the external activities of public libraries, can also mark their internal organization.

Notes

1 Collective management (in Danish: kollektiv ledelse) is stronger than 'participative management', and has a somewhat more precise meaning than a term such as 'industrial democracy'.

2 The Danish word 'samarbejdudvalg' has been translated as 'staff council'. Staff councils resemble similar bodies established by law in several western European countries which give workers a statutory right to be represented on certain decision-making bodies in many different types of organization.

3 The 'amt' is a territorial division somewhat similar to a county.

Obstacles to the modernization of a library system: a case study of France

HENRI COMTE

The ideas expressed in this article are purely personal and do not necessarily represent the views of the Ecole Nationale Supérieure de Bibliothèques.

A peculiarly French model of a library service certainly exists. It can be portrayed simply by comparing the economic and cultural dynamism of a powerful modern state which is France today with the manifest underdevelopment of its library system. This surprising discrepancy has been brought out in many studies and reports, and various theories have been put forward to explain it. Some see the causes as being rooted in the wider society; one theory is that religious, social and political traditions in France have not favoured the act of reading (an activity that is essentially individual, free and potentially critical); another view holds that the education system, which places high value on an oral and authoritarian transmission of knowledge scarcely favours the development of library-based learning; another theory claims that the French social system is very resistant to change and innovation and strongly inhibits the development of self-governing groups or local communities. In short, these theories state that the defects of the French library system can be explained by reference to the unfavourable social environment in which it is embedded.

While this view of the problem has some validity, it also has shortcomings. Its main merit is to emphasize what is obviously true, though sometimes forgotten, namely that every organization is in constant relationship with its environment which will influence and constrain it. And, as shown by Hassenforder in his perceptive study, it can offer a convincing explanation of the development of French libraries in the second half of the nineteenth century.[1]

However the limitations of the 'social environment' theory are also clear. To begin with, if the defects of an organization are always

213

explained in terms of external forces, then it is all too easy to ignore internal weaknesses within the organization itself. More important, however, whatever the validity of these theories when applied to the past, they do not seem tenable at the present. There is no doubt that the demand for a modern library service is as great in France today as in other developed countries. The evidence for this is unambiguous: wherever library services of a satisfactory standard have actually been developed the response has been enormous, with levels of use rapidly reaching those which are to be found in those countries with the most advanced library services.

We must face the fact that the principal reason for the underdevelopment of French libraries today is not due to a lack of 'demand', but to an inadequate 'supply'. To discover why this should be the case we need to examine the way French libraries are controlled, organized and operated.[2]

It is probably easiest and simplest to begin at the beginning and to trace how these libraries have developed from the time of their inception. However, it is important to make clear at the outset that we shall be examining a library system that is *publicly controlled*, not only in the sense that it is available to all, but also that virtually all of it is controlled and organized by the state. As a result, and this is a key element for our argument, the problems of this library system are essentially problems of *public administration*. And, arising from this, the administrative problems can be understood most usefully by reference to the library as an organization. This notion will allow us to emphasize the continuity over time of certain distinctive characteristics of French libraries viewed as organizations. The natural tendency of every organization is to maintain its own identity, and to preserve its values and traditions. So it is no paradox to state that the heritage of the past is an essential element in the present-day organization of the French library system.

As a reaction to this, various reforms and changes have been introduced by the central government in an attempt to modernize the structure or services of the library system. After 1945 the chief agent for change was the French government department called the Direction des Bibliothèques et de la Lecture Publique (DBLP). Indeed, to list the main ways in which French libraries were modernized in this period is tantamount to summarizing the work of the DBLP from its inception to 1975, when it was abolished.

Of the present state of affairs it is difficult to write authoritatively

214

and even less easy to estimate future prospects. Whether French libraries are simply in a transitional period, or whether they are returning to the old ways of the past cannot be decided. What is clear, however, is that they are at the most important crossroads in their history.

In its study of the obstacles to library development, this paper will look firstly at the historical background up to 1945; secondly, it will examine the post-war scene from 1945 to 1975, and finally it will review and comment on the changes of the last few years.

INHERITED BURDENS FROM THE PAST: FRENCH LIBRARIES IN 1945

One of the merits of the new-born Fourth Republic in France was to have started a policy for library development even before the fighting of the Second World War had finally ceased. It was a policy, however, that had to come to terms with the existing patterns of French libraries, inherited from governments of various kinds over the preceding 150 years. The existing pattern was deficient in two ways: in its general administrative structure, and in its resources and activities.

The defects of the administrative structure

A collection of books does not make a library, and a collection of libraries of diverse origin and purpose does not make a library system. The latter can be said to exist only if there is a certain amount of conscious organization, coordination and coherence. This was not the case in France before 1945 where the library system was neither homogeneous nor unified.

Its heterogeneous nature derived from the fact that three quite different and distinct types of library developed at different times and with different aims. The three groups comprised the scholarly libraries, the popular and school libraries, and the university libraries.

The scholarly library was the first to emerge and remained the one with the highest prestige. The Bibliothèque Nationale, the French national library in Paris, symbolizes this pre-eminence. Historically, the Bibliothèque Nationale is the continuation of the Bibliothèque Royale which under the Ancien Régime had already become one of the greatest libraries of the world in the size and quality of its collections. Its purpose, almost from the beginning, was towards conservation of materials. From 1537, when Francis I promulgated the Ordinance of Montpellier, the library had legal deposit rights — rights which of course it still possesses. It grew rapidly at the time of the Revolution when it

215

acquired the best and most valuable of the books and manuscripts confiscated from the clergy and some of the aristocracy and declared to be public property. No less than ten million volumes were confiscated in all. Some 300,000 went direct to the Bibliothèque Nationale, which thereby doubled its collections at a stroke.

The same confiscations were at the origin of the other scholarly libraries which were established throughout France and known as *bibliothèques municipales* ('municipal libraries'). After much hesitation it was decided during the Empire to entrust to the principal towns and cities of France what was left of the mass of confiscated volumes after weeding and various hazards had taken their toll. The selected municipalities could therefore open up a library provided they appointed and paid for a librarian.

The second goup of libraries may be termed 'popular' libraries; they could scarcely be more different from the scholarly type. The latter had acquired a certain prestige by virtue of the value of their collections, but the popular libraries were looked upon at best as minor charitable organizations. They were, indeed, often established for charitable or philanthropic purposes; their aim was to spread a little light among the poor, in the hope of turning them away from vice, crime or moral turpitude. These libraries were characterized by short opening hours, tiny out-of-date collections, inadequate premises and voluntary or unqualified staff.

Though they were all alike in their inadequacy, they varied greatly in their formal status. One group, the smallest, were known as *bibliothèques libres* (independent libraries) and were run by private associations or societies, independent of any public body. More often the libraries were publicly supported institutions, like certain town or school libraries. Some of the town libraries were to develop much later into public libraries of a modern type, but the school libraries provided a classic case, indeed a caricature, of the paternalism and narrowmindedness which often accompanied the organization of this type of library. The school libraries originated in 1862 during the Second Empire, when Rouland, the Minister of Education, decided to set up libraries in every primary school, not only for the children but also for adults. His purpose was both educational and political: he wished to see children developing the ability to read, but also, by carefully controlling the literature available, he wished to promote loyalty to the imperial regime. So the library was closely controlled from the outset. Its collections were made up of items selected and bought by the ministry itself and as a further precaution, the schoolteacher was forbidden to add to the stock on his own initiative.

In 1870 the Third Republic took over the libraries and used them in the same way but for its own purposes. The bonapartist literature was removed and the school library became a tool in the battle against clerical and monarchist ideas. By the end of the century there were some 30,000 school libraries throughout the country standing in ideological opposition to an almost equal number of clerically controlled parish libraries.

The seeds of decline of these libraries were present in the very circumstances which brought them into being. When the book was largely supplanted by the cheap newspaper as the principal means of mass communication, the battle for political influence shifted to control of the press. The library became a place of only minor importance in the political and ideological struggles of the period, and no longer attracted the self-interested attention of public and private power groups. So by 1945 these libraries appear as forgotten relics of the past, virtually unchanged since the separation of Church and State in 1905.

The third type of library, quite separate from the other two, comprised the university libraries. They were created in the early years of the Third Republic. It was stated that their aim was to be 'au service des enseignants et des étudiants', and they were inspired in their structure and outlook by the libraries of the prestigious German universities. Three points may be made about them.

Firstly, they were *university* libraries at a time when the faculty was the all-important unit in higher education. By being conceived of as libraries of the whole university they were able to avoid in principle the rivalries, inequalities and duplication which would have arisen if each faculty or department had its own independent library.

Secondly, they were given, right from the start, an adequate and stable financial base: the library fee which every student had to pay on enrolling in the university.

Thirdly, the running of these libraries was entrusted to staff who, for the first time in the history of French libraries, had to have a professional qualification in librarianship: a diploma entitled *Certificat d'aptitude aux fonctions de bibliothécaire*, set up in 1879.

It can be seen, therefore, that the structure of the library system in 1945 was not functional but simply historical. The system had grown by accretion over the years, and the successive strata which had

217

been laid down were quite separate one from the other. The most 'modern' of the three types of library, the university library, played only a very minor innovating role in respect of the other two types, for the barriers separating the three groups were reproduced in the bureaucratic structure of the central government administration.

The heterogeneous nature of these various types of library would have mattered less if there had been some unity of control at the top, but until 1945 there was none. True, as early as 1832 the ministry of education had been given a general responsibility for libraries, but in practice each type of library came under a different department of the ministry. In 1897, in an attempt to lessen the bureaucratic fragmentation of library administration the various departments dealing with libraries were grouped together under the higher education division of the ministry. But this reform does not seem to have produced any marked results, above all because there was no one whose responsibilities included the libraries as a whole.

Inadequate and unsuitable resources

Not only were French libraries in 1945 ill-organized, but worse, the means at their disposal were quite unsatisfactory. Except in the case of university libraries, there had grown up a particular conception of the library in which the library was identified with its initial stock, and its only purpose was thought to be the proper organization and control of this collection. In other words it was a conception of the library which considered that the purpose of the institution was derived from the means it had at its disposal, and it was directly linked to the historical conditions which existed at the time the libraries were created.

The point can be illustrated most clearly by the case of the older municipal libraries. The original collections of these libraries, as we have seen, derived from the material confiscated at the time of the French Revolution.

In the historical circumstances of their creation we can find a logic which controlled the subsequent organizational development of the library. Given the lack of order prevailing in the initial collection, the first priority for the municipal libraries was to attend to such internal tasks as sorting, accessioning and cataloguing. As a result the library looked inward upon itself, concerned with the books rather than the readers. It was all the more natural for this to happen since the collections were valuable: manuscripts, incunabula, rare and old books. As a precaution against the covetous user there grew up a protective

218

attitude to the stock: direct access was excluded, home lending of books forbidden and even the consultation of certain items greatly restricted. As for the desirable qualifications of the librarians, these seemed to follow logically enough from the nature of the stock: since the collections were essentially of historical interest then it was felt that only a historian was fit to be put in charge of them.

What a paradox! The authors of the French Revolution had wished to use the confiscated materials to set up libraries which would become as they said, 'l'école de tous les citoyens'. In practice, however, by filling the libraries with old and rare books they cut them off from the general public, turning them into museums of books unvisited except by a handful of scholars. And so these libraries, not having the means to fulfil their original purpose, were led by the very nature of their collections to adopt a purpose and outlook in conformity with the means that they had.

Because of the irrelevance of these scholarly libraries to the needs of the people, popular libraries began to be established half a century later. But by this time the idea that a library was nothing more than its original collection of material had become so engrained in the minds of French administrators that the new libraries were all supplied with a basic stock chosen without any real consideration for the desires or the expectations of the readers, and all their activities were subject to a strict political control. In the case of the school libraries, the stock, as we have seen, was chosen directly by the ministry of education. In the popular town libraries (for many towns set up municipal libraries of a 'popular' sort), a rather more subtle system of control was used: inspection and selection committees, set up by the ministry, scrutinized the stock and any additions made to it. And until 1901 even the so-called 'independent' libraries could have their licence to operate revoked at any time by the ministry, which proved a powerful mechanism to ensure conformity.

So the nineteenth and early twentieth century French library, whether of the scholarly or the popular sort, became so to speak a prisoner of its initial collections, collections chosen not by the librarian but by an outside body. And the library was prevented from up-dating its collections or making them more relevant by the control and supervision exercised from above and by a lack of funds.

All this naturally enough, had its effect on the role of librarians. Unable to carry out such basic tasks as choosing and adding to the stock in response to the needs of the users, librarians were little more than caretakers or keepers, looking after a bookstock not of their own making. Indeed it is significant that in France the administrative term for senior professional librarians still remains that of 'keeper' (*conservateur*). Further, the truncated and impoverished role of the librarian removed any justification for the development of proper professional education. The whole logical process of setting up a library was, so to speak, turned upside down. Instead of beginning with an analysis of readers' needs undertaken by professionally qualified librarians, followed by the establishment of a suitable stock to satisfy these needs, the French library as an organization operated in reverse: the nature of the original collection came to determine the whole purpose and functions of the library.

In complete contrast, the university libraries established in the 1870s proved very successful. They began with virtually nothing, but by 1900 they had established themselves as first-class academic libraries, much appreciated and valued by the clientele. Yet by 1945, one of the principal causes of their success was under threat: the students' library fee which had provided a solid acquisitions budget had not increased in line with the cost of books and journals and had become insufficient to finance acquisitions at a satisfactory rate.

This brief sketch of the development of French libraries up to 1945 reveals the magnitude of the tasks which awaited the Direction des Bibliothèques et de la Lecture Publique. Here and there, perhaps, some progress had already been made, but such changes as had occurred remained isolated and were more often in the realm of theory than of practice. So it was only in 1945, with the creation of the DBLP, that a real policy of library modernization could take shape.

THE CREATION OF A DEVELOPMENT POLICY FOR FRENCH LIBRARIES: THE WORK OF THE DIRECTION DES BIBLIOTHEQUES ET DE LA LECTURE PUBLIQUE (DBLP)

The decree of 18 August 1945 which created the DBLP put all matters concerning publicly financed libraries under a specialized government department. This department was not viewed purely as an administrative body but was given the role of promoting new policies to revitalize the whole system. It tried to do this in three different ways: it set up a series of 'central lending libraries' (*Bibliothèques centrales de prêt*), it overhauled the system of professional education, and it promoted and encouraged development in all types of libraries.

The direction of these new policies went partly against tradition, habits and established practices. Often a decision had to be made between the desirable and the possible. For organizations, the past cannot easily be abolished. More than once in its thirty years work the DBLP had to come to terms with this, and so, despite much definite progress, it could not entirely repudiate the heritage of the past.

The Direction des Bibliothèques et de la Lecture Publique (DBLP)

The decree of 1945 gave the DBLP very wide powers, specifically 'toutes les questions concernant l'organisation et le fonctionnement des bibliothèques et de la lecture publique'. Indeed, use of the phrase 'lecture publique' (roughly equivalent to the activities of the Anglo-American type of public library) was itself typical of the rejuvenating spirit which charaterized its work. The phrase implied a new conception of a library; it was no longer to be thought of as a kind of social service to the deprived and imbued with a paternalistic or philanthropic ideology, but as a true public service which would be open to all and capable of responding to the wide-ranging and every-changing needs of the whole population. The preface to the French Constitution of 1946 stressed the rights of the French citizen which included 'égal accès de l'enfant et de l'adulte à l'instruction et à la culture'. The library was to be one of the instruments chosen to make this right a reality.

In the same spirit the DBLP's organization and structure reflected a desire to break with the past and start afresh. Firstly, beside the traditional sections dealing with general administration, finance and personnel, the DBLP established a section on professional and technical services which worked actively to take care of existing facilities as well as to modernize them by encouraging the use of appropriate methods and techniques. Secondly, this new section's sphere of action encompassed all types of state-supported library; the rigid divisions between public, school, university and research libraries were broken down by the creation of new functional departments.

The department's administrative structure, therefore, was quite well adapted to the innovatory role it wished to play. However, even here the heritage of the past made itself felt. Firstly, the administrative head of the department was at the same time the director of the Bibliothèque Nationale. His duties at the DBLP, therefore, could only be part-time and by the same token it meant that the interests of the scholarly research libraries were more than adequately represented in the department. Secondly, and tending to have the same effect, the department never really got the funds it needed to carry out the wide-

221

ranging programmes that it devised. There were never more than forty people (administrators and professional librarians) working for the department at any one time. Nevertheless, these handicaps did not prevent the department from carrying out some radical reforms, as we shall see.

The creation of the Bibliothèques Centrales de Prêt (BCP)
The *bibliothèques centrales de prêt*, or central lending libraries, were established by an ordinance of 2 November 1945, shortly after the founding of the DBLP itself, so the department found that its first major task was the setting up of this new type of library.

To do this, however, involved a major policy change, namely that the public library service outside the larger towns should be undertaken directly by the central government. The basic French unit of local government is the commune. The commune may be a town or city, but more often is nothing more than a village or hamlet. Out of 36,000 communes in France, nearly 33,000 have less than 2000 inhabitants. The rural communes were therefore too small and too poor to run their own library services; these would be undertaken by the *bibliothèques centrales de prêt*. The rule was established that the BCP were to be state-run libraries, established throughout the country and serving all communes with less than 15,000 inhabitants (the figure was raised to 20,000 in 1968).

Their first major task was to take over the innumerable but mostly decrepit small libraries which existed all over France: school libraries, libraries of small towns, and libraries of various public institutions. They all suffered from inadequate bookstocks, insufficient maintenance of the collections, and management by non-professional or volunteer staff. In their place a network of small libraries was set up, or rural depositories were organized in schools, town halls, village centres etc. In order to ensure that the stock of these depository collections would be changed and up-dated regularly a central depot was established at the BCP headquarters which would send out regular consignments of books to each of the local service points. The task of the BCP, therefore, was to establish these local book collections and to keep them up to date by means of regular timetabled visits.

For administrative purposes the French state is divided geographically into 96 *départements*. Except for the *département* of Paris, and for two or three *départements* surrounding Paris, each one is roughly similar in size to an English shire county, and has a similar balance of
222

rural and urban population.[3] It was decided to create one BCP for every department with a rural population. The new service got off the ground quite quickly. In 1945 eight BCPs were started, in 1946, nine; then the rhythm slowed very markedly and only five additional BCPs were established between 1947 and 1961. After that the tempo increased so that today out of 93 *départements* suitable for the installation of a BCP, 78 now have them.

The methods of running these library systems have improved over the years. At first the only method of distributing books to the local depots was by means of bookboxes made up at the central store. Soon, however, the mobile library was introduced, which enabled those who ran the deposit collections to choose material for their libraries themselves. Finally, in the last ten years the mobile libraries of many BCPs have been lending directly to the general public. In 1980 some 188 mobile libraries of all types were operating in the French countryside.

The DBLP's policy on professional training and careers

In 1945 the situation in regard to library personnel cried out for reform. Apart from deciding to increase rapidly the number of library staff, the DBLP set out to do two things: harmonize the career structure and modernize professional education.

The fragmentation of publicly funded libraries into the various categories described earlier had its counterpart in the multiplicity of quite separate career structures, scales of pay and conditions of service for library staff. Besides considerable inequalities of status, mobility of librarians from one type of library service to another was all but impossible. To remedy the situation the DBLP went as far as it could. It brought all librarians working in state-financed libraries into the same career structure, and for those library staff employed entirely by municipal authorities, it unified their conditions of service and made them comparable, as far as possible, with those working in the state sector.

The unification of the career structure of state-employed librarians was completed in the early 1950s. Henceforth, such staff could work successively, if they wished, in the Bibliothèque Nationale, in a university library, in a *bibliothèque centrale de prêt*, or in one of those older municipal libraries still controlled by the state. The reforms encompassed senior professional staff, sub-professional staff and manual staff (caretakers, stack pages etc).

These reforms were important, but nevertheless the heritage of the

223

past influenced their nature and to some extent negated their purpose. One example was the special status still given to the Ecole des Chartes. The Ecole des Chartes is one of France's older *grandes écoles* and has long specialized in the training of experts in the study of medieval manuscripts, paleography and archives. Ever since 1829 graduates of this school have had the right to occupy one-third of the senior library posts in French state-financed libraries, thereby illustrating nicely the dominant view of the library as a museum of books, and the consequent desirability for its curator to be a scholar and historian. The rights enjoyed by graduates of this school were reaffirmed in the statutes of the 1950s, creating therefore something of a paradox. The unified career structure meant that librarians, including those whose studies had been solely at the Ecole des Chartes, could work in any type of state-financed library, thereby widening the opportunities open to such graduates, who might find themselves, after their studies in history and archives, in charge of a scientific research library!

Another heritage of the past lay in the continued existence of the *bibliothèques municipales classées*. While some, and by the 1950s, the majority of municipal libraries were owned and operated outright by the local authority, some 57 of these libraries, usually in the larger towns and cities, had a special status and were termed *bibliothèques municipales classées*. These were the libraries founded after the French revolution to look after some of the millions of works confiscated from the aristocracy and clergy. As we have seen the state had retained certain powers over these libraries, and the DBLP did nothing to change this. These powers could be seen as helpful, since they included paying the salaries of the senior librarians, but were usually felt as a constraint. The city council was not master of its own library, since it had no hand in selecting and appointing the senior staff and therefore was unable to impose its own policies on the library. The situation is in fact a relic of the time when preservation of national property was considered the all-important function of the library. In practice this reluctance to break with the past has slowed the development of a modern library service in a number of these cities.

While the old traditions had only a limited effect on the modernization of the career structure, they have influenced the development of professional education much more seriously. As we have already noted, in many of the 'scholarly' libraries set up after the Revolution the primary tasks were seen as listing and then preserving the collections. Given the nature of the stock, with its wealth of rare books, and the

224

work required in these libraries, the preference given to the appointment of historicans, and especially of graduates of the Ecole des Chartes was a justifiable and praiseworthy act. And given the status of the scholarly libraries, these librarians emerged as the key figures in the profession, the ideal type of the qualified librarian directing the principal libraries of the country.

The pre-eminence of the Ecole des Chartes had no justification outside the scholarly, historical libraries, and attempts were made to create alternative routes to professional competence. In 1879 a separate diploma was established for those wishing to work in the newly founded university libraries, and later new specialist diplomas were established for the large scholarly research libraries in Paris and for the *bibliothèques municipales classées*. Yet such was the prestige and influence of the Ecole des Chartes that graduates from this school were exempt from the new diplomas, which in any case were not taught in a very organized way and were at a rather low level, with none of the status and prestige of that offered by the Ecole des Chartes.

The improvement of professional education for librarians was thought to lie, therefore, in the establishment of a new general diploma of suitable standing. In 1932 one such diploma, the *Diplôme technique de bibliothécaire* was introduced for all types of librarian. Here again, however, the influence of the Ecole des Chartes made itself felt. True, under the new regulations, graduates of this school could not work in a university library or a *bibliothèque municipale classée* without acquiring this additional qualification. But such was the prestige of the school that the school itself was entrusted with the teaching of the new diploma. So for historical reasons, and through the power and influence of one educational establishment, the study of librarianship remained the handmaiden of history right until the 1950s.

The task of the DBLP, therefore, was to try and reverse this century-old tradition in professional education; it proved to be a difficult undertaking. In 1950 it replaced the 1932 diploma by a *Diplôme supérieur de bibliothécaire*. The new diploma admitted students at post-graduate level only (the old one admitted students who had completed only the baccalauréat), and its syllabus placed much more emphasis on professional techniques. Most important of all it was the DBLP which organized the classes in preparation for this diploma. The way was therefore open at last for the establishment of a proper high-level professional course which really met the actual needs of all types of library. However, it was not until 1963 that professional education found a proper home through the creation of the Ecole Nationale Supérieure de Bibliothécaires, an autonomous school specifically providing for the professional education of librarians.

It was established at Villeurbanne, outside Lyon, and its principal mission is to recruit and train librarians for the senior levels of the library service. For those who will be working in state-financed libraries, admission is highly competitive, and can be achieved on one of two ways: recent university graduates may apply, and of a thousand or more who do each year, only twenty are selected, thereby ensuring a very high standard in the school. A second method of entry is reserved for junior professionals (*sous-bibliothécaires*) who have already had considerable working experience in libraries. In addition the school also admits students in a different manner who wish to work outside the state-financed sector (eg in municipally run libraries, or in foreign libraries), and admission requirements here are somewhat less rigorous. All students follow a common one-year course, which is now the normal way of obtaining the *Diplôme supérieur de bibliothécaire*.

Parallel with its work in changing and improving professional education at the senior level, the DBLP tried to develop the qualifications for junior professional staff. For those in the state sector a competitive examination was established in 1950, while a different diploma, the *Certificat d'aptitude à la profession de bibliothécaire* was set up for those who wished to work either in the private sector or in publicly funded libraries outside the state sector. These courses are taught in various parts of France in association with the Ecole Nationale Supérieure de Bibliothécaires.[4]

Viewed from other countries, the DBLP's work in promoting professional education might appear unexceptional or even timid. But, in fact, given the entrenched traditions of French librarianship, and the powerful interests with a stake in these traditions, it brought about a veritable revolution.

The development of French library networks
The considerable achievements of the DBLP in this field were nevertheless limited in two ways. To begin with the department had direct power only over the libraries financed by the state; towards those financed by local authorities or other non-state agencies it could act only indirectly or by persuasion. Secondly, its work was limited by the funds available to it, and in this connection three distinct periods can be discerned. The first, from 1945 to 1946, was characterized by very

226

generous funding; the second, which lasted from 1947 to 1967 was marked by much smaller improvements in its budget but nevertheless with a distinct tendency for funds to increase especially in the later years of the period; the third, from 1967 to 1974, showed another rapid increase in the budget, an increase which ceased in 1975, since when funds allotted to libraries have been distinctly parsimonious.

Within these budgetary constraints the work of the DBLP achieved a remarkable continuity. The three main aspects of its work here comprised technical help; financial help, and the support of cooperative endeavours.

The technical assistance given by the department reflected its desire for the modernization of the French library system. Technical standards based on the best library practice were publicized; the department acted as consultant on many library building projects and systematically encouraged the modernization of library operations and procedures via open access, adoption of the Dewey decimal classification, the simplification of loans procedures and so on.

The financial help, dependent of course on its budgetary allocation, consisted mainly of managing the funds established for the administration of the libraries. That part of the budget attributed to public libraries (*lecture publique*) was for many years very small, but improved after 1968 passing from 15% of the budget in 1967 to 22% in 1972. The DBLP also helped municipal libraries in an important way: top priority was given to the funding of new buildings. At first the DBLP paid 35% of the cost, but after 1968 the proportion rose to 50%. The programme was remarkably successful: in ten years (1965-1975) the surface area of these libraries doubled from 300,000 sq m to 600,000 sq m. Since then the programme has been reduced: from 46,000 sq m in 1974 down to only 6000 sq m in 1981.

Another innovation dating from 1968 was a project to help municipal libraries which were making special efforts to improve their library service. A good idea in principle, it was ineffective in practice as the state aid amounted to an average of only 6% of the municipal library's budget.

Support for cooperative and collective endeavours of various kinds became of growing interest to the department. A regular monthly journal, the *Bulletin des bibliothèques de France*, was started in 1956. The DBLP also encouraged the building up of union catalogues, of which the best known are that on foreign works in French libraries (the *Catalogue collectif des ouvrages étrangers reçus en France*) and that on

227

current periodical holdings (the *Inventaire permanent des périodiques en cours*). Later it sought to harness the power of the computer for more ambitious cooperative projects. Since 1971 an automation office (Bureau d'automatisation des bibliothèques), later expanded to become a whole division in the department (Division de l'informatique de la coopération et de l'automatisation), created, tested and put into operation an automated union catalogue based on the computerized records of the *Bibliographie de la France*.

All in all the work of the DBLP was far from negligible. One could criticize it for being more content to manage than to innovate, for its inability to prevent drastic cuts in the bookfunds of research libraries, or for having waited so long before exploring and utilizing the immense possibilities inherent in library cooperation. Whatever the merits of these criticisms (and we shall return to them in the final section of this paper), these faults certainly did not justify the abolition of the DBLP in September 1975. Problems unsolved by this department, to which we must now add the problems which have arisen as a direct cause of its abolition, are still awaiting solutions today.

FRENCH LIBRARIES AT THE CROSSROADS: PRESENT-DAY PROBLEMS

In the summer of 1981 *Le monde* published two articles devoted to the difficulties experienced by French libraries, thereby bringing to the attention of informed public opinion and of the political decision-makers the crisis which libraries are now facing.[5]

The measures to be taken will depend, however, upon the diagnosis made on the present state of the library service. Depending on the results of this diagnosis, there are two alternative strategies. The easier one is to increase the resources available to the existing system. The other way is more difficult and more contentious and would involve further substantial structural reforms, but which would ensure a long-term future for the library system. The financial crisis which affects French libraries is there for all to see, but it might simply hide a more deep-seated and dangerous fault. In other words what will be important in the future under the new French government will be to see not so much the *amount* of effort put in to help libraries, but the *ways* this help will be given.[6] More specifically three key questions must be answered: what should be the future organization of the central government's role in the library system; how can the academic libraries be rejuvenated, and what is the future of the public library?

228

Some of the answers will be suggested in the final sections of this paper.

The crisis in the central administration for libraries

When a new building is finally completed, no one bothers when the scaffolding surrounding it is removed. But when a building is only half-finished, and the scaffolding is taken down and removed from the site, then the prospects for the early completion of this building are dim. This is what has happened in the case of government support for library development. Thanks to the scaffolding provided by the DBLP, the construction of a coherent library system for France was proceeding more or less satisfactorily, even if a good way from completion. The abrupt abolition of this department in 1975 has called into question, once again, the whole basis of government support for libraries.

There was no mystique about the DBLP, and we could well imagine that when the French library service came to maturity, this department could well have been dispensed with. As things are, however, the break-up of this body is, at the very least, premature, and although an attempt has been made to use some of the pieces of this scaffolding on quite a different building site, there are very strong doubts about the effectiveness of this action.

The other building site is that of the book. French publishers, booksellers and authors are facing a difficult economic situation, though France is not alone in this. In September 1974 the prime minister appointed a junior minister, Paul Granet, to investigate the problem. A well-researched document was produced as a result of his enquiry and which became known as the Granet report. Its principal recommendations were accepted by the French cabinet on 16th April 1975. Among these recommendations was one which proposed that public library services be brought under the control of the ministry of culture, as part of a general regrouping of all administrative departments connected with the book trade. The recommendations were put into effect in the autumn of 1975, and the changes are shown in figure 1.

The DBLP was thereby split in two. Academic and research libraries, unaffected by the reorganization, remained in the department of universities. Public libraries, however, were henceforth to be the responsibility of the new government department called the Direction du livre, part of the ministry of culture.

In an attempt to limit the drawbacks of this division for libraries

229

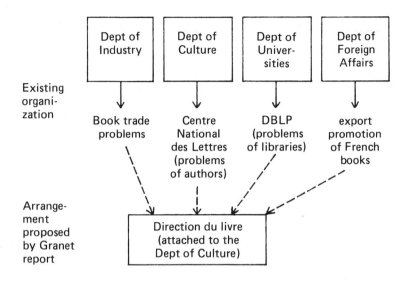

Existing organization	Dept of Industry	Dept of Culture	Dept of Universities	Dept of Foreign Affairs

Existing organization

Book trade problems   Centre National des Lettres (problems of authors)   DBLP (problems of libraries)   export promotion of French books

Arrangement proposed by Granet report

Direction du livre (attached to the Dept of Culture)

Fig 1 Administrative reorganization proposed by the Granet Report

certain services remained applicable to all state-supported libraries, such as the state library inspectorate and the unified career structure. Nevertheless, this reform broke up and scattered the state's responsibilities for the library system. In the ministry for universities a division was made between the head of the libraries section and the direction of the Bibliothèque Nationale, these responsibilities being henceforth undertaken by two different people. This change endangered the cooperative arrangements existing among the scholarly and academic libraries. Further, in January 1981, all matters concerning automation were removed from the libraries section and given to a separate body, the Direction de l'Information Scientifique et Technique, while in June 1981 the responsibility for the Bibliothèque Nationale was transferred to the ministry of culture. Today, therefore, the functions of setting up a nationwide libraries policy have been split up among four distinct and perhaps rival decision-making bodies.

Unity of control of French publicly supported libraries has now well and truly gone, and if we remember that in the past this unity was the *sine qua non* of any coherent development, we can only conclude that the new arrangements are a step backwards. If a new policy for the development of French libraries is to be found, then an adminis-

230

trative body must be given the powers to put it into practice. It is not necessarily desirable to return to the pre-1975 pattern, but somebody must be given the necessary powers if only to deal with the pressing problems of academic libraries on the one hand and those of public libraries on the other.

The collapse of the academic library sector

The principal research collections of the country are to be found in the national library and the university libraries. The former has not escaped its own problems, but has not suffered to the extent of the university libraries. Before the Second World War the latter were the finest flowers of the French library system, but are today near to complete collapse. This is true in terms of their organization, of their finance, and of their structure.

University libraries were never considered to be open solely to the staff and students of the institution in which they were situated. Being paid for directly by the state, they were in principle open to members of the public. Still less were they regarded as libraries of the faculties or institutes making up the university, but today the organizational aspect of the present crisis revolves around the relationship of the central library to the institute libraries. One hundred years ago the principle of a single university library implied at the same time that such a library would have a monopoly of the information resources within the university. As time passed this policy was often applied too rigidly, for example by concentrating all the collections in one central library building, and this left certain information needs unsatisfied. For example, laboratories and research institutes needed to have control over some of the literature relevant to them, and immediate access to it. These specific needs were not met by the main library, so many laboratories and research centres developed their own collections, some of which have since become very large. Even the more elementary function of provision of students' materials fell far short of meeting their basic but massive need for textbooks, and this led, in the same way, to the provision of specialized services for them in the shape of reading rooms (*salles de travail*), physically separate from, and quite independent of, the main university library. There developed an uncontrolled proliferation of independent libraries, some of which required very considerable resources and which amounted to a great deal of waste and duplication.

It would be impractical today just to close down these independent

231

libraries, nor could they simply be taken over by the central university library. The solution would seem to lie in a completely new definition of the role and function of a university library which would enable all the libraries and documentation centres within the university gradually to come together. In 1976 the libraries section of the ministry for universities undertook a detailed investigation of the matter, but has not, so far as we know, given any indication of its future policy on this problem.

The financial crisis of the university library derives from the collapse of their acquisitions budgets. Here again the original principle has gone wrong. The 'library fee' has not risen in line with inflation and more and more exemptions have been granted to particular categories of student. By 1981 it was estimated that the revenue derived from this fee amounted to only one-fifth of what it ought to be. As for that part of the library's funds supplied direct by the ministry, this has never fully compensated for the decline in the purchasing power of the library fee, and in recent years has gone more and more into the general administration of the library. As a result the acquisition rate in university libraries has declined drastically. The official enquiry of 1976 showed that university libraries in the provinces were buying material at the rate of only 0.24 books per library user per annum (the rate for the libraries of the Parisian universities was at twice this figure). Compare this with the Unesco standard of five books per year per student, or even with the standard of three books per year per student recommended by the government when compiling its sixth national plan. The libraries have been forced to cut their periodical subscriptions wholesale, and to buy only a tiny part of what they need to keep their bookstocks up to date. Indeed, by a strange reversal of history, it is the university libraries which are being forced to become concerned mainly with the preservation of their stock, and already half the students and the academic staff have ceased to make use of them.

Things have now reached such a state that the university libraries can only be rescued and then brought back to health through a complete reappraisal of their role and methods. In this respect two fundamental changes seem to be necessary: cooperation and computerization. Unfortunately, in both these fields much remains to be done. The great advantage of cooperation is that costs and benefits may be shared, but the process is still very much at an embryonic stage. Its best known form is the inter-library loan, which is still based on the antiquated method of passing slips from one library to another. It is slow and

232

uncertain, though it does result in the lending of about 200,000 documents a year.

As for the union catalogues mentioned earlier, they cover only a small part of the library's requirements. The use of automated data bases, it is true, has greatly increased in the last few years, but although this method can provide the user with the titles of potentially useful documents, it cannot provide the documents themselves. One innovation made in 1980 attempted to deal with this problem. A certain number of libraries were to be designated centres of excellence in certain fields (Centres d'acquisition et de diffusion de l'information scientifique et technique). The operation has only just started but to many librarians it seems less like the beginnings of an era of plenty than a system of rationing in a time of famine. Programmes for a national acquisitions policy, for the provision of bibliographical information about existing collections, for cooperative acquisition in certain fields, for the construction of specialized computerized data bases, for a modern inter-library loan system, all, and more, still remain to be thought out, organized and put into effect.

Since 1981 a separate government department, the Direction de l'information scientifique et technique, has assumed responsibility for these kinds of programmes, and is quite distinct from the libraries section. There is some doubt as to how far the new department will associate the practising librarian in the formulation and execution of its policies, and this doubt seems indicative of the way that academic libraries seem to have lost control of the forces that will decide their future.

New problems in the public library service
It was earlier pointed out that the present organization of the public library service rests on the dichotomy between city and country. In the larger towns and cities (those of over 20,000 population) the library service is the responsibility of the commune (municipality). In the small towns and throughout the countryside it is the central government that provides the library service through the *bibliothèques centrales de prêt*. Does this arrangement still have some value? The experience of the last couple of decades makes one doubt it.

The municipal libraries have developed most encouragingly. In 1942 an enquiry showed that only 136 towns of more than 10,000 population had a municipal library. By 1977, the last year for which statistics are available, 767 towns with a population of 10,000 or over had

233

their own public library. Today all towns of over 50,000 inhabitants have a public library as do 93% of those with 20,000 population or more. Their services have increased correspondingly: in 1942 municipal libraries lent an average of only 0.4 volumes per year per inhabitant. By 1966 the figure was 0.8 rising to 1.0 in 1968, 1.5 in 1972 and 2.0 in 1978. As for the important figure of library membership, here again a rapid increase in recent years can be seen. In 1942 only an estimated 1.5% of the population were members of a municipal library; by 1966 this had reached 4.6%, rising to 6.3% in 1972 and to 9% by 1978. Within these general figures there are great variations from town to town, and some municipalities which have made a real effort to develop their services have membership levels at over 20% of the population, showing that in France, given the opportunity, there is a large clientele for the public library service.

The *bibliothèques centrales de prêt*, on the other hand, seem to have lagged behind. According to the latest available statistics they lent 25 million items to an estimated one million readers (out of 24 million potentially served). These figures show that both the number of items lent and the number of readers are half that of the municipal libraries. But the real picture is even more disturbing than these figures suggest. A more detailed analysis of the libraries' collections and of the population served show that children and juvenile literature play a preponderant part in the libraries' activities. More than 70% of the BCP's depositories are in schools, and often half the stock consists of children's books. Children, therefore, may be reasonably well served by these libraries, for sometimes 50% or even 70% of schoolchildren are members. Adults, on the other hand, seem scarcely touched by the service. The depository collections in schools are little more than school libraries, used by children while they are still at school, but abandoned by them as soon as they leave. The work of these libraries, therefore, is without any lasting effect on the children and has virtually no effect at all on the adults.

Given the unsatisfactory nature of the situation, what can be done? Would extra funds solve these problems? Some believe that they would, but not the present writer who believes that only a complete reassessment of the whole service can lead to a real improvement.

In the first place the present service is haphazard. In order to establish a depository in the village or small town a volunteer must be found willing to look after it; sometimes no one comes forward, which is why even in the *départements* where BCPs have been set up, a quarter of the population remains unserved.

In the second place the present system cannot provide a regular continuous service. It cannot do so in part because the deliveries to the depositories are so infrequent (the stock is changed on an average only 2.8 times a year). Even more serious there is a lack of continuity in access to collections. When the collections are lodged in the school and looked after by a schoolteacher, then they are not accessible to adults during school hours. And even for the pupils the library may well be shut during the school holidays, that is to say at the very time when children have most opportunity to read! In short the system of volunteers means that the opening hours reflect the availability of the volunteer librarian, not of the needs of the users. The question of opening hours is less crucial, it is true, when the library is housed in the local council offices or when the collections are fortunate enough to be housed in a building expressly set apart for them. But the problem occurs even more acutely with the mobile libraries for when they lend direct to the public their stops in any one place are of the order of just a few hours every month.

In the third place the level of service is bound to remain limited. A library will only attract people if it offers a reasonable choice of material. But the average size of a depository library run by the BCP is only 500 volumes! Even the mobiles which lend direct to the public offer a far better choice. But the mobile library, given its high costs can only operate in the more densely populated parts of the countryside — in those very areas where a purpose-built library is a possibility.

So whichever way we look at the BCPs, there are serious constraints and limits on their activities. Indeed, in addition to all the specific criticisms that have been made, one can question the whole basic philosophy of these libraries, and to suggest other, and perhaps better ones. In France two principal strategies are in operation as a means of bringing a library service to the general public.

One strategy can be termed 'institutional', for the library reaches its clientele by utilizing an already existing institution: a school, a youth centre, an association, a firm etc. The BCPs use this strategy, for their local depots can only be placed in the buildings of institutions ready to receive them.

The other strategy we may term 'sectorial'; it is the one used by the modern municipal libraries, and here, quite simply, the library reaches the reader directly, and irrespective of any institutional affiliations the reader may have. No longer does the library try to reach the child only through the school, the teenager only through the youth club, or the worker only through the factory. Instead the whole population is served directly through a system of autonomous libraries offering a variety of service to children, young people, workers and all other social categories.

In our view the real solution to the question of the rural public library service would be to change from the 'institutional' to the 'sectorial' strategy. Indeed a project along these lines, termed the 'sectorial media centre' (*médiathèque de secteur*) has already started.[7] It calls into question the traditional division between town and country, and presupposes a mixed geographical area comprising a town together with all its rural hinterland. Within each sector a hierarchy of provision would be established with a central library, branch libraries (urban or rural) and mobile libraries.

The principal practical benefits of this new type of rural library service would include a more rational distribution of resources, easier access to them and shorter runs for the mobile libraries. The difficulties, given the traditional pattern of administration and of local government in France, should not be underestimated, but the future of the rural public libary service surely lies in this direction.

The French poet Paul Claudel once said, 'le pire n'est pas toujours sur' (one cannot even be sure that the worst will happen), and yet the worst may well be what will happen to French libraries in the future, and this despite the efforts made to give them the influence and prestige of those to be found in English-speaking countries. From this point of view to list the obstacles and to identify the constraints is not pessimism, but realism. This paper has analysed some of these impediments, but we can affirm that no irreversible destiny lies in store for French libraries; the only dangers they face are policies with the wrong purpose.

References and notes

1 Hassenforder, J *Développement comparé des bibliothèques en France, en Grande-Bretagne et aux Etats-Unis dans la seconde moitié du 19e siècle* Paris, Cercle de la Librairie, 1967.

2 Comte, H *Les bibliothèques publiques en France* Lyon, Presses de l'Ecole Nationale Supérieure de Bibliothécaires, 1977.

3 The density of population, however, will normally be much less. In France as a whole there are 95 people per sq km. In the United Kingdom the figure is 230, and for England alone, 355 per sq km. (Editor's note.)

4 For readers unfamiliar with professional education in France it

may be useful to point out, as is suggested from the above account, that the simple division into 'professional' and 'non-professional' library staff does not occur in French state-supported libraries. Instead there is a tripartite structure consisting of senior professionals (*personnel scientifique*), junior professional or library technicians (*personnel technique*) and manual staff (*personnel de service*), and entry to each of these branches is quite separate. The division reflects the general structure of the French civil service (and is paralleled in British civil service with its division into administrative, executive and clerical branches). Hence the small intake into the ENSB, which recruits only for those who will occupy the most senior positions (Editor's note).

5 *Le monde*, 6 June 1981, 2 and 22 July 1981, 2.

6 The Minister of Culture in the new French government, Jack Lang, in one of his first public statements, announced his intention of developing a new policy for French libraries.

7 For a more extended analysis see *Mediathèques publiques* 49, 1979.